# E-LEARNING
## Uncovered℠

# Lectora© 11

D1305924

Diane Elkins
Desirée Pinder

E-Learning Uncovered: Lectora 11

By Diane Elkins and Desirée Pinder

Alcorn, Ward, & Partners, Inc. dba Artisan E-Learning

2771-29 Monument Road #329

Jacksonville, FL 32225

www.artisanelearning.com

Trademarks

Lectora and CourseMill are registered trademarks of Trivantis Corporation.  Microsoft is a registered trademark of Microsoft Corporation.  iPad and iPhone are trademarks of Apple Inc., registered in the U.S. and other countries.

Other product and company names mentioned herein may be trademarks of their respective owners.  Use of trademarks or product names is not intended to convey endorsement or affiliation in this book.

Warning and Disclaimer

The information provided is on an "as is" basis.  Every effort has been made to make this book as complete and as accurate as possible, but no warranty or fitness is implied.  The authors and the publisher shall have neither liability nor responsibility to any person or entity with respect to any loss or damages arising from the information contained in this book.

# Chapter Table of Contents

## Detailed Table of Contents

## Detailed Table of Contents

# Detailed Table of Contents

# Detailed Table of Contents

# Detailed Table of Contents

# Detailed Table of Contents

# Detailed Table of Contents

## 16. Preferences & Customization ............................................. 241

## Detailed Table of Contents

# Introduction

We've been using Lectora since 2005. I still remember the first branching scenario I made. I was so proud of it! I've come a long way since then, and so has Lectora. Lectora remains one of the more powerful rapid development tools on the market. Since 2005, I've always appreciated the design flexibility it gave me – letting me create truly custom interactions and navigation.

While Lectora has always been advanced, some people have found it not to be as simple or user-friendly as other authoring tools. Version 11 has gone a long way in addressing those concerns. This release helps make things easier. The redesigned interface is similar to other software most users are familiar with, commonly used features are now easier to find, and logic that used to be set up manually is now done automatically.

Be sure to look for the "new" symbol throughout the book. Because of the interface redesign, everything is pretty much in a different place. Because of this, the "new" symbol is reserved for features that are completely new or significantly enhanced, rather than simply in a different place.

Enjoy!

# Acknowledgments

As always, many people helped make this book possible. Special thanks to the extended production team, including Leslie Harrison and Lucie Haskins. This book would not have been possibly without the support (and comma-finding expertise) of my husband, Steve. Writing a book is a huge undertaking, and he was instrumental in keeping me focused and motivated.

Diane Elkins

# Getting the Most Out of This Book

This book assumes you are a functional user of Windows software. If you are familiar with how to use dialog boxes, drop-down menus, and other standard Windows conventions, then you'll be fine. This book covers the core Lectora software available as Lectora Publisher or as part of the larger Lectora Inspire suite. The additional tools in the Inspire suite are only mentioned briefly in this book.

Use the detailed table of contents and comprehensive index to help you find what you are looking for. In addition to procedures, look for all the hints, tips, and cautions that can help you save time, avoid problems, and make your courses more engaging.

 **DESIGN TIP**

Design Tips give you insight on how to implement the different features and include everything from graphic design to instructional design to usability.

 **CAUTION**

Pay special attention to the Cautions (which are full of "lessons learned the hard way") so you can avoid some common problems.

 **BRIGHT IDEA**

Bright Ideas are special explanations and ideas for getting more out of the software.

 **POWER TIP**

Power Tips are advanced tips and secrets that can help you take your production to the next level.

 **TIME SAVER**

Time Savers...well...save you time. These tips include software shortcuts and ways to streamline your production efforts.

 This symbol indicates a cross-reference to another part of the book.

 This symbol indicates a feature that is new or significantly enhanced in Lectora version 11.

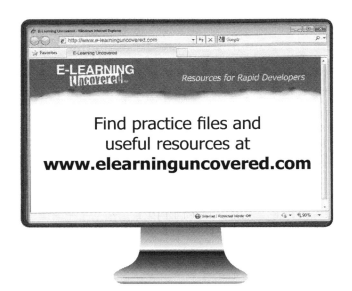

Find practice files and useful resources at **www.elearninguncovered.com**

# Getting to Know Lectora

## Introduction

Lectora by Trivantis Corporation Inc. is a rapid development (meaning no programming required) e-learning development tool. It is available in three versions:

- Lectora Publisher: This is the core e-learning software and is what this book covers. This is the tool you need to create a full e-learning course with interactions, quizzing, tracking, etc.

- Lectora Inspire: Inspire is a suite of tools that starts with Lector Publisher and then adds some additional tools to create media: Camtasia (for capturing screen simulations), Snagit (for taking screen captures and editing images), and Flypaper (for creating template-based interactions). The core Lectora e-learning software covered in this book is the same in both Inspire and Publisher. (The extra media tools are not covered in this book.)

- Lectora Online: This is an online version of Lectora Publisher that is especially useful in a collaborative team environment. Rather than installing the software and saving the course files to your computer, both the software and your development files reside online. This lets more than one person at a time work on a course. While this book does not specifically teach Lectora Online, many of the features are the same as Lectora Publisher.

In this first chapter, you'll learn your way around the Lectora interface, which is significantly different for version 11. In this version, Lectora moves away from the menu/toolbar design to a tab/ribbon design that makes it easier to find what you need.

### In This Chapter

- The Lectora Interface
- Opening, Closing, and Saving Titles

# Notes

# The Lectora Interface

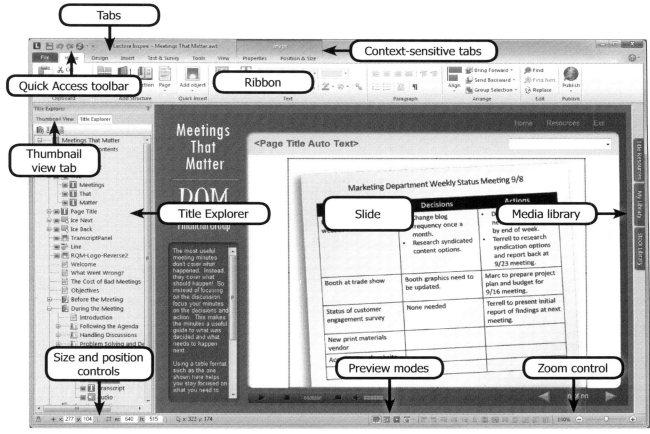

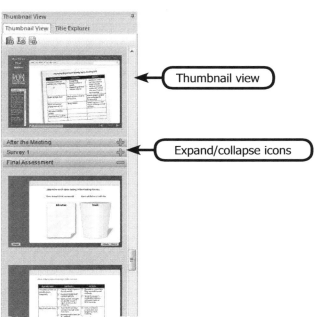

# The Title Explorer

The elements of a Lectora course, known as a title, are organized much like a book. The title is the highest level and contains individual pages that can be organized into chapters. These chapters can be further divided into sections and sub-sections.

The title, chapters, sections, and pages are all organized in a tree-style outline menu in the **Title Explorer**. Objects, such as images, media elements, and actions, live at the title, chapter, section, or page level.

- Click a page to show that page in the work area. While in **Edit** mode, use your **Page Up** and **Page Down** keys to move between pages.
- Click the plus or minus icons to expand or collapse chapters, sections, pages, and objects.
- Click the gray box next to an object to hide it from view on the page. Click the box again to return it to view. (This does not affect how the objects are published—just how it appears in **Edit** mode.)
- Click in a text label, and then click in it again to rename it.

 **BRIGHT IDEAS**

- Take the time to name your objects logically. This makes it easier to work with certain functions and easier for you or someone else to come back and make changes later.
- To quickly expand or collapse multiple objects, right-click a page, section, or chapter, and select **Expand All** or **Collapse All**. For example, if you do this on a chapter, it expands all sections, pages, and objects in that chapter.
- If you'd rather not have the **Title Explorer** showing at all times, click the pushpin icon at the top of the pane. This collapses the pane to a tab on the side of the interface that only appears when you roll over the tab. Click the pushpin again to lock it back into place.

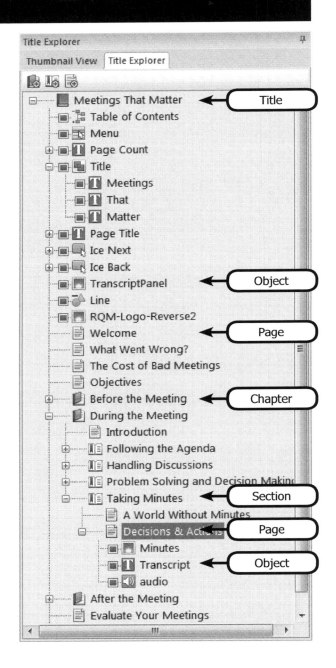

# View Modes

Whether you want to edit your project or see how the finished course will look, there are several different view modes to work in. You can access these modes from the **View** tab or from the buttons at the bottom of the interface.

### Edit Mode

This is the default mode, and it is where you create and edit your content. When you are in **Edit** mode, buttons, links, and other actions are not active.

### Preview Mode

In this mode, the buttons, links, and other actions are functioning. The Lectora interface is still visible, but you cannot make any changes. You can still use the **Title Explorer** to navigate around the course.

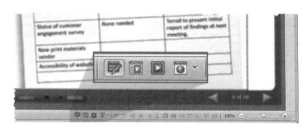

### Run Mode

This mode is similar to **Preview** mode, but the Lectora interface is hidden. Once in **Run** mode, press the **Esc** key to return to **Edit** mode.

### Debug Mode

Debug mode runs the title in **Run** mode with a separate window that tells you what is happening. As you navigate through the course, the **Debug** window logs all actions as they happen, along with any variables. This helps you make sure everything is working properly and can help you troubleshoot any problems, especially on advanced interactions.

Debug window

### Preview Page in Browser Mode

This option shows the current page in your default browser. If you click the drop-down arrow below or next to the button, you can choose from the different browsers installed on your computer.

If you are publishing your course for the web, it's a good idea to preview it in a browser, because the browser may create a slightly different result than **Run** mode. If you need to preview more than one page in a browser, publish the course to HTML and click the **Preview** button in the final dialog box.

 Publishing, ch. 17

## ⚠ CAUTION

When you use the **Preview Page in Browser** mode, only the page you are working on gets generated. Because of this, any links to other pages are inactive.

# Opening, Closing, and Saving Titles

## Open an Existing Title

**If the Getting Started dialog box is open:**

1. Find and select the title you want in the **Recent Titles** section. **(A)**

——— or ———

1. Click the **Browse** button. **(B)**
2. Find and select the title you want.
3. Click the **Open** button.

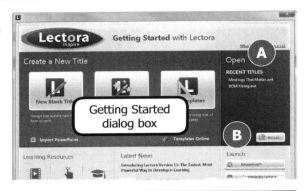

**If the Getting Started dialog box is not open:**

1. Go to the **File** tab.
2. Select **Open Existing Title. (C)**
3. Find and select the title you want.
4. Click the **Open** button.

——— or ———

1. Go to the **File** tab.
2. Select **Recent Titles. (D)**
3. Find and select the title you want.

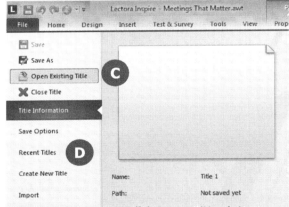

## Close a Title

**To close a title:**

1. Click the red **X** button in the top-right corner of the interface.

——— or ———

1. Go to the **File** tab.
2. Click **Close Title**.

If you have unsaved changes, Lectora will ask if you want to save changes before closing the title.

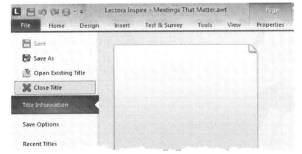

# Save a Title

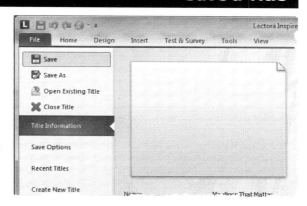

**To save with the same name in the same location:**

1. Press **Ctrl + S**.

—— or ——

1. Click the **Save** button on the **Quick Access** toolbar.

—— or ——

1. Go to the **File** menu.
2. Click **Save**.

If this is the first time you are saving, Lectora asks for a title name and location.

**To save with a different name or location:**

1. Go to the **File** menu.
2. Click **Save As**.
3. Enter a new name and/or location.
4. Click the **Save** button.

# Save Options

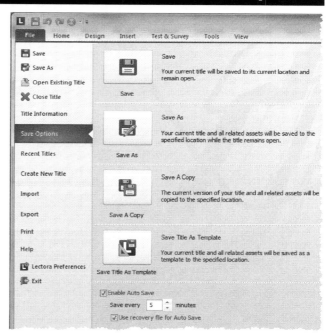

If you select **Save Options** from the **File** menu, there are a few additional options for saving.

### Save a Copy

This option is similar to **Save As**. The difference is which file remains open. When you use **Save As**, the newly saved file remains open, rather than the original. When you use **Save a Copy**, the original file stays open, rather than the newly saved version.

### Save Title as a Template

This option saves the title properties and title-level objects as a template, making it easier to create new titles with the same properties.

 Templates p. 238

### Auto Save

By default, Lectora auto saves your title every 5 minutes. If the software or your system fails, then the next time you open that title, a dialog box appears asking if you want to open the recovered files.

- Uncheck the **Enable Auto Save** box if you don't want the backup copy to be saved.

- Change the frequency of the backup by entering the number of minutes you want.

- Your "live" version only gets saved when YOU save it, and the backup version is saved as a separate file (with ~$ in front) that you only restore if you need to. Uncheck the bottom check box if you'd like the live version to auto save over itself.

## File Structure

When you create or save a copy of a title, Lectora automatically sets up a file structure for you. It is important that you keep these files together and do not rename them.

- **Extern** folder: If you have an action that launches a document or you added a file in the title properties, it is kept here.

- **Images** folder: All photos, graphics, and animations you place in the title are kept here.

- **Media** folder: All audio and video elements you place in the title are kept here.

- **~$Filename.awt** (Lectora Title): If you see a copy of your title document with ~$ in front of it, it means there is an auto-save version of the course.

- **Filename.awt** (Lectora Title): The **.awt** file is the main Lectora file that you open to edit or publish your course.

- **Filename.ini** (Configuration settings): This file is automatically generated. You do not need to do anything with it.

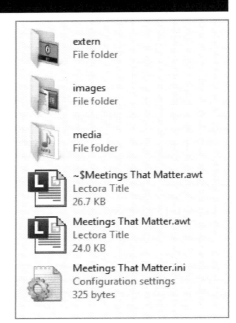

 **BRIGHT IDEA**

You generally won't need to directly open up the auto save version (~$) from your project files. If Lectora crashes, reopen Lectora and you will be asked if you want to restore the auto save version.

# Setting up a Title

## Introduction

In this chapter, you'll learn about the structure of a Lectora course, referred to as a title. Just like a book, your title can be organized into chapters, sections, and pages. Lectora gives you a high level of control over features and properties at each level of the course. You can manually configure all of your settings or use the various template and wizard options to help you get started.

Taking the time up front to think about the important design considerations of your course structure is like starting a house with a detailed blueprint--it makes everything else that much easier to build.

### In This Chapter

- New Title Options
- Title Properties and Options
- Chapters, Sections, and Sub-Sections
- Assignable Units
- Adding Pages

# Notes

# New Title Options

When you are ready to set up a new title (new course), you have several options.

**Blank Title**: When you use this option, you get a completely blank title with one page in it. This is best when you want to create completely custom navigation, interface, structure, etc.

**Themes**: This option gives you a one-page title with a set of formatted elements such as a header bar and buttons. The theme can be changed after you have created the title.

**Templates**: When you select this option, you can choose from hundreds of templates, including templates for mobile, tablet, and Section 508 courses. Each template has one or more pages with basic navigation and graphic elements in place, and you create the structure from scratch.

**Design Wizard**: The **Design Wizard** walks you through the setup process, creating a title that has the structure and even the text you enter in the wizard. There are several formats and designs to choose from. This option is best when you know what you want in advance and want some help setting up the structure. This option will be taught at the end of this chapter.

**Title Wizard**: The **Title Wizard** is like a cross between templates and the design wizard. It is like templates because the titles come with navigation and design elements. It is like the design wizard in that you can make some choices to customize your title.

**Import PowerPoint**: You can create a new title by importing a PowerPoint file. (Covered in chapter 15.)

Some of these options can be found on both the **File** tab and the **Getting Started** window, which appears anytime you start Lectora. Others can be found in only one of those places.

## Create a New Blank Title

**To create a new blank title:**

1. Launch Lectora.
2. In the **Getting Started window**, click **Create New Title**.

———— or ————

1. Go to the **File** tab.
2. Select **Create New Title**.
3. Click **Blank Title**.

 **CAUTION**

In previous versions of Lectora, you had to save your title as part of the creation process. In Lectora 11, you do not. So be sure to save your title after creating it.

 Saving, p. 7

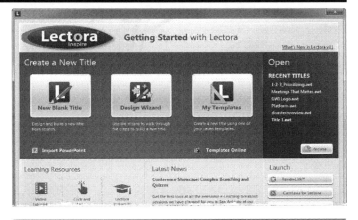

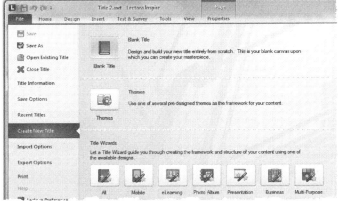

# Create a New Title With a Theme

A theme is a pre-designed layout with some combination of a header, footer, title, and navigation buttons. You can design a new title from a theme, change the theme after you create the title, create a blank title and add a theme later, or add a theme as part of the **Design Wizard** or **Title Wizard**.

**To create a new title with a theme:**

1. Go to the **File** menu.
2. Select **Create New Title**.
3. Click the **Themes** button. **(A)**
4. In the panel that appears on the right, select the size you want. **(B)**
5. Select the thumbnail for the color theme you want.
6. Click the **Create from Theme** button.

 Page size, p. 16

Once your title is created, you can change the theme from the **Design** tab. **(C)**

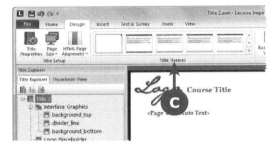

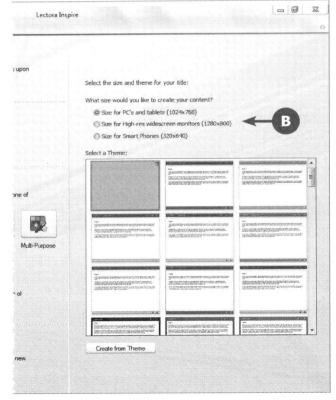

# Create a New Title From a Template

You can create a new title from a template that you've created or imported yourself, or from one from the online template library.

**To create a new title from a template:**

1. Launch Lectora to bring up the **Launch Pad**.

— or —

1. Go to the **File** tab.
2. Select **Create New Title**.

— then —

3. Click the **My Templates** or the **Templates Online** button. **(A)**
4. Find and select the template you want. **(B)**
5. Click the **Create From Template** button. **(C)**

 Saving a title as a template, p. 238

 **TIME SAVER**

If you are creating a tablet-friendly, mobile-friendly, or Section 508 course, be sure to look for templates that are already configured for those purposes.

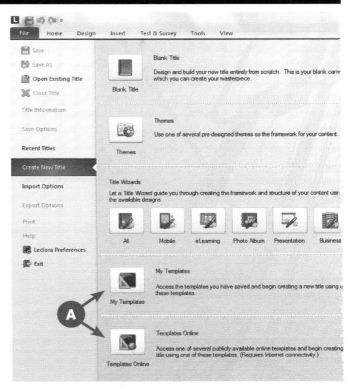

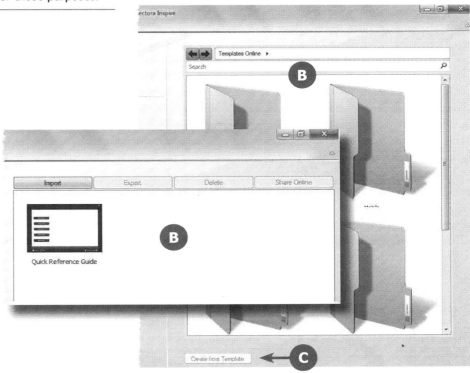

# Create a New Title From the Title Wizard

**To create a new title from the Title Wizard:**

1. Go to the **File** menu.

2. Select **Create New Title**.

3. In the **Title Wizards** section, select the type of title you want. **(A)**

4. In the panel that appears, find and select the format you want. **(B)**

5. Click the **Start Wizard** button. **(C)**

6. Enter a name for the title. **(D)**

7. Click the **Choose Folder** button.

8. Find and select the location where you want to save the title.

9. Click the **OK** button.

10. Click the **Next** button.

11. Answer the questions about the design and structure of your course. The questions will vary based on the type of title you chose. **(E)**

12. Repeat steps 10 and 11 until there are no more options.

13. Click the **Finish** button. **(F)**

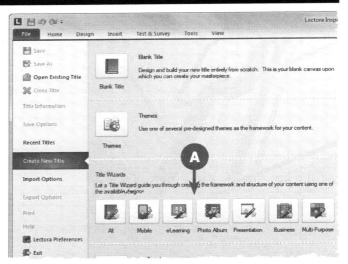

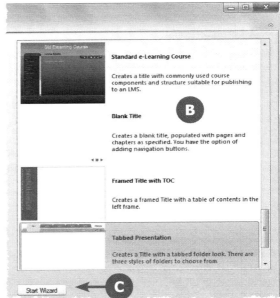

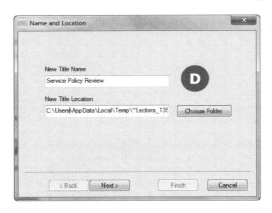

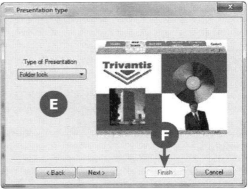

# Title Properties and Options

Before setting up individual chapters and pages, it is a good idea to configure your title-level properties and settings first.  These include logic settings, such as whether the course will integrate with a learning management system, and design settings, such as the page size and background color.  These options are found on the **Design** tab.

## Change Title Options

### To change the title options:
1. Go to the **Design** tab.
2. Click the **Title Properties** button.
3. Change the settings you want.
4. Click the **OK** button.

## Title Properties Options

### Name
Here you can change the name of the title.  You can also do this from the title explorer.

### Title Type
This field governs whether or not logic is included for the course to "talk" to a learning management system (LMS) or a learning record store (LRS).  Select **Standard** if you will not be integrating with one of these databases.

 Publishing, ch. 17

### Enable Dynamic Text Option
If you check this box, you can designate text boxes as dynamic text.  When you do this, the text is copied to an associated XML file that you can update without opening Lectora or republishing.

 Dynamic text, p. 48

### Use Web Accessibility Settings
If you are designing your course to be accessible to those with disabilities, you may want to check this box to disable some of the Lectora features that are not accessible, including lightbox pop-up windows and enabling ALT tags.

 Accessibility, p. 215

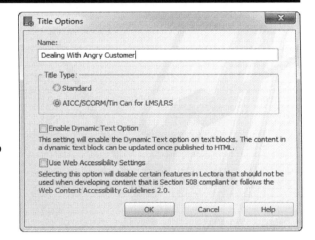

###  BRIGHT IDEA

#### What are AICC, SCORM, and Tin Can?

These are industry standards for how e-learning courses and learning management systems communicate.  If you have a SCORM-compliant course, it should be able to "talk" successfully to a SCORM-compliant LMS.  Similarly, an AICC-compliant course should talk to an AICC-compliant LMS, Tin Can would talk to Tin Can, etc.

**AICC**: Aviation Industry CBT Committee

**SCORM**: Shareable Content Object Reference Model

**Tin Can**: This is the newest generation of SCORM, which includes both learning management systems and learning record stores.

# Adjust Page Size

One of the first things you do when setting up your title is to get the page size the way you want it.  You can change the page size later, but you may need to resize and reposition all of your elements.

When you change the page size on the **Design** tab, it affects all pages in the title.  You can then override it on individual chapters, sections, or pages on the Properties tab for that object.

**To change the page size:**

1. Go to the **Design** tab.
2. Click the **Page Size** button.
3. Select the pre-set page size you want.

———— or ————

3. Select **Custom Size**.
4. Enter the width and height.
5. Click the **OK** button.

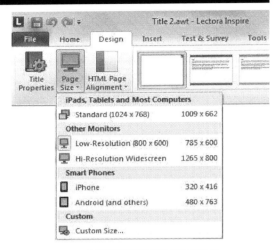

## DESIGN TIP

With HTML courses for PC, mobile, or tablets, consider the size of the display plus the space needed for the browser.  If you set the page size to 1024 x 768 for a 1024 x 768 monitor, the course still scrolls, because of the space needed for the browser.

If students were using the browser shown below, your page would need to be about 995 x 616 to prevent scrolling.

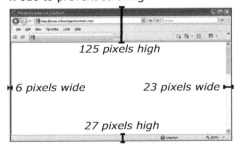

*125 pixels high*

*6 pixels wide*          *23 pixels wide*

*27 pixels high*

Check your title on the target devices before you get too far into the design process.  It's a lot easier to resize a course at the beginning than at the end.

## Adjust Page Alignment

You can determine how you want your pages aligned if the user's browser window is bigger than the course. This setting controls the alignment of the entire page and does not affect the elements on the page.

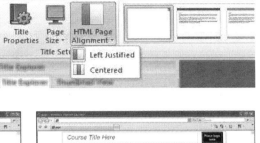

**To change page alignment:**
1. Go to the **Design** tab.
2. Click the **HTML Page Alignment** button.
3. Select **Left Justified** or **Centered**.

*Left justified*

*Centered*

## Apply or Change Themes

Themes are sets of objects and formatting that apply to the entire title. A theme includes:

- Page size
- Interface graphics
- Navigational elements

You can apply a theme at any time to your project, and can even change it after you've already started to build your course.

**To apply or change themes:**
1. Go to the **Design** tab.
2. Select the theme you want.

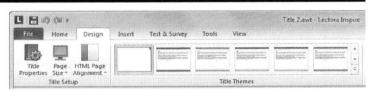

### CAUTION

If you change your theme after you've started adding content, be sure to go back through your pages to make sure that all of your page elements look good. Since some themes have more/larger graphics than others, you'll want to make sure your page objects don't interfere with the new theme graphics.

# Create a Background With the Background Wizard

The **Background Wizard** lets you create a custom page background very quickly. If you use the **Design** tab, the background will apply to the whole title. This can be overridden at the chapter, section, or page level, using that object's **Properties** tab.

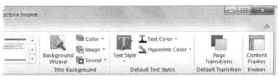

**To create a background with the Background Wizard:**

1. Go to the **Design** tab.
2. Click the **Background Wizard** button.
3. Select the range of pages you want to apply the background to.
4. Click the **Next** button.
5. Select the type of background you want.
6. Click the **Next** button.
7. Configure formatting options such as size, color, and placement. (Options vary based on the type of background you choose.)
8. Click the **Finish** button.

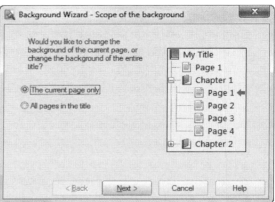

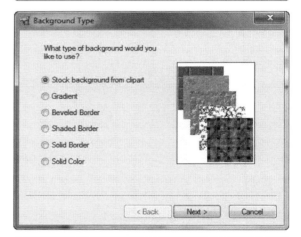

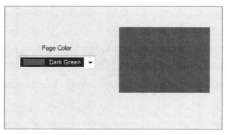

*Solid color options*

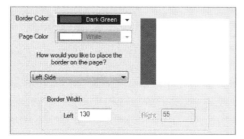

*Gradient, beveled, shaded, and solid border options*

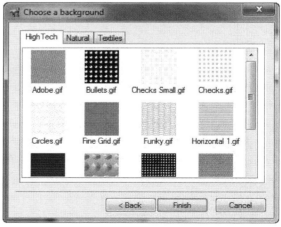

*Stock background from clipart*

# Apply a Background Color, Image, or Sound

You can also add individual elements to your page backgrounds. These elements apply to the whole title, but can be overridden at the chapter, section, or page level. You can pull images and sounds from a file on your computer or from your media library in Lectora.

 Media library, p. 218

**To apply a background color:**
1. Go to the **Design** tab.
2. Click the **Color** button.
3. Select the color you want.

 Selecting colors, p. 64

**To add a background image:**
1. Go to the **Design** tab.
2. Click the **Image** button.
3. Select **Browse for File** or **Browse My Media**.
4. Find and select the image you want.
5. Click the **Open** button.

**To add a background sound:**
1. Go to the **Design** tab.
2. Click the **Sound** button.
3. Select **Browse for File** or **Browse My Media**.
4. Find and select the sound file you want.
5. Click the **Open** button.

**To remove a background image or sound:**
1. Go to the **Design** tab.
2. Click the **Image** or **Sound** button.
3. Select **None**.

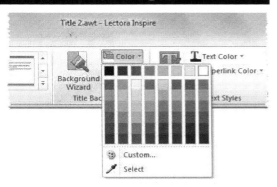

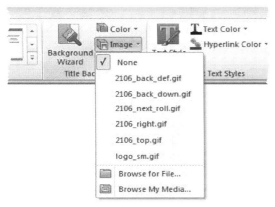

 ## CAUTION

When you add a background color or image using the methods on this page or the previous page, the background may fill the entire HTML page. So if the page is bigger than the course, the background may extend beyond the course. Preview your course to make sure this is what you want.

 ## DESIGN TIP

Just because you can, doesn't mean you should. Use these design options with care.

- Strong background colors can make it difficult to read text and see other elements on a page.
- Background images can take the focus away from where it should be—your page's content.
- Background audio is played each time a new page loads. This can get annoying if you aren't careful.

There can be a time and a place to use all of these design options. Make sure your design choices support your message instead of competing with it.

# Apply Page Transitions

On the **Design** tab, you can designate a transition to use when every new page loads, similar to the slide transitions in PowerPoint. These can be overridden at the chapter, section, or page level.

**To apply page transitions to all pages in the title:**

1. Go to the **Design** tab.
2. Click the **Page Transitions** button.
3. From the **Transitions** menu, select the transition you want.
4. From the **Transition Options** menu, select the option (such as **Up** or **Down**) you want.
5. Using the slider, select the speed you want.
6. Click the **OK** button.

 **CAUTION**

Page transitions can slow down a course. Buttons and links don't work until the page transition is finished, and the transition doesn't even start until the whole page is loaded. If a connection is slow, your students can get frustrated if they have to wait that extra time to get their content.

# Enable Frames

When you use frames, the page is divided into parts that can be built and navigated separately. For example, you can have a frame on the left with a table of contents and a frame on the right with your content pages. If the user changes the page or scrolls down on the right, the frame on the left stays the same. If you decide to add frames, your page and your **Title Explorer** are split up.

**To enable frames for your title:**

1. Go to the **Design** tab.
2. Click the **Content Frames** button.
3. Select the frame structure you want.
4. Select the frame border option you want.
5. Enter the sizes you want.
6. Click **OK**.

## Frame Options

**Use Thick Visible Frames**: If you check this option, a visible border is added between the frames. If you leave it unchecked, there is no visual indication where one frame stops and another one starts.

**Specify Size in Percentages**: If you will be adjusting the size of the frames, check this box if you prefer to work with a percentage of the screen instead of pixels.

**Top Row Height/Left Column Width**: Each frame comes pre-set with certain widths and heights for the frames. In these two fields, you can change the pixel size (or percentage) of the different frames to customize the overall page layout.

## Building Content in Your Frames

The **Title Explorer** contains one area for each of the panes, much like a section or chapter, that can have its own objects, chapters, sections, pages, etc.

The page is split up also. You can only place objects on the part of the page that's active in the **Title Explorer**.

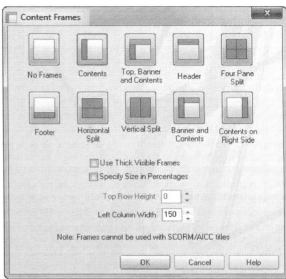

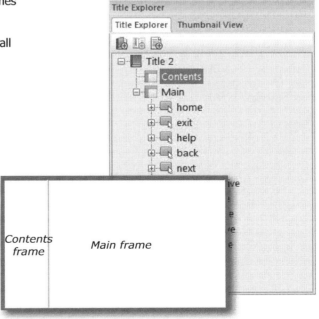

 **CAUTION**

Frames are not AICC- or SCORM-compatible.

# Set Default Text Attributes

On the **Design** tab, you can set default text attributes for your title. These include:

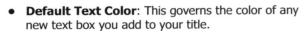

- **Default Text Style**: this governs the text attributes of any new text box you add to your title.

 Text styles, p. 40

- **Default Text Color**: This governs the color of any new text box you add to your title.

- **Hyperlink Color**: By default, hyperlinks are blue before they have been clicked and purple after they have been clicked. Here you can designate the "pre-click" color for a hyperlink.

 Selecting colors, p. 64

**To change the default text style:**
1. Go to the **Design** tab.
2. Click the **Text Style** drop-down button. **(A)**
3. Select the style you want.

**To change the default text color:**
1. Go to the **Design** tab.
2. Click the **Text Color** drop-down button. **(B)**
3. Select the color you want.

**To change the hyperlink color:**
1. Go to the **Design** tab.
2. Click the **Hyperlink Color** drop-down button. **(C)**
3. Select the color you want.

# Create a New Title With the Design Wizard

**To create a new title with the Design Wizard:**

1. Launch Lectora to bring up the **Getting Started** window.
2. Click the **Design Wizard** button.

3. Enter a name for your title.
4. Click the **Browse** button.
5. Find and select the folder where you want to save the title.
6. Click the **OK** button.
7. Select **No** or **Yes** based on whether the course will integrate with an AICC/SCORM learning management system or Learning Record Store.

    Title properties, p. 15

8. Click the **Next** button.

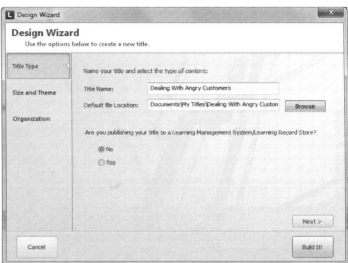

9. Select the page size you want.

    Page size, p. 16

10. Select a theme.

     Themes, p. 17

11. Click the **Next** button.

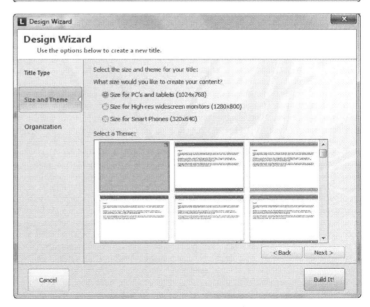

# Create a New Title With the Design Wizard (cont'd)

12. Select **Pages only** or **Chapters and Pages**, based on what structure you want to give your title.

13. In the table, enter the names for the chapters or pages. (Click the **X** button to delete a line. Click in the last row to add a new one.)

14. Check the box if you want to include a graded test.

15. Click the **Build It** button.

You can change any of these decisions after the title has been created. For example, you can go to the **Design** tab to change page size, theme, etc.

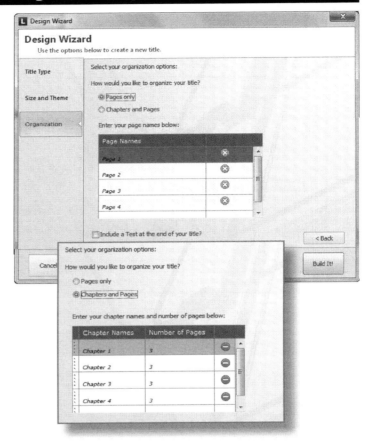

# Chapters, Sections, and Sub-Sections

Once your title is set up, you can add pages to it that can be organized in chapters, sections, and sub-sections. Organizing your pages this way has several benefits.

- Each unit (chapter, section, or sub-section) can have its own properties. This means the pages in that unit can have a different size, color, default font, etc.

- You can place an object at the highest level of a unit to make it appear on every page in that unit. For example, if you put a section title text box at the section level, it appears automatically on every page in the section, but not anywhere else in the title. You only have to place that text box once.

- Any unit can exclude items found elsewhere in the title. For example, if you want to have a section that doesn't have the next and back buttons, you can remove them at the section level. They won't appear on the pages of that section, and you didn't have to go to the trouble of removing them from every single page.

- When working on your title in Lectora, these units can help keep your **Title Explorer** organized, making it easier to find everything. Plus, if you need to select a page or object from a dialog box, it will be easier to find there as well.

- Chapter/page structure and names are shown in the table of contents feature. Your students may benefit from seeing the organizational structure as well.

## Understanding Inheritance

When you add an object at a certain level, that object appears on every page in that level. In the image on the right:

- The top seven objects are "attached" to the title level, meaning they appear on every page in the title. These are the interface and navigational elements.

- The **Chapter Title** text box lives at the chapter level. This means it appears on every page in that chapter. The second chapter is broken into sections and sub-sections. The text box appears on all of them.

- In contrast, the **Page Title** text box and **1-2 audio** file live on an individual page. That means those items only appear on that page.

By default, objects appear on every page at or below that level in the hierarchy. This is known as inheritance. However, it is possible to "disinherit" certain objects if you don't want them. For example:

- On the very last page of the course, you wouldn't want a **Next** button since there isn't a page to go to. So you can turn off the inheritance of the button on that one page.

- You may have an entire chapter (such as a test chapter) in which you don't want the students to be able to go back. You can turn off the inheritance of the **Back** button at the chapter level, meaning nothing in that chapter will show the button.

Inheritance is controlled on the **Properties** tab for the chapters, sections, sub-sections, and pages.

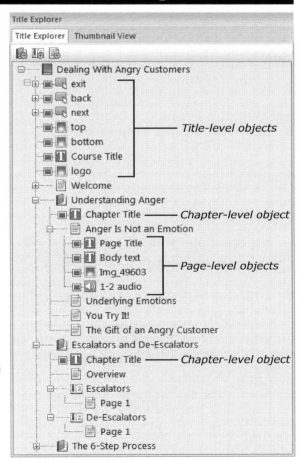

## Add a New Chapter

**To add a chapter to the title:**

1. In the **Title Explorer**, select the object you want the new chapter to come after.
2. Go to the **Home** tab.
3. Click the **Chapter** button.

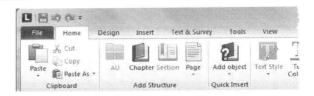

## Add a New Section

**To add a section to a chapter:**

1. In the **Title Explorer**, select the chapter or page in a chapter you want the new section to come after.
2. Go to the **Home** tab.
3. Click the **Section** button.

 **BRIGHT IDEAS**

- You can only add a section if you are in a chapter. Otherwise, the **Section** button is inactive.
- You can only add a sub-section if you are in a section.
- Your sub-sections can have sub-sections, too.

## Add a New Sub-Section

Sub-sections can be added to sections and other sub-sections. They don't have their own button, but rather rely on the regular **Section** button. Sub-sections have all the same features and properties as regular sections. Throughout the book, if you see anything related to a section, it applies to sub-sections as well.

**To add a sub-section to a section:**

1. In the **Title Explorer**, select the section, sub-section, or page you want the new sub-section to come after.
2. Go to the **Home** tab.
3. Click the **Section** button.

# Chapter and Section Properties

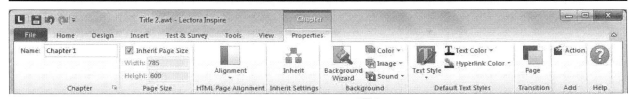

When you select a chapter or section icon in the **Title Explorer**, the corresponding **Properties** tab appears. The options are the same for both and mimic the **Design** tab, where the title-level properties are set.

 Title-level properties and settings, pp. 15-20
Actions, ch. 8

By default, all of the properties are set to the same as the level above them. (Chapter properties are the same as the title; section properties are the same as the chapter; etc.) You can change/override the properties using this tab.

## DESIGN TIP

Why might you want to override some of these settings? You might want to:

- Use a different background color for your quiz chapter.
- Create a glossary that has long scrolling pages.
- Create a chapter of pop-up pages that are smaller than the main course page.

# Disinheriting Objects

By default, chapters and sections (except test/survey chapters) inherit all objects from the level above them. Chapters show all title-level objects; sections show all title and chapter objects. You can change that with inheritance.

If you disinherit an object at the chapter level, it does not appear in any sections or pages in that chapter.

**To disinherit all objects from higher levels:**
1. Select the chapter, section, or page you want to disinherit objects for.
2. Go to the **Properties** tab.
3. Click the **Inherit** button.
4. From the drop-down menu, select **ALL objects from parents**.
5. Click the **OK** button.

**To disinherit specific objects from higher levels:**
   *Perform steps 1–3 above.*
4. From the drop-down menu, select **Specific objects from parents**.
5. Select the objects on the left that you want to disinherit.
6. Click the button with the right-facing arrows.
7. Click the **OK** button.

**To re-inherit all objects:**
   *Perform steps 1–4 above.*
5. Select the objects on the right that you want to re-inherit.
6. Click the button with the left-facing arrows.
7. Click the **OK** button.

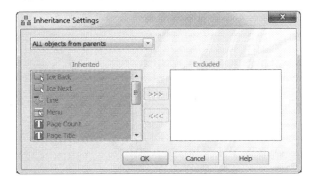

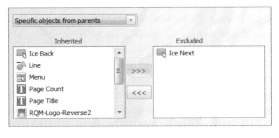

# Assignable Units

Lectora defines an assignable unit as "the largest unit of organization in an AICC/SCORM published title." When you select **AICC/ SCORM for LMS** in the title properties, an assignable unit (AU) is automatically added to your title, and all the objects in the title fall under it.

You have the option of keeping just the one AU, or adding several AUs. Each AU will be launched and tracked separately in your LMS. You can also configure properties for the AU, which impacts how it works with your LMS. (If you are not working with an LMS, you don't need assignable units.)

 Title properties and settings, p. 15

 **BRIGHT IDEA**

"Assignable unit" is a term that comes from the AICC standard. It is the same as a SCO (Shareable Content Object) in the SCORM standard.

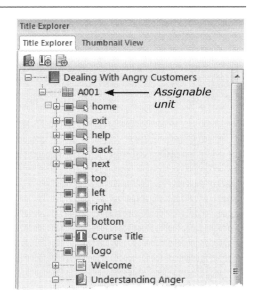

# Assignable Unit Properties

On an assignable unit's **Properties** tab, you'll find many of the same property options as for chapters and sections: page size, alignment, background, etc. If you just have one AU, you won't need to change any of these, because the title-level properties apply. If you have more than one AU and you want each one to have its own properties, then this is where you would change them.

# Assignable Unit Information

The assignable unit's Information tab is where you would enter information about how the AU interacts with the learning management system or learning record store.

**System ID**: An automatically-generated system identifier.

**Developer ID**: The developer of the assignable unit. Some LMSs keep track of the developer of the course, letting users search for a course by developer.

**AU Type**: A description of the type of assignable unit within the LMS. For example, one LMS may differentiate between a curriculum, a course, and a lesson. Another might use a course, a module, and a chapter.

**Description**: A text description of the assignable unit.

**Maximum Point Score**: The total number of points possible in the assignable unit. If you leave it blank, it assumes 100 points for each graded test.

**Mastery Score**: The minimum score required to pass.

**Time Limit**: The maximum amount of time the student is allowed to spend in the assignable unit. If you want to have a time limit, first check the **Enable** box, and then set the hours and minutes for the limit. Then set the action to be taken when the student uses the allotted time.

**Prerequisites**: Other AUs within the same title that are required before the student can take this AU.

## POWER TIPS

- When publishing to AICC/SCORM, there must be at least one assignable unit.
- If it is your first time publishing a course to a certain LMS, do a test early with a sample course.
- You may find it is easier to set and change properties such as a description and minimum passing score directly in the LMS, rather than here in your title.
- When you have multiple assignable units in one title, you cannot have links that go back and forth between the different AUs. (Although you can if you publish using the SCORM (disconnected) option.)

# Add Extra Assignable Units

If you have enabled AICC/SCORM/Tin Can for your project, you an add more than one assignable unit to your title so that each AU is tracked separately in the LMS.

**To add an extra assignable unit:**

1. Go to the **Home** tab.
2. Click the **AU** button.

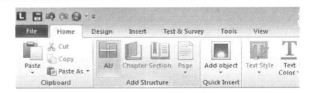

# Adding Pages

When you add a chapter or section, one page is automatically added. You can add as many additional pages as you want with the **Page** button.

By default, a page uses the properties of the section or chapter it is in. However, you can click the page icon in the **Title Explorer** to enable the **Properties** tab. Just change the settings on the **Properties** tab to override the default settings on that particular page.

For example, you may want to:

- Add a background sound to play music or sound effects for that page.
- Disinherit the **Back** button on the first page of the title.
- Change the page size of your FAQ page to make it longer.

Page properties are very similar to chapter and section properties, with the exception of **Metadata**, covered on the next page.

 **BRIGHT IDEA**

Looking for how to exclude a chapter, section, or page from a table of contents? That feature is now on the **Properties** tab of the table of contents object itself.

 Table of Contents, p. 138

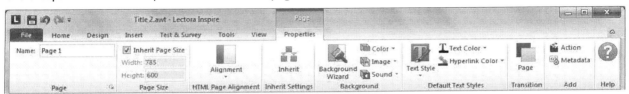

## Add a New Page

**To add a new page:**

1. In the **Title Explorer**, select the object you want the new section to come after.
2. Go to the **Home** tab.
3. Click the **Page** drop-down menu.
4. Select the page layout you want.

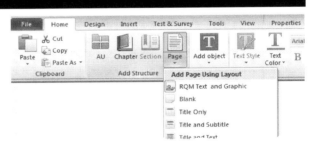

 **BRIGHT IDEA**

Version 11 now has dynamic buttons. Some buttons, like the **Page** button are split, with an icon at the top and a drop-down arrow at the bottom. Click the drop-down arrow for a full menu of options. Click the icon portion at the top for the most recently used option. The icon at the top changes based on the choice you last made.

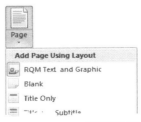

# Adding Metadata to a Page

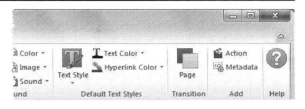

Metadata is data about data.  Search engines (including an LMS' search function) use metadata when they conduct searches.  So if you want search engines to find your pages, you might want to add metadata.  There are three options: custom, external, or IMS data elements. When you select one of these options, the bottom portion of the dialog box changes accordingly.

**To add metadata to a page:**

1. Select the page in the **Title Explorer**.
2. Go to the **Home** tab.
3. Click the **Metadata** button.
4. Check the **Use metadata** box.
5. Select the source for the metadata.
6. Enter your metadata.
7. Click the **OK** button.

## Metadata Sources

### Custom Metadata

Select this option if you want to add your own information.  Simply type it in the **Custom Metadata** field.

### Use External XML File for Custom Metadata

You can keep your metadata in an external XML file. Once you select this option, load the file at the bottom of the dialog box.

### IMS Metadata Elements (IEEE LTSC LCOM)

The IMS metadata option comes with pre-defined fields that you can add, edit, and remove.

- To add an item, click the **Add** button, select an element from the menu, and enter a value.
- To remove an item, select it, and click **Remove**.
- To edit an item, select it, click **Edit**, and change the value.

### Publish This Object's Metadata

If you uncheck this box, the metadata will be kept with the Lectora title, but will not be published with the page. You might use this if you want the term to bring up this course in a search, but not necessarily that particular page.

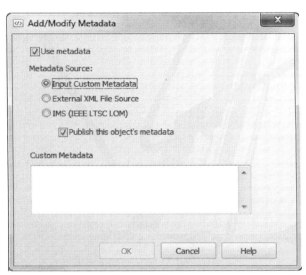

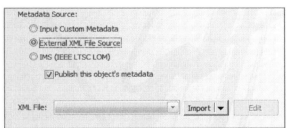

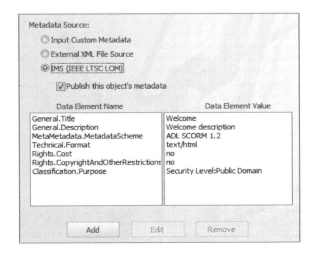

# Notes

# Working With Text

## Introduction

Text in Lectora works much like it does in PowerPoint. You can create as many moveable, resizable text boxes as you want to put text on your pages.

A text box obviously contains text, but it is also an object like any other, such as a graphic or a line. In this chapter, you'll learn about the features specific to text. Refer to chapter 5 for properties common to all objects, such as moving, resizing, selecting colors, etc.

### In This Chapter

- Adding and Editing Text
- Formatting Text
- Text Styles
- Text Block Properties
- Working With Tables
- Dynamic Text

# Notes

# Adding and Editing Text

Text boxes operate in two modes: object mode and edit mode.

- When you click a text box on a page or select it from the **Title Explorer**, you are in object mode. That means you can move, resize, or copy/paste the entire box.

- When you double-click in a text box on a page, you are in edit mode. This gives you a cursor to select, edit, and format individual bits of text.

For example, if you copy and paste in object mode, you paste the entire text box. If you copy and paste in edit mode, you paste just the selected text.

Each mode has a different right-click menu. Make sure you are in the right mode to do what you want to do.

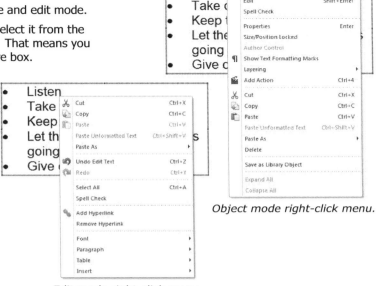

*Object mode right-click menu.*

*Edit mode right-click menu.*

---

## Add a Text Box

**To add a text box:**
1. Select the object (page, chapter, etc.) that you want to add the text to.
2. Go to the **Home** tab.
3. Click the **Add object** button.
4. Select the text icon. **(A)**

——— or ———

2. Go to the **Insert** tab.
3. Click the **Text Block** button.

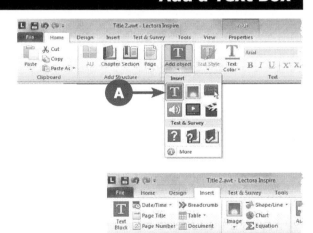

---

## Edit Text

**To edit a text box:**
1. Double-click the text box to enter **Edit** mode.
2. Make text changes as you would with any other text editing software.

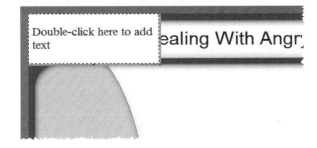

# Editing Options

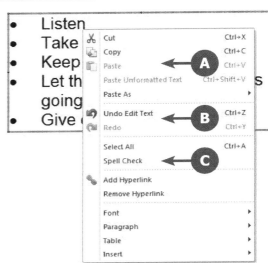

## Cut, Copy, and Paste (A)

Cut, copy, and paste text using the **Home** tab, right-click menu, or keyboard shortcuts (**Ctrl + X**, **Ctrl + C**, and **Ctrl + V**).

 **DESIGN TIP**

When you copy text from another document, there may be formatting that isn't supported by HTML. In this case, your page might look good in **Preview** mode, but not when viewed in a browser. To avoid this, you can paste in several different unformatted text options, which strip the text from any formatting. Find this option from the right-click menu or the **Paste As** drop-down menu on the **Home** tab.

## Undo and Redo (B)

Undo and redo actions from the **Quick Access** toolbar, right-click menu, or keyboard shortcuts (**Ctrl + Z** and **Ctrl + Y**).

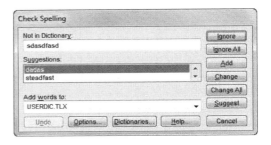

## Spell Check (C)

Run spell check either from the **Tools** tab, right-click menu, or keyboard shortcut (**F7**).

## Find and Replace (D)

Find and replace text from the **Home** tab or keyboard shortcuts (**Ctrl + F** and **Ctrl + H**).

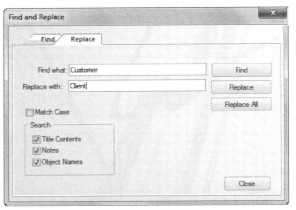

# Formatting Text

Formatting text in Lectora is much like formatting text in other word processing software. All you have to do is select the text you want to format, and then use the **Home** tab to apply the formatting. If you want to apply the formatting to the entire text box, select the whole box instead of the text itself.

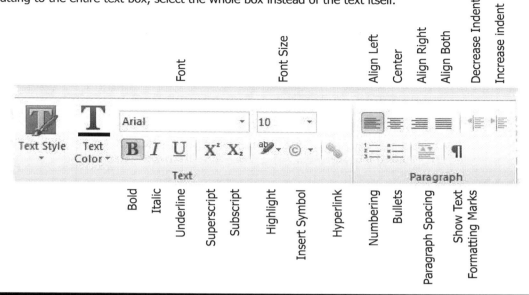

## Text Formatting Features

### Numbered Lists

If you want to change the style of the numbering or change the starting number of the list, select **Paragraph** from the right-click menu and then **Numbering Options**.

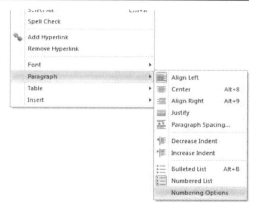

### Bulleted Lists

The **Bullet** button offers just the standard round bullet. If you want to use a special symbol or image as a bullet, consider creating a table where the first column contains the image and the second column contains the text.

### Formatting Marks

Use this option to see formatting commands in your text (such as spaces, tabs, and hard returns).

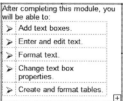

# Text Formatting Features (cont'd)

## Paragraph Spacing

If you want to put space between your paragraphs, you can do that with hard returns. However, if you instead set the paragraph spacing, you have more control over how much space is between the paragraphs – an important consideration when working with limited space on a page.

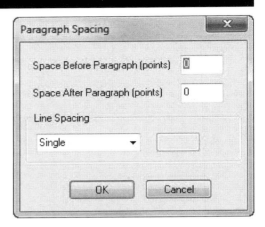

If it is your job to lead the meeting, then LEAD the meeting. This means it is your responsibility to make sure that the meeting stays focused and productive and that the participants stay engaged and professional. Sometimes this means saying what everyone thinks but no one else is willing to say. For example, when a person keeps taking the conversation off topic, it is your job to bring the conversation back on topic.
At first, it may feel like you are playing the role of the "bad guy," but in the end, everyone will appreciate

*regular spacing*

If it is your job to lead the meeting, then LEAD the meeting. This means it is your responsibility to make sure that the meeting stays focused and productive and that the participants stay engaged and professional. Sometimes this means saying what everyone thinks but no one else is willing to say. For example, when a person keeps taking the conversation off topic, it is your job to bring the conversation back on topic.

At first, it may feel like you are playing the role of the "bad guy," but in the end, everyone will appreciate

*space and a half*

If it is your job to lead the meeting, then LEAD the meeting. This means it is your responsibility to make sure that the meeting stays focused and productive and that the participants stay engaged and professional.

Sometimes this means saying what everyone thinks but no one else is willing to say. For example, when a person keeps taking the conversation off topic, it is your job to bring the conversation back on topic.

At first, it may feel like you are playing the role of the "bad guy," but in the end, everyone will appreciate

*6 points before each paragraph*

**DESIGN TIPS**

### Working With Fonts

- Typically, a sans-serif font is easier to read online, making it the best choice for your body text. Verdana, Tahoma, and Arial all make good choices for body text. Times New Roman is an example of a serif font, which works better in print.

## Verdana, Tahoma, Arial

## Times New Roman

*serifs*

- If you are publishing to HTML, use a common system font—one that is installed with most systems. (Go to www.e-learninguncovered.com for a link to a list of standard system fonts.)

- If users don't have the font you are using, their system replaces it with the font of its choice—with unpredictable results. If you want to use a non-standard font, there is an option to render it as an image to avoid that problem.

 Convert text to an image, p. 42

- Make sure your text is easy to read. Provide enough color contrast between the text and the background, and be careful about putting patterns behind text.

- Make sure your fonts are big enough for everyone to read. You may be able to read it well, but that doesn't mean everyone else can!

- A good rule of thumb is to go no lower than 11 or 12 point for body text. However, different fonts actually look bigger or smaller even if they are the same point size. Times New Roman really needs 12 point, but Verdana can often work at 10 point.

Times New Roman 12 pt

Verdana 10 pt

### Fonts and HTML

- If you are publishing your title to HTML, be sure to preview your text in a browser.

- Fonts are interpreted differently in some browsers, so the flow of your text may change.

- Some formatting attributes copied over from Word or other software may not be supported in HTML. The text would look fine in Lectora, but not in the final published course when viewed in a browser.

- Some formatting attributes offered in Lectora may not work well in HTML. For example, some browsers may have trouble with right-justified text. That formatting would look fine in a CD-published course, but not an HTML-published course.

# Text Styles

Text styles let you group together formatting attributes that you use regularly, such as font style, size, color, etc.  When you create a style for all those attributes, you can simply apply the style to your text instead of applying each attribute individually, saving you a lot of time.

In addition, styles can be updated instantly throughout your title. For example, if you hear from the marketing department that all of your screen headings are in the wrong shade of blue, all you have to do is change the style used for those headings – instead of changing each and every screen individually.

 **DESIGN TIP**

What are good uses for styles?
- Screen headings
- Instructions
- Cautions, tips, etc.
- Body text
- Captions

What are the advantages of styles?
- Save time in applying formatting.
- Ensure consistency.
- Reduce formatting mistakes.
- Make global changes quickly.

## Apply a Text Style

**To apply a text style to text:**

1. Select the text or text box you want to format.
2. Go to the **Home** tab.
3. Click the **Text Style** button.
4. Select the style you want.

 Set default text style, p. 22

## Change the Formatting of an Existing Text Style

If you want to update the formatting of text throughout your title, all you have to do is change the style once.

**To change the formatting of a text style:**

1. Select any text box.
2. Go to the **Home** tab.
3. Click the **Text Style** button.
4. Select **Manage Styles**.
5. Select the style you want to change.
6. Click the **Edit** button.
7. Make your formatting changes.
8. Click **OK**.
9. Click **Yes** to confirm you want to change the formatting throughout your title.
10. Click **Done**.

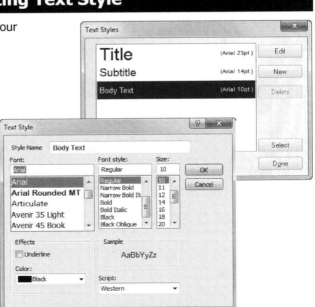

## Create a New Text Style

**To create a new text style:**

1. Select any text box.
2. Click the **Text Style** button.
3. Select **Manage Styles**.
4. Click the **New** button.
5. Enter a style name for this new style.
6. Select whatever formatting attributes you want.
7. Click **OK**.
8. Click **Done**.

 **CAUTION**

Styles are tied to your computer, not to the title. If you change a style in one title, it changes the style in other titles as well. If you don't want that to happen, you may want separate styles for each course. For example, instead of using the **Title** style, create **HR Screen Heading** and **IT Screen Heading** to use on two different projects.

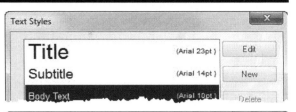

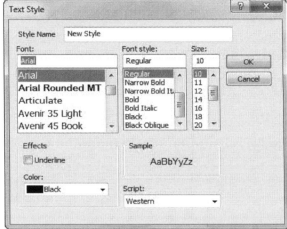

## Import and Export Styles

You can export styles and put them on a shared drive or e-mail them to other developers to import on their computers.

**To export a style:**

1. Select any text box.
2. Go to the **Home** tab.
3. Click the **Text Style** button.
4. Select **Manage Styles**.
5. Select the style you want to export.
6. Click the **Export Styles** button.
7. Navigate to where you want to save the style.
8. Change the file name, if needed.
9. Click **Save**.

**To import a style:**

1. Select any text box.
2. Go to the **Home** tab.
3. Click the **Text Style** button.
4. Select **Manage Styles**.
5. Click the **Import Styles** button.
6. Find and select the style you want.
7. Click **Open**.

*Exported styles have an .als extension.*

# Text Block Properties

Whereas you use the **Home** tab to format your text, you use the **Text Properties** tab to configure settings to the object itself. The **Properties** tab becomes available any time you select a text block. Properties that are unique to text boxes are covered here. Properties common to all objects are covered in chapter 5.

## Text Block Properties: Text Section

### Name

This is what the text block is called in the **Title Explorer**. The student does not see this name. You can change the name either here or in the **Title Explorer**.

### Label For

If you have a form element on the page, you can link your text block to be the label for that form element. This field is only active if you have a form element on the page.

 Form labels, p. 206

### Wrap Text

With this option, the text wraps around any object on top of it. Objects under the text do not change how the text flows.

### Vertical Scroll

When you want to include a lot of text in a small space, you can use a scrolling text box. This is a great way to include an on-screen transcript without taking up a lot of space.

### Convert to Image

If you want to make sure your text appears EXACTLY the way you want it to, you may want to convert your text to an image when you are publishing to HTML.

When you do this, you can still edit it like any other text box while working in Lectora. When you publish, an image is created and put in the **Images** folder.

 **CAUTION**

When you convert text to an image, you lose the option of using some of the text-related features, such as hyperlinks, vertical scroll bars, dynamic text, embedded images, or a **Change Contents** action for it. Watch for error messages when you publish.

If it is your job to lead the meeting, then LEAD the meeting. This means it is your responsibility to make sure that the meeting stays focused and productive and that the participants stay engaged and professional.

Sometimes this means saying what everyone thinks but no one else is willing to say. For example, when a person keeps taking the conversation off topic, it is your job to bring the conversation back on topic.

**LEAD MEETING**

At first, it may feel like you are playing the role of the "bad guy," but in the end, everyone will appreciate shorter, more productive meetings that don't waste anyone's time.

*Text box wrapped around a graphic.*

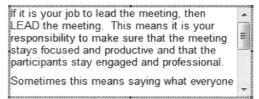

*Text box with a vertical scroll bar.*

 **DESIGN TIP**

When would you want to convert text to an image?

- You are using a non-standard font that your users are not likely to have.

- The text is very carefully lined up with objects on the page where a slight change in text flow could compromise the design or even the meaning.

Realize that converting to an image means it takes a little more bandwidth, students can't copy and paste the text, and you may lose some resolution.

# Text Block Properties: Style Section

## Background
Here you can select the background color for the text block.

## Margin Size
If you have a colored background, border, and/or outline, you may want to add a margin. This keeps the text from going all the way to the edge by adding a "buffer" area around the inside of the text box. Type in the pixel width or use the arrow buttons to designate how big you want the margin. The margin will be applied on all four sides.

## Outline
An outline is a one-pixel line around the text block. Here you can set the color for the outline.

## Border Weight
The border settings create an outline around the inside edge of your text box. Here you designate a point size to determine the weight/width of the border.

## Border
If you have designated a border weight, use this menu to select a color for the border.

## Border Style
If you have designated a border weight, use this menu to select a border style. Choose from **Cutout Bevel**, **Flat**, or **Raised Bevel**.

## Appearance and Transition Sections
The properties in these two sections are the same for most objects. You can find details in chapter 5.

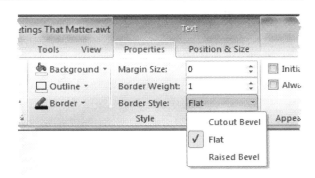

*Default setting*

*6-pixel margin*
*Beveled 3-point border*

*Black outline*
*5-point light blue border*

## Text Box Properties: Web Options Section

### Web Options Section

#### Empty ALT Tag

If you are converting the text to an image, Lectora uses the object name as the ALT tag. Check this box to use an empty ALT tag instead. This option is only active if **Convert to Image** is selected.

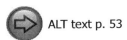

ALT text p. 53

#### Dynamic Text

If you check this box, the text will be added to the title's **dyntitle.xml** file that publishes with the course, letting you update the text outside of Lectora. This field is only active if dynamic text is enabled in the **Title Properties** dialog box.

Dynamic text p. 48

#### HTML Text Type

Changing the **HTML Text Type** can help you if you are interested in having search engines find your page. By changing the type to **Heading 1** or **Heading 2**, the text is given a higher priority by search engines.

This setting also helps screen reader users to interpret the hierarchy of your content because the screen reader recognizes the text block as a heading.

It does not change the visible formatting of your text.

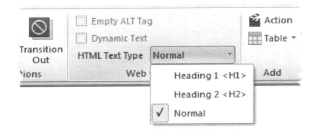

## Text Box Properties: Web Options Section

#### Action

If you click the **Action** button, it adds an action to your text box. This is the same as going to the Insert tab and selecting **Action**.

Actions, ch. 8

#### Table

Use this drop-down menu to add a table to the text box. Full details on working with tables follow on the next two pages.

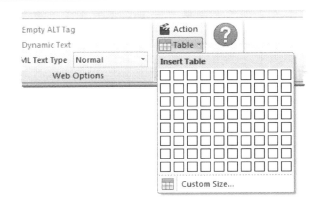

# Working With Tables

Unlike many other authoring tools, Lectora gives you the ability to make tables. You can either add a table into an existing text box or create a table in its own, new text box.

## TIME SAVER

If you already have a table in Word or if you are more comfortable creating tables in Word, you can copy and paste a table created in Word into Lectora. Just be sure to preview it in a browser if you are publishing to HTML to make sure all structure and formatting works properly.

## Create a Table

**To create a table in an existing text box:**

1. Double click in an existing text box and place the cursor where you want to insert the table.
2. Go to the **Properties** tab.
3. Click the **Table** drop-down button.
4. Click the cell that represents the number of rows and columns you want.

———— or ————

4. Select **Custom Size**.
5. Enter the number of rows and columns you want.
6. Click the **OK** button.

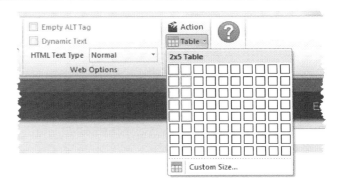

**To create a table in its own, new text box:**

1. Go to the **Insert** tab.
2. Click the **Table** drop-down button.
3. Continue with step 4 above.

## Moving Around the Table

- Just as in word processing software, click in a cell to start typing. You can also use the **Tab** key to move from cell to cell.

- To select a range of cells, click and drag your mouse across the cells you want.

- To select a column, hover your mouse over the top of a column until you see a black arrow. Then click your mouse.

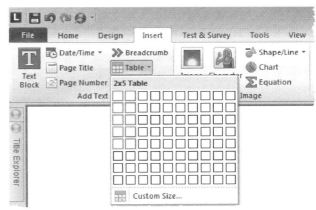

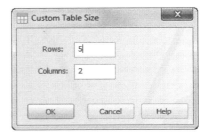

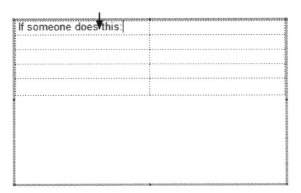

# Edit Table Structure

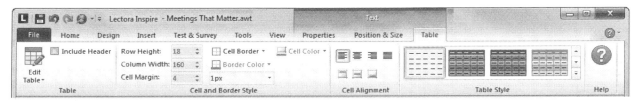

When your cursor is in any of the cells in a table, a new **Table** tab appears on the ribbon. This is where you can edit and format your table properties.

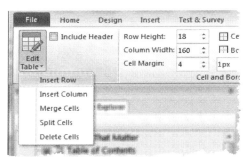

**To add rows or columns:**

1. Select the row below or the column to the right of where you want the new one.
2. Go to the **Table** tab.
3. Click the **Edit Table** drop-down button.
4. Select **Insert Row** or **Insert Column**.

**To delete rows or columns:**

1. Select the row(s) or column(s) you want to delete.
2. Go to the **Table** tab.
3. Click the **Edit Table** drop-down button.
4. Select **Delete Cells**.
5. Select **Delete Columns** or **Delete Rows** as appropriate.
6. Click the **OK** button.

**To merge or split cells:**

1. Select the cells you want to merge or split.
2. Go to the **Table** tab.
3. Click the **Edit Table** drop-down button.
4. Select **Merge Cells** or **Split Cells**.

**To change the height or width of rows or columns:**

1. Select the cells you want to modify.
2. Go to the **Table** tab.
3. Enter a new value in the **Row Height** or **Column Width** field.

———— or ————

1. Position your mouse on the edge of a row or column until you see the cursor shown to the right.
2. Click and drag your mouse to change the size.

*Merged cells*

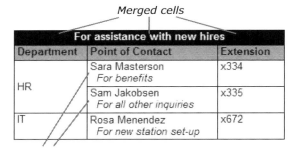

| For assistance with new hires | | |
|---|---|---|
| **Department** | **Point of Contact** | **Extension** |
| HR | Sara Masterson <br> *For benefits* | x334 |
| | Sam Jakobsen <br> *For all other inquiries* | x335 |
| IT | Rosa Menendez <br> *For new station set-up* | x672 |

*Split cells*

| If someone does this: | Try this: |
|---|---|
| Takes a discussion off topic for a minute. | Allow it for a minute or so to see if it runs its course. Sometimes it is quicker to let a tangent die on its own then start a discussion about why you shouldn't be discussing it. |

## TIME SAVER

You can access many of the same functions from the table's right-click menu.

# Format a Table

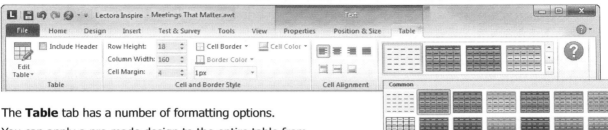

The **Table** tab has a number of formatting options.

You can apply a pre-made design to the entire table from the **Table Style** gallery. Click the drop-down arrow to see the full gallery.

Or you can select individual cells and use the **Cell and Border Style** and **Cell Alignment** sections to set up individual formatting elements on the cells selected.

 Selecting Colors, p. 64

Most of the formatting elements are self-explanatory. Here are details on a few options that do require an explanation.

### Include Header

If you have a header row in your table, such as the one in the example to the right, check the **Include Header** box. This adds some extra HTML code to help with Section 508 compliance in making it easier for assistive technology (such as a screen reader) to interpret the table.

 Accessibility, p. 215

### Cell Margin

Margin determines how much space is between the cell edges and the text. Increase this number when you don't want text to rest right against the edge of the cell.

| If someone does this: | Try this: |
|---|---|
| Takes a discussion off topic for a minute. | Allow it for a minute or so to see if it runs its course. Sometimes it is quicker to let a tangent die on its own then start a discussion about why you shouldn't be discussing it. |
| | |
| | |

*Table with table style applied*

 **DESIGN TIP**

If you want even more control over the cell borders, right-click the table, select **Table**, and then **Cell Properties**. The **Cell Properties** dialog box has most of the same options as the **Table** tab (and the **Table** tab is easier to use). However, this dialog box does give you a little more control over some features, such as the width of borders.

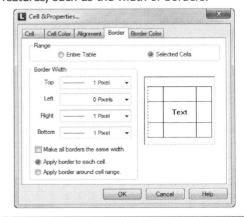

# Dynamic Text

Dynamic text lets you update text in your published course without opening Lectora or republishing the course.  You don't have to have Lectora on your computer or even have the **.awt** file.  You just need the published files and a text editor such as Notepad or Wordpad.

When you enable a text box for dynamic text, the text is included in an **.xml** file that's published with the course.  Any change to the text in that **.xml** file is updated in the course automatically.

## Add/Edit Dynamic Text

**To convert a text box to dynamic text:**

1. In **Title Options**, enable the dynamic text option for the title.  (See page 15.)
2. Select the text box you want to make dynamic.
3. Go to the **Properties** tab.
4. Check the **Dynamic Text** box. **(A)**

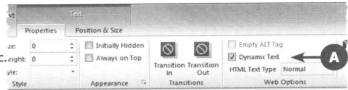

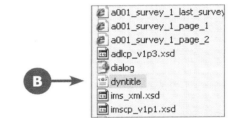

**To edit dynamic text in the published files:**

1. Open the **dyntitle.xml** file that is included in your published files.  **(B)**
2. Make the changes to the text. **(C)**
3. Save the **dyntitle.xml** file.

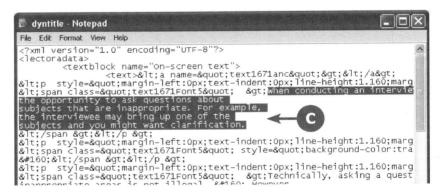

## BRIGHT IDEAS

- Even though you don't need to republish your title for the changes to appear, you may need to re-post them.  So if your course is on a learning management system or company intranet site, don't just update the .xml file on your desktop.  Be sure to put the updated file with the files that are online.

- If you've never worked with XML before, that's OK.  If you look through the file carefully, you can see where the text is.  Be careful when you make your changes that you don't change anything other than the text in question.

- You can use a text editor such as Notepad to edit the XML file.

# Adding Graphics

## Introduction

In this chapter, you'll learn how to add graphics such as photos, clipart, shapes, characters, and screen captures. Lectora provides a number of ways to add images, such as from files on your computer, stock photos and characters from the Lectora library, and, if you have Lectora Inspire, from Snagit.

## In This Chapter

- Adding Images
- Adding Shapes
- Using the Inspire Suite for Graphics

# Notes

# Adding Images

Images can help explain a concept, set a mood, or simply provide visual interest. Lectora accepts the following image formats:

- Bitmap > .bmp
- GIF > .gif
- JPEG > .jpg or .jpeg
- Portable Network Graphics > .png
- TIFF > .tif
- Windows Metafiles > .wmf
- Windows Enhanced Metafiles >.emf

When you place an image into your title, a copy of it is added to the Images folder associated with your title.

 **DESIGN TIP**

Pick the right file type to get the best combination of quality and file size.

- Try using **.jpg** format for photos and **.gif** or **.png** for simpler images. (But go ahead and try a photo as a **.gif** and see if it still looks good – it usually is a smaller file size.)
- Stay away from bitmaps as they have a large file size—often 10 times as much as a **.gif**.

## Add an Image

**To add an image from a file:**

1. On the **Home** tab, click the **Add object** drop-down button.
2. Click the **Image** icon.
3. Find and select the image file you want.
4. Click **Open**.

**To add an image already associated with your title.**

1. Click the **Title Resources** tab.
2. Click and drag the image you want onto the page.

**To add an image saved to your personal library:**

1. Click the **My Library** tab.
2. Navigate to the image you want.
3. Drag the image onto the page.

**To add an image from the Lectora stock library:**

1. Click the **Stock Library** tab.
2. Navigate to the image you want.
3. Drag the image onto the page.

## TIME SAVERS

- On your desktop, open the folder with the media file you want (image, audio, etc.), and then drag it onto the Lectora page.
- You can copy and paste an image from another document (such as a Word or PowerPoint document). If you do a regular paste, the image is added as a bitmap, which is a large file type. So instead, right-click the page and select **Paste As**. This lets you pick the best file format.

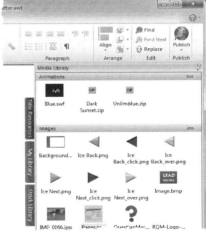

*Media libraries collapsed*    *Media libraries expanded*

 Media Libraries, p. 218

# Add a Character Image

Lectora 11 comes with a library of photographic characters in different poses that you can add to your title.  You can access them from the **Stock Library** or from the **Insert** tab.

**To add a character:**

1. Go to the **Insert** tab.
2. Click the **Character** button.
3. In the **Stock Library**, double-click the folder for the pose you want.
4. Select the character you want.
5. Click the **OK** button.

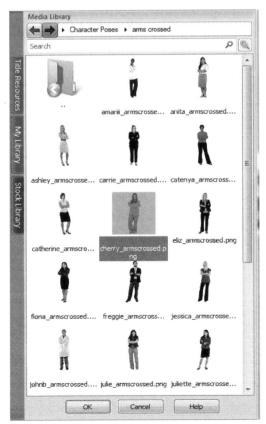

# Image Properties

Many of the properties for an image are the same as for most other types of objects (size, position, etc.). These common features are covered in the next chapter. Here are some image-specific features worth noting.

## Name

As with any other object, the **Name** field is the same as the object's name in the **Title Explorer**. It can be changed either here or in the **Title Explorer**. This field is especially important for images in that it also serves as the image's ALT text.

## Edit the Image

You can click the **Edit the Image** button to edit the image in photo-editing software. If you are using Lectora Inspire, the image opens in Snagit. If you want to use your own software such as Photoshop, you can set that up in **Preferences**. Without either, the **Edit the Image** button will be grayed out.

 Preferences, p. 245

## Empty ALT Tag

By default, Lectora uses the image name as the text for the ALT tag if you choose to publish ALT tags with your title. If you check this box, then this particular image will not have any ALT text associated with it. This is useful for lines or other images that don't have any real content associated with them.

## Preload

With this box checked, the image loads as soon as it is ready, rather than waiting for the entire page to load. Uncheck this box if you'd like the whole page to load at once.

## DESIGN TIP

### What is ALT text?

If you hover your mouse over an image on a Website and see a small yellow caption, that's ALT text.

Good, descriptive ALT text is most important for visually-impaired people using screen readers, such as JAWS. The screen reader reads the ALT text to the person, so he or she can tell what is in the object.

The object name field is limited to 128 characters.

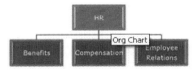

*ALT text that isn't very descriptive*

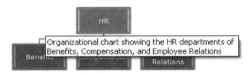

*Useful, descriptive ALT text.*

 Accessibility, p. 215

## BRIGHT IDEA

Did you know you can add images in text boxes? Double-click in the text box to get the cursor, and then insert the image like you normally would. An image in a text box moves and scrolls with the text.

# Change an Image

You may need to change an image because you want to use a different image completely or because the image has changed in some way. You can delete the current image and place the new image. However, sometimes it is better to change the image instead. That way, the placement is the same, and any actions related to that image stay in place.

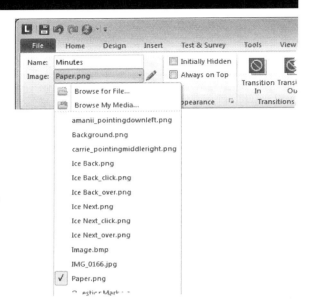

**To change to a new image:**

1. Go to the **Properties** tab.
2. Click the **Image** drop-down arrow.
3. Select an image from the list that's already in the title, or use the browsing options to find and add the image you want.

## TIME SAVER

You can swap out an image by copying it over in the **Images** folder, without even opening Lectora! Just copy the new or revised image into the **Images** folder, and make sure it has the same name (including file type) as the original. As soon as you do, it is automatically updated on the page.

You may need to adjust the size of the new image if it is a different size or proportion.

# Adding Shapes

You can add a number of graphical elements right from Lectora using the various shape, line, and arrow tools. Shapes can be used for interface elements, diagrams, or to add visual interest to a page.

## Add a Shape

**To add a shape:**
1. Go to the **Insert** tab.
2. Click the **Shape/Line** drop-down button.
3. Select the shape type you want.
4. Click and drag your mouse on the page to draw the shape.

### DESIGN TIPS

- Press and hold **Shift** while drawing a rectangle or ellipse to create a perfect square or circle.

- Press and hold **Shift** while drawing a line to keep it at a 0, 90, or 45 degree angle.

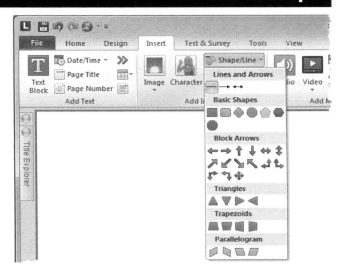

## Change the Color of a Shape

**To change the color of a shape:**
1. Go to the shape's **Properties** tab.
2. In the **Fill Color** field, change the fill color.
3. In the **Outline Color** field, change the outline color.
4. In the **Weight** field, indicate how many pixels wide you want the outline to be.

**Fill Color** is not available on lines.

Selecting Colors, p. 64

# Using the Inspire Suite for Graphics

If you have the full Lectora Inspire suite (as opposed to just Lectora Publisher), you have additional tools for working with graphics in SnagIt.

## Create a New Image in SnagIt

**To create a new image in SnagIt from Lectora:**

1. Go to the **Insert** tab.
2. Click the **Image** drop-down button.
3. Select **New Image**.
4. Create a new image in SnagIt.
5. Save your image in SnagIt.
6. Add your saved image in Lectora as you would any other image.

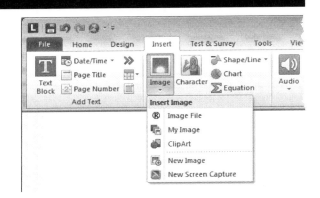

## Add a Screen Capture From SnagIt

**To add a screen capture:**

1. Go to the **Insert** tab.
2. Click the **Image** drop-down menu.
3. Select **New Screen Capture**.
4. Click the large red **Capture** button.
5. Click and drag around the area of your screen you want to capture.
6. Make any edits to your capture you might need (such as cropping or callouts).
7. Save your image.
8. Add the new image to your title as you would any other image.

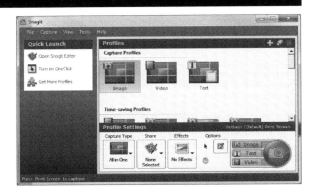

# Working With Objects

## Introduction

You've already learned how to add text boxes, images, and shapes as well as some of the properties specific to those object types. Now it is time to look at some of the options and properties that apply to these and other object types, such as selecting and moving objects, selecting colors, etc.

## In This Chapter

- Managing Objects
- Additional Object Properties
- Selecting Colors

# Notes

# Managing Objects

## Select Objects

You can select an object in the **Title Explorer** or on the slide, if it appears there.

- To select more than one object in the **Title Explorer**, press and hold the **Ctrl** key while you select each object; or when selecting consecutive items, click the first item, and then hold down the **Shift** key while selecting the last item.

- To select more than one object on the slide, press and hold the **Ctrl** key while you select each object, or click and drag your mouse around the items. (**Shift** does not work in the work area.)

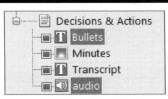

*Ctrl used on first and last object*

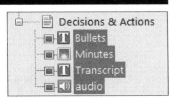

*Shift used on first and last object*

## Cut, Copy, and Paste Objects

You can cut, copy, and paste objects in the **Title Explorer** or on the slide by using the Home tab, right-click menu, or keyboard shortcuts.

You can copy more than one object, but you can't paste while more than one is still selected. Select just a single object or the page before pasting.

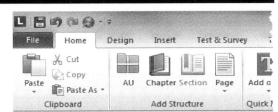

### 🕐 TIME SAVER

You can drag and drop items to move them from one page to the other in the **Title Explorer**. As you drag an object, watch for the black line to make sure you are moving the object to the right place.

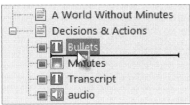

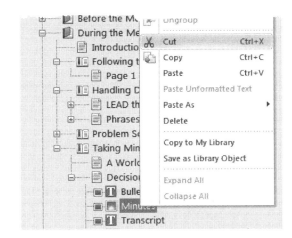

## Delete Objects

Delete a selected object by pressing the **Delete** key on your keyboard or by right-clicking and selecting **Delete**.

# Resize Objects

There are three options for resizing objects such as text boxes or graphics.

**Option 1:**
1. Click and drag the handles of the object.

**Option 2:**
1. Go to the **Position & Size** tab.
2. Enter the pixel dimensions in the **Width** and **Height** fields.

**Option 3:**
1. Enter the pixel dimensions in the **w** and **h** fields in the **Status Bar**.

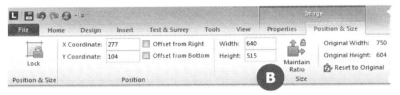

---

 **CAUTION**

- When resizing text boxes, you can end up making it too small and cutting off some of the text. Look for a small plus sign in the bottom-right corner **(A)** to let you know there is cut-off text. Either manually resize the text box or double-click it to have it automatically resized for you.

- It's great that you can resize an image right from Lectora. However, if you resize a photo larger than its underlying file, you will lose some quality.

  And if you shrink a large photo down, realize the underlying photo is still as big. That means your users are having to download a much larger image than what they are seeing. If the image is significantly larger than you need, save some file size by resizing it first in your photo-editing software.

 **DESIGN TIPS**

- By default, graphics are set to maintain their aspect ratio when you resize them, meaning they won't skew or stretch in one direction or the other. If you want to resize in only one direction, click the **Maintain Ratio** button on the **Position & Size** tab. **(B)**

- To return an image to its original size, click the **Reset to Original** button on the **Position & Size** tab.

- If you want to make an object the same size as another object, select the one that is the size you want first. Then select the other objects you want to be the same size. Finally, go to the **Alignment** toolbar in the **Status Bar** and click one of the resize options.

Make Same Width
Make Same Height
Make Same Width and Height

# Move Objects

There are also three options for moving objects on a slide.

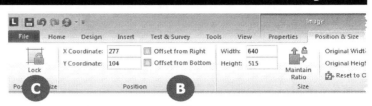

**Option 1:**

1. Click and drag the object to its new location.

**Option 2:**

1. Go to the **Position & Size** tab.
2. Enter the number of pixels from the right in the **X Coordinate** field and the pixels from the top in the **Y Coordinate** field.

**Option 3:**

1. Change enter the pixel location in the **x** and **y** fields in the **Status Bar**. **(A)**

## DESIGN TIPS

- When moving an object with your mouse, hold and press the **Shift** key to move it evenly across or down.

- Use the arrow keys on your keyboard to move an object one pixel. Use **Shift** plus an arrow key to move it 10 pixels.

- By default, the x and y coordinates are measured from the left and top. However, you can also use measurements from the right and/or bottom. Check the **Offset from Right** or **Offset from Bottom** check boxes on the **Position & Size** tab. **(B)** This also "anchors" your object to the bottom/right. For example, if you have a Next button anchored to the bottom right and then make your page size bigger or smaller, the button will still be in the same location relative to the bottom right corner.

- If you want to keep yourself (or someone else) from accidentally moving or resizing an object, you can lock it by clicking the **Lock** button on the **Position & Size** tab. **(C)** The system will make an error sound if you try to move it. Click the button again to unlock it.

# Additional Object Properties

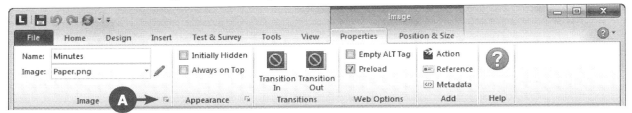

## Description

If you click the small arrow in the bottom of the **Image** section for an image **(A)** or the **Text** section for a text box, you get the **Description** dialog box. Here you can add information about the object for internal purposes, such as notes about where it is from or how it is structured. This description serves a similar purpose as the **Notes** feature. The difference is that a note lives on a page whereas this description can be attached to individual objects.

 Notes, p. 212

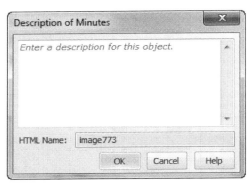

## HTML Name

You'll find the HTML name for a given object in the Description dialog box. This is useful to know if you are adding your own HTML or JavaScript and need to reference a page or an object.

## Initially Hidden

By default, all objects appear on the page in the published course. If you don't want that to happen, check this box. You'll still see it in Edit mode, but not in the published course. You would need to set up some sort of action to make it appear. For example, the student might need to click a button for it to appear.

## Always on Top

If you check this box, the text box always appears on top of overlapping objects, even if it isn't on top in the **Title Explorer**. However, if overlapping items are all marked to appear on top, Lectora uses the order in the **Title Explorer** to decide what actually appears on top.

 Layering, p. 68

## CSS Classes

If you click the small arrow in the bottom of the **Appearance** section, you get the **CSS Classes** dialog box. If you are using your own cascading style sheets (CSS) for the course, use this feature to link an item to a given style sheet.

 **CAUTION**

The phrasing on this feature is different in version 11. In previous versions, the field was called **Initially Visible** and was checked by default. Now it is called **Initially Hidden** and is unchecked by default. The net result is the same, but just make sure you are considering the new phrasing when deciding if you need to check the box.

 **TIME SAVER**

In version 11, you can change the properties of multiple objects at once. Simply select the objects you want to change, go to the **Properties** tab, and make the change once. The **Properties** tab will only display the features that can be changed for the selected object types.

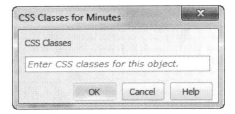

## Additional Object Properties (cont'd)

### Transitions

Just as you can add page transitions, you can add similar transitions to individual objects, with several additional features.

You can set one transition for when the object appears and one for when it disappears (when the student goes to the next page or when an action hides it).

In the dialog box that appears, you can set a delay before the transition takes effect.

 **CAUTION**

Be careful about using delayed transitions to time your text to the audio if you are publishing to HTML. If the audio takes a little bit longer to download, then the timing will be off. Instead, you can work with audio events.

 Audio events p. 121

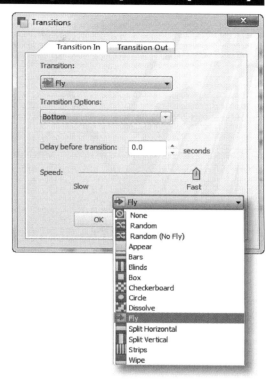

### Action

If you click the **Action** button, it adds an action to your text box. This is the same as going to the Insert tab and selecting **Action**.

 Actions, ch. 8

### Reference

Click the **Reference** button to bring up the **Add/Modify Reference** dialog box where you can include important reference information about the object. The advantage of putting information here is that you can add a list of all the references in your title to create an easy photo credits page or similar feature.

To add reference information, check the box at the top to open up the fields for editing.

 Display references, p. 160

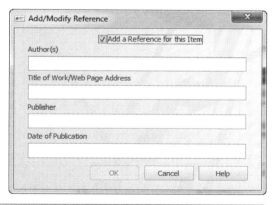

### Metadata

The **Metadata** button works just like the one in the **Page Properties** tab, except that the data is associated with the object instead of the whole page.

 Page metadata, p. 31

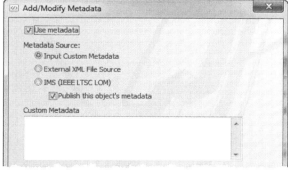

# Selecting Colors

Whether you want to format text, create a shape, or make a colored background, the options for how to select colors are the same anywhere you see a color menu.

## Select a Color

**To select a standard color:**
1. Click a color drop-down menu (such as **Text Color**, **Outline Color**, etc.)
2. Select the color you want.

**To select a standard color from a larger palette:**
1. Click a color drop-down menu.
2. Select **Custom**.
3. On the **Standard** tab, click on the color you want.

**To match a color used somewhere in your title:**
1. Click a color drop-down menu.
2. Click **Select**.
3. Click on an item that is the color you want to use.

**To create a custom color:**
1. Click a color drop-down menu.
2. Select **Custom**.
3. Click the **Custom** tab.
4. Select or create the color you want.
   - Enter your own hue, saturation, and luminosity values if you know them.
   - Enter your own red, green, and blue values if you know them.
   - Mix your own color:

     Click in the color mixer on the color you want. (Left versus right changes the hue; up versus down changes the intensity.)

     Click in the value slider on the right to determine how dark or light that color is.
5. Click **OK**.

 **TIME SAVER**

You don't have to enter custom colors over and over again if you add them to the **Saved Colors** palette. On the **Custom** tab, click first in a blank square at the bottom of the dialog box. Then mix your color. And finally, click the **Add to Saved Colors** button. To use that color, come back to this dialog box and click on the custom color swatch you want.

Custom colors are saved to your computer, not to the title. You'll want to share the color values with other developers to set up their own palette.

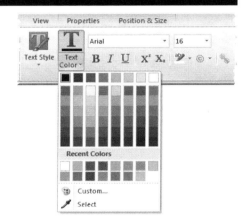

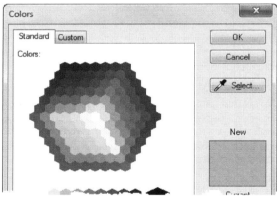

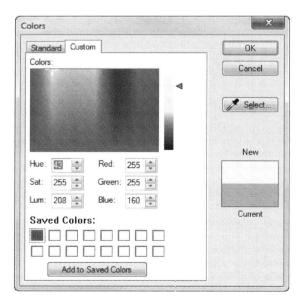

# Page Layout and Design

## Introduction

Whereas the last chapter dealt with the properties of individual objects, this chapter provides tips on working with multiple objects at once (such as alignment and layering) and overall layout design.

## In This Chapter

- Arranging Objects
- Page Layouts

# Notes

# Arranging Objects

To help you create a professional look in less time, Lectora provides a number of tools to help you arrange your objects. You can:

**Group**: Group items together so that when you move or copy the items, they always stay together.

**Layer**: Adjust the layering of overlapping objects so you have the correct ones on top.

**Align**: Line up the top, bottom, right, left, or middle of objects for a polished look; space items evenly; or center them on the page.

**Snap**: Snap items to a standard grid or custom guide lines to make sure items are in the right place.

**To group items together:**
1. Select the items you want to group.
2. On the Home tab, click the **Group Selection** button.

**To add objects to an existing group:**
1. In the Title Explorer, drag the objects(s) into the group.

**To ungroup items:**
1. Select the group.
2. On the Home tab, click the **Group Selection** drop-down arrow.
3. Select **Ungroup Selection**.

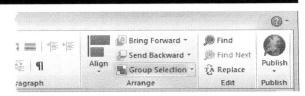

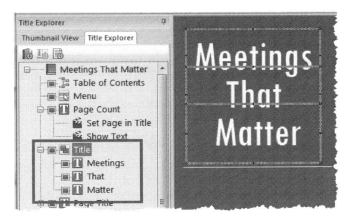

 **BRIGHT IDEAS**

- The group and ungroup options are also available on an object's right-click menu.
- If you want to reposition an individual object in a group without moving the others, press the **Alt** key while you drag it.
- Select the group icon in the **Title Explorer** to rename it or apply transitions to it in the Properties window.
- Groups of actions are called **Action Groups**.

 Action Groups, p. 119

# Layering Objects

In the **Title Explorer**, the objects listed last are the ones that appear on the top layer. The ones listed first are the ones on the bottom layer. Seem backwards?

Think of it this way. Lectora builds each page from top to bottom in the **Title Explorer**. It puts the first item it finds on the page first, and then the next item, etc. The last items are added to the top layer of the page. It's like a hot fudge sundae. The last items added are on the top.

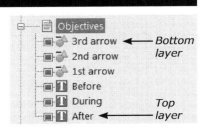

**To bring an item forward one layer:**
1. Go to the **Home** tab.
2. Click the **Bring Forward** button.

**To bring an item to the very top layer:**
1. Go to the **Home** tab.
2. Click the **Bring Forward** drop-down arrow.
3. Select **Bring to Front**.

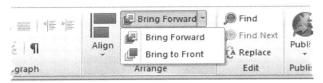

**To send an item back one layer:**
1. Go to the **Home** tab.
2. Click the **Send Backward** button.

**To bring an item to the very bottom layer:**
1. Go to the **Home** tab.
2. Click the **Send Backward** drop-down arrow.
3. Select **Send to Back**.

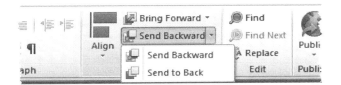

**To change the order in the Title Explorer:**
1. Click and drag an object to the position you want.

**To "lock" an item to stay on top:**
1. Go to the **Properties** tab.
2. Check the **Always on Top** box.

 **CAUTION**

- If you check **Always on Top**, the item does not change position in the **Title Explorer**, which may make troubleshooting difficult. You may want to layer it on the top first, and then check the box as a safety.

- If more than one overlapping object is marked to be on top, only one can actually be on top. Lectora uses the layering in the **Title Explorer** to decide what to show on top.

- Buttons from the **Button Wizard** are automatically set to **Always on Top**.

- The layering order determines the order in which the items are read by screen readers. If you are creating a Section 508-compliant course, be sure to put your objects in a logical order. For example, you might want the main text to be read before an image.

 Accessibility, p. 215

# Aligning Objects

You've already learned how to set the x and y coordinates for an object, which you can use to help line them up (i.e., putting two objects at the same x coordinate lines them up on the right). You can also use the alignment tools to line up items in relation to the slide or in relation to each other.

The **Alignment** toolbar is found in the **Status Bar** at the bottom of the Lectora interface.

**To align objects:**
1. Select the objects you want to align.
2. Click the appropriate button on the **Alignment** toolbar.

Align Right
Align Left
Align Top
Align Bottom
Align Horizontal Center
Align Vertical Center
Center Horizontal on Page
Center Vertical on Page
Space Horizontal
Space Vertical
Make Same Width
Make Same Height
Make Same Width and Height

## BRIGHT IDEA

These same options are available from the **Align** drop-down button on the **Home** tab.

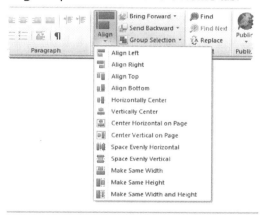

# Using Grids and Guides

Grids and guides can be visual references for you to use when manually moving and arranging objects. Or, if you turn on the "snap" features, the objects snap in place if you get close to the grid or guide. This means you are more likely to place the object where you want it and less likely to be off by a pixel or two.

Grids are automatic, and guides are added manually. If you haven't added any guides, you won't see anything when you first try to show them. Guides appear on every page in the title, which makes it easier to be consistent with layout.

**To show grids or guides:**

1. Go to the **View** tab.
2. Click the **Show Grids** or **Show Guides** button.

Click the same buttons to hide them.

**To manually add guides:**

1. Go to the **View** menu.
2. Click the **Show Rulers** button.
3. Click and drag your mouse down from the top ruler for a horizontal guide or to the right from a side ruler for a vertical guide.
4. Release the mouse where you want the ruler.

Move an existing guide by pressing the **Ctrl** key while dragging it to a new location. Press **Ctrl** and drag it back to a ruler to remove it completely. Click **Clear Guides** on the **View** tab to remove all of the guides.

**To turn on the snap features:**

1. Go to the **View** menu.
2. Select **Snap to Grid** or **Snap to Guides**.

Select the same options to turn off the snap features. Check marks let you know if the features are on or off.

Once the snap feature is turned on, simply move the item with your mouse towards the gridline or guide you want, and the object snaps in place when it gets within a few pixels.

**To change grid and guide options:**

1. Go to the **View** tab.
2. Click the **Options** button.
3. Make the changes to the color of the guides or the color and spacing of the grid.
4. Click the **OK** button.

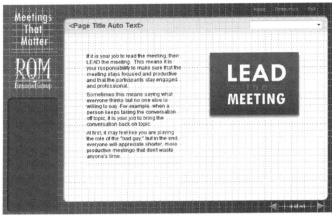

*Grid*

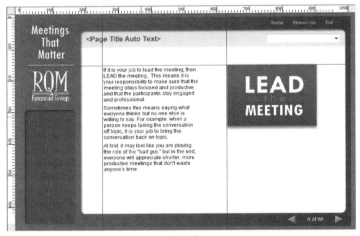

*Guides*

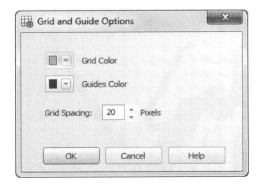

# Page Layouts

To help save time and create a consistent look in your titles, you can use page layouts to build your pages. A page layout is similar to a master slide in PowerPoint that contains placeholders for your text and media elements.

You can either use a pre-made layout, create your own, or import and export them to share with your team.

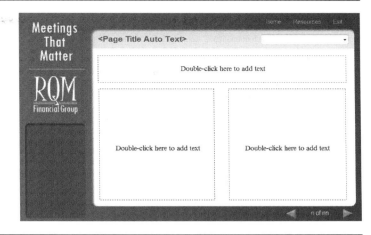

## Apply a Page Layout

**To create a new page using a page layout:**
1. Go to the **Home** tab.
2. Click the **Page** drop-down arrow.
3. Select the layout you want.

The icon for the most recently selected page layout takes the place of the **Page** button. The next time you click the **Page** button (not the **Page** drop-down arrow), you'll get a new page using that layout.

**To apply a layout to an existing page:**
1. Go to the **Home** tab.
2. Click the **Page** drop-down arrow.
3. Select **Manage Page Layout**.
4. Select the layout you want.
5. Click the **Apply Layout to Current Page** button.
6. Click the **Done** button.

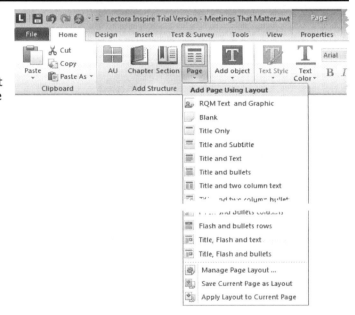

## POWER TIP

Page layouts can be big time-savers because they put object placeholders on a page. But what if you have specific text, images, formatting, or actions that you want to include? If that is the case, you might be better off creating your own page templates using **Library Objects**.

Library Objects, p. 221

## Create a New Page Layout

The page layouts provided may not fit with your particular interface design.  Fortunately, you can create your own layouts.

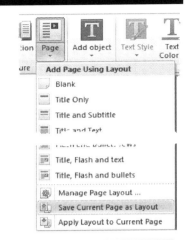

**To create a new page layout:**

1. Design a page with the layout you want.
2. Go to the **Home** tab.
3. Click the **Page** drop-down menu.
4. Select **Save Current Page as Layout**.
5. Type a new name for the layout.
6. Click the **OK** button.

## Export and Import Page Layouts

You can export page layouts so other developers can import and use them.

**To export a page layout:**

1. Go to the **Home** tab.
2. Click the **Page** drop-down menu.
3. Select **Manage Page Layout**.
4. Select the layout you want to export.
5. Click the **Export Layout** button.
6. Navigate to where you want to save the layout.
7. Change the file name, if needed.
8. Click **Save**.
9. Click **Done**.

**To import a page layout:**

1. Go to the **Home** tab.
2. Click the **Page** drop-down menu.
3. Select **Manage Page Layout**.
4. Click the **Import Layout** button.
5. Find and select the layout you want.
6. Click **Open**.
7. Click **Done**.

# Audio, Video, and Flash

## Introduction

You've already learned how to add text and images. Now it's time to learn how to add other forms of media: audio, video, and animations, such as Flash. In addition, you'll learn about properties unique to these object types (in addition to the common properties taught in chapters 5 and 6), as well as how to take advantage of the Flash activities that come as part of the Lectora stock library.

## In This Chapter

- Adding Audio and Video
- Adding Animation Files

# Notes

# Adding Audio and Video

Lectora supports a wide variety of audio and video types and gives you many options for how they are controlled.

You can add audio/video from a file; insert an online file, such as from a streaming media service or YouTube; or, if you have the full Inspire suite, you can create your own.

When you place an audio or video file into your title, a copy of it is placed in the **Media** folder for your title.

**All Supported Audio Files**
AIFF (*.aiff,*.aif)
AU Format (*.au)
M4A (*.m4a)
MIDI (*.mid,*.midi,*.rmi)
MP3 (*.mp3)
RealAudio (*.ra,*.ram,*.rm,*.mmm)
Wave (*.wav)
Windows Media Audio (*.wma)
Advanced Streaming Format (*.asf)
Flash Video (*.flv)

**All Supported Video Files**
Windows Video (*.avi)
Quicktime Movie (*.mov)
MPEG (*.mpg,*.mpeg,*.mpa,*.mp4,*.m4v)
Real Video (*.ram,*.rm)
Windows Media Video (*.wmv)
Advanced Streaming Format (*.asf)
Flash Video (*.flv,*.f4v)

## Add an Audio or Video File

**To add audio or video from a file on your computer:**
1. Go to the **Home** tab.
2. Click the **Add object** drop-down button.
3. Click the **Add Audio** or **Add Video** icon.
4. Find and select the file you want.
5. Click the **Open** button.

**To add a file already associated with your title:**
1. Click the **Title Resources** tab.
2. Drag the file you want onto the page.

**To add a file saved to your personal library:**
1. Click the **My Library** tab.
2. Navigate to the file you want.
3. Drag the file onto the page.

**To add a file from the Lectora stock library:**
1. Click the **Stock Library** tab.
2. Navigate to the folder and file you want.
3. Drag the image onto the page.

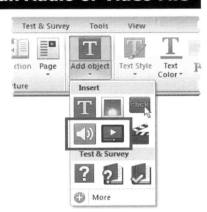

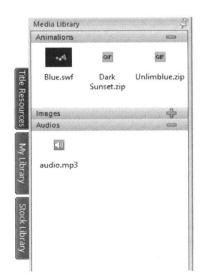

# Add Streaming Media

**To add streaming audio or video:**

1. Go to the **Insert tab.**
2. Click the **Audio** or **Video** drop-down button.
3. Select **Streaming Audio** or **Streaming Video**.
4. In the drop-down menu, select the type of streaming you will be using.
5. In the **URL** field, enter the web address for the media.
6. Click the **OK** button.

## BRIGHT IDEA

What is streaming media?

Streaming media is stored separately on a server, rather than in your course. The file is presented gradually to the user while it is still downloading, rather than waiting for the file to finish downloading completely. This means the user can watch/listen much more quickly, even if it is a very large media file.

## DESIGN TIPS

### Modifying Audio and Video Clips

Just as with images, you can:

- Go to the **Properties** tab to change the file or any of the properties.
- Copy over the file in the **Media** folder if you have an updated version.

### Tips for Mobile Publishing

If you are publishing your course to play in an iPhone or iPad, FLV audio and media will not work. You'll need to convert your FLV media to a different file format and bring it into Lectora.

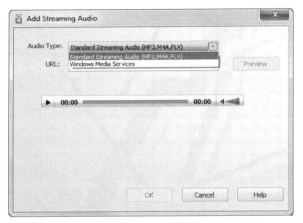

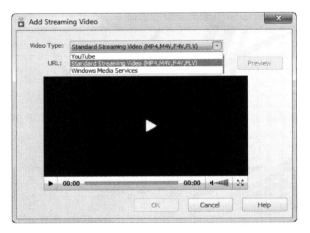

# Create New Audio With Lectora Inspire

If you have the full Lectora Inspire license, you can create new audio and video files from the Inspire suite of tools.

**To create a new audio file:**

1. Go to the **Insert** tab.
2. Click the **Audio** drop-down button.
3. Select **New Audio Recording**.
4. Click the **Settings** button to select which system microphone you want to use. **(A)**
5. Click the big red button to begin your recording.
6. Click the same button again (now a stop button) to stop recording.
7. Click the **Save** button that appears.

# Create New Video From Lectora Inspire

**To create a new video file:**

1. Go to the **Insert tab.**
2. Click the **Video** drop-down button.
3. Select **New Video Recording**.
4. Click the **Settings** button to select which system microphone and camera you want to use. **(B)**
5. Click the big red button to begin your recording.
6. Click the same button again (now a stop button) to stop recording.
7. Click the **Save** button that appears.

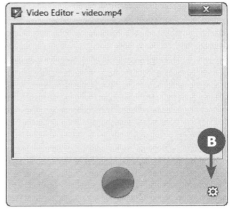

# Audio Properties

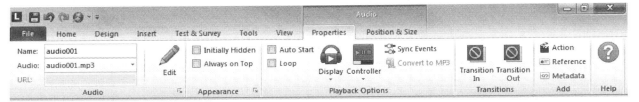

When you select an audio file (either on the page or in the **Title Explorer**), you get a **Properties** tab and a **Position & Size** tab. Any of the properties that are visual in nature (**Initially Hidden**, x and y coordinates, etc.) refer to the audio controller that appears on your page. You learned about many object properties in chapters 5 and 6. Here are additional properties that are unique to audio files.

## Edit

If you have the Lectora Inspire suite or if you have "attached" your own audio editor to Lectora, you can click this button to edit your audio file.

 Editors, p. 245

## Auto Start

Check this box to have the audio play as soon as the page loads. Leave it unchecked if you want the student to click the control bar or want to add an action that plays it.

## Loop

Check this box to have the audio start over again every time it finishes; otherwise it plays once.

## Display

This determines whether or not to include controls for playing and pausing the audio clip. You can choose to have no controller, a speaker button, a full playbar, or a file that you add yourself.

## Controller

If you enable the controller on the **Display** menu, you can use this drop-down menu to select the style for the control toolbar.

## Sync Events

This feature lets you time certain events (such as objects appearing and disappearing) to the audio.

 Events, p. 120

## Convert to MP3

If your audio file is not already in **.mp3** format, you can click this button to convert it. The **.mp3** format is often a smaller file size and is iPad compatible. (This option is not available for FLV audio files.)

# The Audio Editor

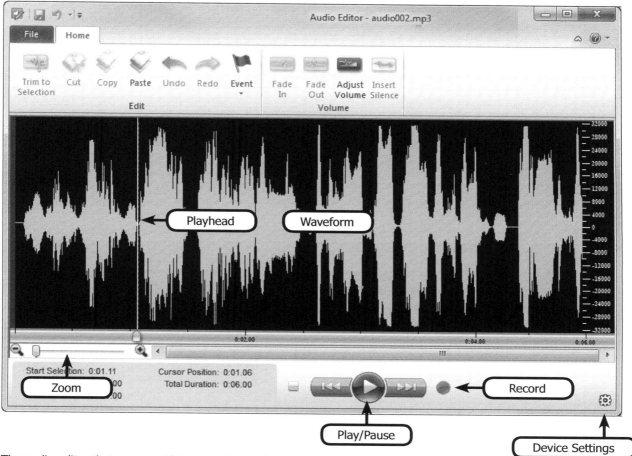

The audio editor that comes with Lectora Inspire is very straightforward. Here are a few tips.

- Click in the **Waveform** to position the **Playhead**. Many functions are based on where the **Playhead** is, such as play, record, paste, etc.

- Click and drag in the **Waveform** to select a section of text. This is useful for deleting an outtake, increasing volume on just that portion, etc.

- The **File** menu lets you save your audio file into different formats, including **.mp3**, **.flv**, **.wma**, **.asf**, and **.wav**.

- The **Event** button lets you add triggers to the audio that cause actions to happen when that point of the audio is reached.

 Events, p. 120

# Video Properties

Video properties are very similar to audio properties. Here are the properties not covered in chapters 5 and 6.

## Edit

If you have the Lectora Inspire suite or if you have "attached" your own video editor to Lectora, you can click this button to edit your video file.

 Editors, p. 245

## Auto Start

Check this box to have the video play as soon as the page loads. Leave it unchecked if you want the student to click the control bar or want to add an action that plays it.

## Loop

Check this box to have the video start over again every time it finishes; otherwise it plays once.

## Rollover

Check this box if you want the video controller to appear only when the student's mouse hovers over the video, instead of having it show at all times.

## Controller

By default, a control toolbar is added to all video files. Use this drop-down menu to select the style or to remove it completely.

## Sync Events

This feature lets you time certain events (such as objects appearing and disappearing) to the audio.

 Events, p. 120

## Convert to MP4

If your video file is not already in **.mp4** format, you can click this button to convert it. The **.mp4** format is often a smaller file size and is iPad compatible. (This option is not available on FLV video.)

## Add Captions

If you are working with FLV video, you can use an XML file to add closed captioning, which helps with accessibility. See the next page for more details.

 **POWER TIP**

You can import and export custom skins. Select **Manage Custom Skins** from the bottom of the Controller drop-down menu for an audio or video file.

# Add Closed Captioning to FLV Video

**To add closed captioning to an FLV Video:**

1. Go to the **Properties** tab.
2. Click the **Add Captions** button.
3. Click the **Sample XML File** button.
4. In the XML file that opens, change the existing caption text and timing with your own, adding additional lines, as needed.
5. Save the XML file.
6. Repeat steps 1 and 2 if the **Add Captions** dialog box is not still open.
7. Click the **XML Caption File** drop-down menu.
8. Select **Browse for File**.
9. Find and select your caption file.
10. Click the **Open** button.
11. Click the **OK** button.

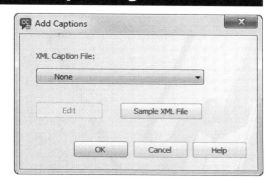

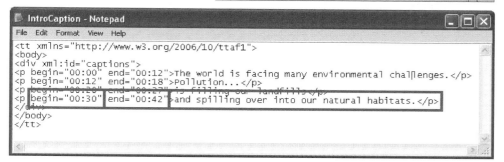

## POWER TIP

If you are comfortable with XML code, you can change the font formatting of the captions. Search the Lectora user's guide for "closed-captioning video" to find the specific parameters to use.

## The Video Editor

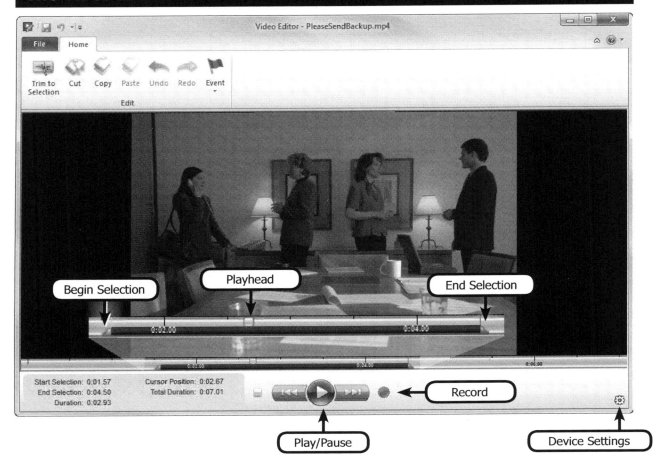

The video editor that comes with Lectora Inspire is very straightforward. Here are a few tips.

- Drag the green and red sliders to create a selection. From there, you can cut, copy, or trim to that selection.
- Drag the **Playhead** to create an insertion point for recording/pasting or where to start playing when clicking the editor's Play button.
- The **File** menu lets you save your audio file into different formats.
- The **Event** button lets you add triggers to the audio that cause actions to happen when that point of the audio is reached.

 Events, p. 120

 **CAUTION**

Not all video file types can be edited in this manner. The video editor accepts **.avi**, **.wmv**, **.flv**, and **.mp4**. Other formats can be included in your title, but can't be edited with the Lectora Inspire tools.

# Adding Animation Files

Animations can be anything from a simple, spinning graphic, such as animated GIFs to full-scale simulations and interactions created in Adobe Flash or Captivate.

When you add an animation to your title, a copy of it is placed in your **Images** folder.

| Type | Description |
|------|-------------|
| .gif | GIFs are image files. However, they can be animated by having several different frames that run successively – like an old-fashioned "flip book" cartoon. You might create them in Photoshop or purchase them from a stock image collection. |
| .swf | SWF files (Shockwave Flash) are published files that play in the Adobe Flash player. They may have been created in Flash, Adobe Captivate, Raptivity, or any number of other tools that output to the Flash Player format. |
| .spl | These are animations made with FutureSplash Animator, the software that later became Flash. |

## Add an Animated GIF File

**To add an animated GIF file:**

1. Go to the **Insert** tab.
2. Click **Animation**.
3. Find and select the file you want.
4. Click the **Open** button.

 **BRIGHT IDEA**

You can also add animation files from the three libraries: **Title Resources**, **My Library**, and **Stock Library**.

## Animated GIF Properties

The **Properties** tab for an animation is identical to that for an image with the following exception.

### Auto Start

By default, your animation will play when the object loads. Leave it unchecked if you want to create some sort of action that causes the animation to start.

# Add a Flash File

**To add a Flash file (.swf or .spl):**

1. Go to the **Insert** tab.
2. Click the **Flash** button.
3. Find and select the file you want.
4. Click the **Open** button.

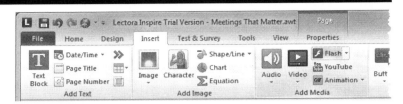

 **CAUTION**

If you add your own Flash file or one from the Lectora library, the file will not play on iOS devices, such as iPhones and iPads.

# Flash Properties

Here are the properties not covered in chapters 5 and 6.

## Additional Files

Some Flash files require other files in order to function. For example, they might need to get information from a text file. If your Flash file requires other files, click this button to add those files to the title. Flash animation files are added to the **Images** folder, but these additional files go in the **Extern** folder. You might need to move them into the **Images** folder if everything needs to be in the same folder to work.

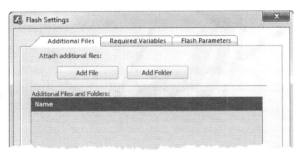

## Required Variables

Click this button to indicate which variables are needed for the Flash file to work. For example, the Flash developer might set up the Flash file to be configurable with certain custom variables.

 Variables, p. 124

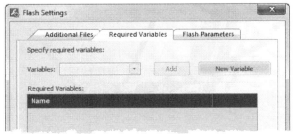

## Flash Parameters

There are two types of Flash parameters you can add to control your flash file.

- **Standard Flash parameters**: The **Name** drop-down menu contains common parameters that you can control right in Lectora, such as background color and scale. To set these parameters, select it from the drop-down menu, enter the value in the **Values** field, and then click **Add parameter**.

- **Custom Flash parameters**: When your Flash file was built, it might have been built with options that could be configured outside of Flash, making it more flexible. For example a quiz show animation might allow for 4, 5, or 6 questions. If your file was set up this way, click the **Add parameter** button to add these custom configuration parameters and the values you want. You'll need to work with your Flash programmer to know what the parameters and the acceptable values are.

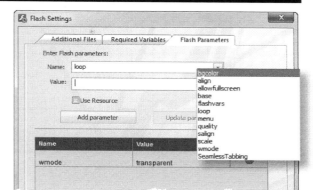

## Transparent

Check this box to automatically set up one of the most common parameters: transparent. The main reason to do this is if you want an object to appear on top of the Flash file.

## Fit to Browser

Check this box if you want your Flash animation to fit to the dimensions of a student's browser.

## Create a Simulation in Camtasia

If you have the full Lectora Inspire license, you can computer simulations with Camtasia.

**To create a new simulation with Camtasia:**

1. Go to the **Tools** tab.
2. Click the **Screen Recording** button.
3. Create your simulation in Camtasia.
4. Click the **Produce and Share** button.
5. Configure the publish settings.
6. Click Next.
7. Find and select the location where you want the file saved.
8. Click the **Finish** button.
9. In Lectora, go to the **Insert** tab.
10. Click the **Video** button. (You may need to click a different button based on the publishing format you chose.)
11. Find and select your newly published Camtasia simulation.
12. Click the **Open** button.

Refer to the help documentation in Camtasia for details on how to use the software.

## Create a Flash Interaction in Flypaper

If you have the full Lectora Inspire license, you can create custom Flash interactions with Flypaper.

**To create a new interaction with Flypaper:**

1. Go to the **Tools** tab.
2. Click the **Flash Animation** button.
3. Create your animation in Flypaper.
4. Click the **Publish** drop-down button.
5. Select **Publish to Lectora as Single SWF**.
6. Configure the publish settings.
7. Click the **Publish** button.
8. Find and select the location where you want the file saved.
9. Click the **Save** button.
10. In Lectora, go to the **Insert** tab.
11. Click the **Flash** button. (You may need to click a different button based on the publishing format you chose.)
12. Find and select your newly published Flypaper animation.
13. Click the **Open** button.

Refer to the help documentation in Flypaper for details on how to use the software.

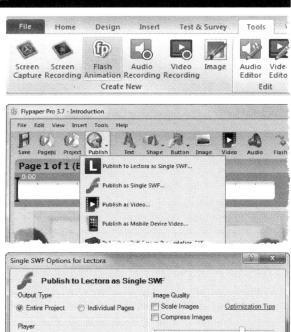

# Add a Lectora Flash Activity

Lectora versions 9 and later come with a library of easy-to-configure Flash animations and games. You can insert them from the Lectora stock library and then customize them with your own images, text, etc.

**To add a Lectora Flash Activity:**

1. Click the **Stock Library** tab.
2. Double-click the **Flash Activities** folder.
3. Drag the activity you want onto the page.
4. Configure the settings in the wizard, clicking the **Next** button to get to the next setting.
5. Click the **Finish** button when you are done.

The configuration window uses a variety of drop-down menus, buttons, text entry fields, and other methods to set up the animation. The options vary based on which animation you choose.

Click the **Edit** button in the **Properties** tab to change any of the settings.

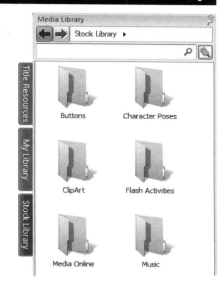

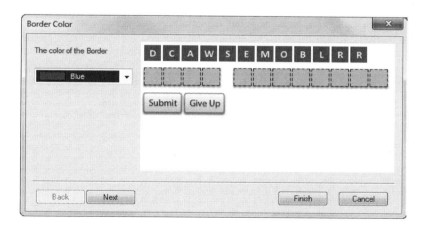

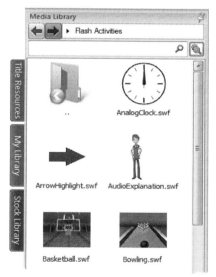

**POWER TIP**

Many of the animations have associated variables that you can use to either track results or control the interaction. Refer to **Specifying Flash Parameters** in the Lectora user guide for more information.

# Lectora Flash Activity Gallery

| Animation | Description | Useful Options |
|---|---|---|
| AnalogClock.swf | Analog clock that displays the current time | 5 styles to choose from:<br><br>Classic    Modern    Gel    No Hands    Pocket Watch |
| ArrowHighlight.swf | Animated arrow | • Color, size, direction, animation style, looping.<br>• Animation styles:<br><br>No animation       Grow<br>Fade                    Spin<br>Shift Horizontal     Stretch Horizontal<br>Shift Vertical         Stretch Vertical |
| AudioExplanation.swf | Animated character with mouth movements and gestures | Male and female characters in different professions and ethnicities.<br>• AudioExplanation: single audio file with no text<br>• BulletsWithOneAudio: Single audio file with bulleted list<br>• BulletsSyncWithAudio: Multiple audio files (up to 10), each timed with their own bullets |
| Basketball.swf | Students make baskets by answering multiple-choice questions correctly. | • Number of questions (up to 15)<br>• Four choices per question |
| Bowling.swf | Students get strikes or gutter balls by answering multiple-choice questions correctly or incorrectly. | • Number of questions (up to 15)<br>• Four choices per question |
| CardFlip.swf | Double-sided card that flips over when the user clicks it | Image or text on front and back.  (Back is the side the students see first.  Front is what they see when they flip it over.) |
| Categories.swf | Jeopardy-style game with questions organized into categories. | • Number of categories (up to 8)<br>• Number of questions per category (up to 5)<br>• Number of choices per question (up to 4)<br>• Color of the squares |

## Lectora Flash Activity Gallery

| Animation | Description | Useful Options |
|---|---|---|
| CharacterRace.swf | Students answer questions to finish the race before a computer-generated opponent does. | • Image for each character<br>• Number of questions (up to 10)<br>• Number of answers the student can get wrong and still beat the opponent |
| Crazycans.swf | Students answer multiple-choice questions to knock down a stack of cans. | • Number of questions (up to 5)<br>• Four choices per question |
| 12:00:00 PM<br><br>DigitalClock.swf | Digital clock that displays the current time. | 5 styles to choose from:<br><br>08:17:37 AM    08:17:48 AM    **08:17:59 AM**    08:18:35    08:19:07 AM<br>*Classic        Modern        Crisp        Flip        Odometer* |
| Dunkingbooth.swf | Students answer multiple-choice questions to try to dunk the person in the dunk tank. | • Number of questions (up to 5)<br>• Four choices per question |
| Golf.swf | Students answer multiple-choice questions to try to get a hole in one. | • Number of questions (up to 15)<br>• Four choices per question |
| Hangman.swf | Word puzzle where students guess one letter at a time | • Paper type<br>• Number of questions (up to 10)<br>• Randomization of questions |
| Horserace.swf | Students answer multiple-choice questions to get their horse to win the race. | • Number of questions (up to 5)<br>• Four choices per question |
| JigsawPuzzle.swf | Jigsaw puzzle where the student assembles the image of your choice. | Level of difficulty (number of pieces):<br>1= 4 pieces<br>2= 9 pieces<br>3= 16 pieces<br>4= 25 pieces |

# Lectora Flash Activity Gallery

| Animation | Description | Useful Options |
|---|---|---|
| MatchingPairGame.swf | "Concentration" style game where students flip over two cards at a time to match up a pair. | • Color, text, and image on the back of all cards<br>• Format, text, and image on the front of all cards |
| MillionDollarQuestio... | "Who Wants to Be a Millionaire"-style game. | • Number of questions (up to 15)<br>• Four choices per question<br>• Background color<br>• Currency type |
| Mountainclimb.swf | Students answer multiple-choice questions to help a climber climb up a mountain. | • Number of questions (up to 5)<br>• Four choices per question |
| PhotoViewer.swf | Slide show display with captions. | • Number of images (up to 20)<br>• Controls: auto play, buttons, arrow keys |
| Reveal.swf | Students answer true/false questions to reveal an image. | • Image to reveal<br>• Randomization of questions<br>• Number of tiles/questions (4, 9, or 16) |
| Slotmachine.swf | Students get a chance to play the slot machine when they answer multiple-choice questions correctly. | • Number of questions (up to 9)<br>• Four choices per question |
| Soccer.swf | Students make or miss a soccer penalty kick based on answers to multiple-choice questions. | • Number of questions (up to 15)<br>• Four choices per question |

# Lectora Flash Activity Gallery

| Animation | Description | Useful Options |
|---|---|---|
| **Lorem i**<br><br>TextAnimation.swf | Animated text where individual letters animate in | • Font, color, speed<br>• 10 animation styles to choose from. Individual letters:<br>  Pop up<br>  Shift right<br>  Stretch<br>  Grow<br>  Shrink<br>  Spin<br>  Bounce<br>  Fade<br>  Blink<br>  Drop |
| TicTacToe.swf | Tic-Tac-Toe game with true/false questions. Correct answers give an "O" and incorrect answers give an "X". | • Nine questions<br>• Text on the True/False buttons<br>• Feedback messages |
| Walktheplank.swf | Students answer multiple-choice questions, moving closer to the end of the plank with each missed question. | • Number of questions (up to 5)<br>• Four choices per question |
| WordScramble.swf | Word game where students drag letters into the correct order to unscramble a word | • Size and color of the tiles<br>• Number of tries<br>• "Give up" button |

# Notes

# Actions and Interactions

## Introduction

Actions are the building blocks used to create interactions and custom features. Once you understand how these building blocks work, it is up to you and your imagination to create the interactions, games, and custom features you want.

For example, you would use actions to:

- Take students to a glossary when they click a button.
- Branch to different pages based on how students answer a question.
- Create a game with points and scores.
- Launch a document or go to a website.
- Bring up a pop-up explanation when students roll the mouse over an image.
- Hide the **Next** button until the student clicks all the options on the page.

You can "layer" actions so that several things happen on a single click (such as show an image, play a sound, add a point to a score, etc.). They can be grouped together (action groups) to keep them organized. You can make actions conditional, so that they only "fire" when certain conditions are met. These conditions are based on variables – stored bits of information in a title, such as whether or not a question was answered correctly, a test was passed, etc.

In this chapter, you'll learn about basic actions. In the next chapter, you'll learn about advanced interactions, including conditions and variables.

## In This Chapter

- Understanding Actions
- Simple Action Types
- Adding Buttons and Hyperlinks

# Notes

# Understanding Actions

An action can involve up to six parts.  You will learn about them gradually over the next two chapters.

| Object | Trigger | Action | Target | Condition | Alternate Action |
|---|---|---|---|---|---|
| The object that the action is attached to: | The event that causes the action to run: | The step performed when the trigger initiates the action: | The object that is acted upon: | Any special requirements needed for the action to happen: | The action that happens instead if the condition is not met: |
| • Chapter<br>• Section<br>• Page<br>• Image<br>• Text box<br>• Media<br>• Etc | • Click<br>• Double-click<br>• Mouse enter<br>• Keystroke<br>• No trigger (automatic)<br>• Etc. | • Go to a page<br>• Add a point<br>• Print<br>• Play/Pause/ Stop<br>• Etc. | • Page<br>• Graphic<br>• Text box<br>• Media<br>• Etc. | • Only if a question is correct<br>• Only if a score isn't 0<br>• Only if the student entered "yes"<br>• Etc. | • Otherwise, go to that page<br>• Otherwise, subtract a point<br>• Etc. |

The specific action types are covered throughout the book, based on the type of function they perform. The table on page 97 gives a brief overview of each action and tells you where you can find detailed information about that action.

 **BRIGHT IDEA**

Actions can be attached to just about any object in your title. When attached to a title, chapter, section, or sub-section, actions use the same inheritance as any other object. For example, an action attached at the title level "fires" when any page in the title loads.

 Inheritance, p. 27

## Create an Action

**To add an action to an object:**

1. Select the object you want to attach the action to.

2. Go to the **Insert** tab.

3. Click the **Action** button.

4. Go to the **Properties** tab.

5. In the **Trigger** section, click the drop-down button to select the trigger you want. **(A)**

6. Enter a number of seconds if you want a delay for the action.

7. In the **Action and Target** section, click the **Action** drop-down button to select the action you want. **(B)**

8. Complete the rest of the fields based on the action you chose.

When you add an action, it appears in the **Title Explorer** under the object you attached it to. In the example on the bottom-right, there are four actions attached to one of the graphics.

To delete an action, select it in the **Title Explorer**, and press the **Delete** key.

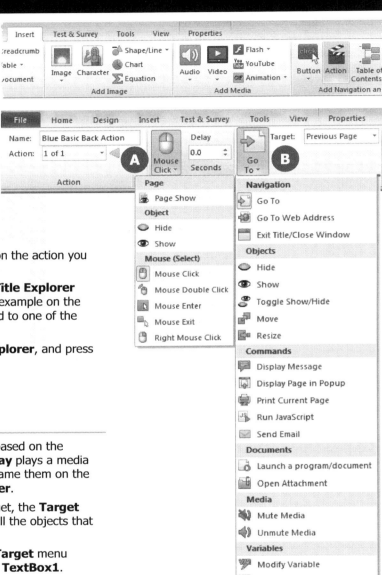

 **BRIGHT IDEAS**

- Actions are named automatically based on the trigger and the action. **OnMClkPlay** plays a media clip on a mouse click. You can rename them on the **Action** tab or in the **Title Explorer**.

- If a given action type needs a target, the **Target** drop-down menu populates with all the objects that are "eligible" for that action.

- It's hard to find an object on the **Target** menu if they all have generic names like **TextBox1**. Instead, name objects with meaning, like **Page heading**, **Left bullet list**, **Pop-up 1**, etc.

- If the object you are attaching the action to is also the target of that action (hide this object when the student clicks it), you can simply select **This Object** from the **Target** menu. This way, you don't have to hunt for the right object. Plus, it makes the action portable – if you paste the action on another object, it works on that object the same way.

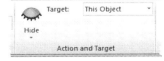

*Multiple actions as seen in the Title Explorer*

# Action Types

| | Action | Description | Covered in | Pg |
|---|---|---|---|---|
| **Navigation** | Go To | Navigate to another page in the title. | 8: Actions | 100 |
| | Go to Web Address | Launch a website. | 8: Actions | 101 |
| | Exit Title/Close Window | Exit the course or close a pop-up window. | 8: Actions | 101 |
| **Objects** | Hide | Hide an object on the page. | 8: Actions | 102 |
| | Show | Show an object on the page. | 8: Actions | 102 |
| | Toggle Show/Hide | Switch between show and hide. | 8: Actions | 102 |
| | Move | Move an object somewhere on the page. | 8: Actions | 103 |
| | Resize | Resize an object smaller or larger. | 8: Actions | 104 |
| | Change Contents | Swap out a graphic, media clip, or text box. | 9: Adv. Actions | 131 |
| | Set Character Pose **11 NEW!** | Change the pose of a character object. | 8: Actions | 104 |
| **Commands** | Display Message | Display a custom pop-up message. | 8: Actions | 105 |
| | Display Page in Popup | Show page from the title in a pop-up window. | 8: Actions | 106 |
| | Run Action Group | Run the actions in an action group. | 9: Adv. Actions | 119 |
| | Print Current Page | Bring up a Print dialog box. | 8: Actions | 107 |
| | Flash Command **11 NEW!** | Communicate with a Flash file. | 9: Adv. Actions | 122 |
| | Run JavaScript | Add your own JavaScript code to run. | 9: Adv. Actions | 104 |
| | Send Email | Bring up a blank e-mail message. | 8: Actions | 107 |
| | Tin Can Statement **11 NEW!** | Track information about a specific activity. | 9: Adv. Actions | 123 |
| **Docs** | Launch a Program/Doc. | Open document such as a PDF or run a program. | 8: Actions | 108 |
| | Open Attachment **11 NEW!** | Open a document such as a PDF. | 8: Actions | 108 |
| **Media** | Pause | Pause an audio, video, or animation. | 8: Actions | 109 |
| | Play | Play an audio, video, or animation. | 8: Actions | 109 |
| | Stop | Stop an audio, video, or animation. | 8: Actions | 109 |
| | Toggle Play Mode | Switch between play and pause. | 8: Actions | 109 |
| | Mute Media | Stop the audio on all Flash media in the title. | 8: Actions | 109 |
| | Unmute Media | Play the audio on all Flash media in the title. | 8: Actions | 109 |
| **Variables** | Modify Variable | Change the value of a variable. | 9: Adv. Actions | 126 |
| | Submit Variable Values | Send the value for all variables. | 9: Adv. Actions | 127 |
| | Reset All Variables | Reset all variables to their initial value. | 9: Adv. Actions | 127 |
| **Questions, Tests & Surveys** | Process Question | Grade a question. | 12: Tests | 188 |
| | Reset Question | Clear a question. | 12: Tests | 188 |
| | Process Test/Survey | Grade a test; send test or survey data. | 12: Tests | 188 |
| | Reset Test/Survey | Reset all questions; set score to 0. | 12: Tests | 188 |
| | Cancel Test/Survey | Cancel a test or a survey. | 12: Tests | 188 |
| **Forms** | Submit Form | Send form data. | 14: Forms | 208 |
| | Reset Form | Clear all responses on a form. | 14: Forms | 208 |
| **Progress Bars** | Set Progress Bar Position | Set the location on a progress bar. | 10: Interface | 145 |
| | Step Progress Bar Position | Move a progress bar forward one step. | 10: Interface | 145 |

# Action Triggers

Actions have 11 different trigger options. The options vary based on the object you attach the action to. For example, if you are working with a media clip, you can use the **Done Playing** trigger, which is not available on non-media objects. The table on the next page explains each of the trigger types and what types of objects you can attach them to.

When you attach an action to the title or a chapter, section, or sub-section, it fires on every page in that title, chapter, etc.

 **CAUTION**

- The **Show** and **Hide** triggers can be confusing because they are also the names of actions. For example, when the page loads (**Show** *trigger*), you can show (**Show** *action*) a text box. Double-check your work to make sure you are setting up the right options in the right fields.

- Some of the trigger types have special restrictions when publishing to the Web:

- The **Mouse Click** and **Right Mouse Click** triggers cannot be attached to a title, chapter, section, or page.

- The **Done Playing** trigger only work when the media element is a Flash file and you are publishing to HTML.

# Timed Interval and On Keystroke Triggers

When you select the **Keystroke** or **Timed Interval** triggers, there are additional fields to fill in.

**Keystroke:** Click the **Next Key Typed** button, and type the keystroke you want to have trigger the action. You can type any letter, number, or special character, as well as use any **Shift**, **Alt**, or **Ctrl** combination.

**Timed Interval:** Enter the number of seconds you want to use as the interval for the timer. The action fires every time it reaches that interval.

 **CAUTION**

If you are publishing to the Web, avoid using keystrokes that work in the student's browser. If a student presses **Ctrl** + **P** when viewing the course in Internet Explorer, the browser's **Print** dialog box appears. **Ctrl** + **W** closes the browser window completely! Be sure to test your actions in the browser(s) the students will be using.

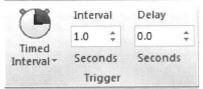

# Trigger Types

| Trigger | Description<br>*Action is performed when:* | Example Application | Title/Chapter/Section/Page | Text Box | Image | Audio/Video | Animation | Button | Hyperlink |
|---|---|---|---|---|---|---|---|---|---|
| **Page** | | | | | | | | | |
| **Page Show** | The page loads. | When the page loads, the student's point total is refreshed. | ✓ | ✓ | ✓ | ✓ | ✓ | | |
| **Object** | | | | | | | | | |
| **Done Playing** | The media element or timer is done playing. | When the audio is done playing, the Next button appears. | | | | ✓ | ✓ | | |
| **Hide** | The object is hidden or the student leaves the page. | When a pop-up text box goes away, the audio stops playing. When a user leaves any page in a chapter, a point is added to his or her game score. | ✓ | ✓ | ✓ | ✓ | ✓ | | |
| **Show** | The object appears. | When an image appears, the corresponding audio plays. | ✓ | ✓ | ✓ | ✓ | ✓ | | |
| **Select/ Change** | A form element is selected or changes. | Run if/then logic based on the student's answer to a form | form | | | | | | |
| **Mouse (Select)** | | | | | | | | | |
| **Mouse Click** | The user clicks the page/object. | The user clicks a button or link to go to another page. The user clicks an object to get more information. | ✓ | ✓ | ✓ | ✓ | | ✓ | ✓ |
| **Mouse Double Click** | The user double-clicks the object. | The user double-clicks a graphic to see a larger version of it. | | | | ✓ | ✓ | | |
| **Mouse Enter** | The user hovers the mouse over the object. | The user rolls over an item to see a pop-up description. | | | | ✓ | ✓ | | |
| **Mouse Exit** | The user moves the mouse off of the object. | Pop-up description goes away when the user pulls the mouse away. | | | | ✓ | ✓ | | |
| **Right Mouse Click** | The user clicks the page/object with the right mouse button. | The user right-clicks an image to see a pop-up description. | ✓ | ✓ | ✓ | ✓ | | | |
| **Keyboard** | | | | | | | | | |
| **Any Key** | The user presses any key on the keyboard. | The user presses any key to stop an animation. | ✓ | | | | | | |
| **Keystroke** | The user presses the pre-defined key on the keyboard. | The user presses the right arrow to go to the next page. The user presses **F12** in a game about keyboard shortcuts. | ✓ | | | | | | |
| **Other** | | | | | | | | | |
| **Timed Interval** | The timer interval is reached. | An item flashes on and off at set intervals. | ✓ | | | | | | |

# Simple Action Types

The action types on the next few pages are easy to set up and use, even if you are a first-time Lectora user.   See page 97 for a list of where the other action types are taught.

## Navigation: Go To

Use the **Go To** action when you want the student to go to a different page in the title.  Once you select the action, the **Target** drop-down menu is populated with pre-set pages (such as first page, next page, etc.) or the specific pages in the title.  Simply select the page you want from the menu.

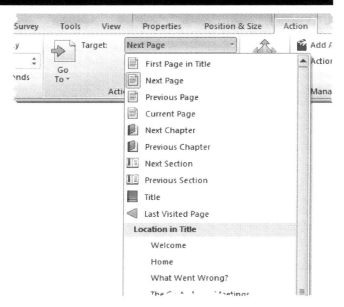

## BRIGHT IDEAS

- In previous versions of Lectora, the **Go To** action also included the options for going to a website or bringing up a page in a pop-up window.  Those options are now their own actions.

- If you select **Current Page** or one of the specific pages, you have the option of taking the student to a specific object on the page.  This is useful for long, scrolling pages.

- The **Title** option is useful if you want to create a menu that links to multiple titles on a CD.

- If you want to link to the first page in a title, chapter, or section, don't link directly to the first page itself.  Instead, link to the title, chapter, or section itself.  That way, if you delete or rearrange the pages, the link will still be good.

## TIME SAVER

The **Home**, **Back**, and **Next** buttons in the Lectora Stock Library come pre-populated with actions going to the first page in the title, next page, and previous page **Go To** actions.

## Navigation: Go to Web Address Action

Use this option to take the student to an Internet or intranet website. Enter the url in the **Address** field. In the **Open In** field, indicate if you want the website to appear in the course window or in a new, pop-up window.

If you select the **New Window** option, you click the **Edit** button next to the menu to set properties for the pop-up window.

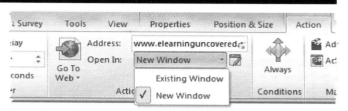

### New Window Properties

**Window Name**: Type the name you want to have appear in the header bar of the pop-up window.

**Window Style**: Select **New Browser Window** for a standard browser window, **Lightbox** to use the style shown on page 105, and **Use Publish Option** to use whatever settings you select during publishing.

**Window Size and Screen Position**: By default, Lectora uses the target page size as the window size and places the window in the middle of the user's screen. Uncheck the boxes if you want to enter your own width and height or x/y position.

**HTML Properties**: If publishing to the Web, use these checkboxes to "lock down" the browser, such as hiding the address bar (Location Bar).

## Navigation: Exit Title/Close Window Action

This action is one of the easiest to set up, with no additional fields other than the trigger and action.

- If the action is on a pop-up window, this action closes the window.
- If the action is on the main course page, it closes the course.

 **TIME SAVER**

If you use one of the pre-made exit buttons from the Lectora Stock Library, this action is already attached.

# Objects: Hide, Show, and Toggle Hide/Show Actions

### Hide

The **Hide** action hides the target you choose. When you select this action, the **Target** menu populates with every object on the page, including any that are inherited. For example, you might want text instructions that you hide once a video starts playing.

The **Hide** action is different than inheritance. If you disinherit something, it doesn't show at all. The **Hide** action takes something that does appear on the page and hides it based on a trigger.

### Show

The **Show** action shows an object. The **Target** menu shows all the items on the page, including those that are inherited. For example, you may want to show a text box with a description when the student clicks a hyperlink, or you may want to show the **Next** button when the audio is done.

### Toggle Hide/Show

This action switches back and forth between show and hide. If the object is hidden, it will be shown. If it is showing, then it will become hidden. This action works well with the **Timed Interval** trigger, creating a flashing effect, such as a flashing arrow or a flashing border around an item to draw attention to it.

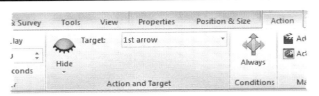

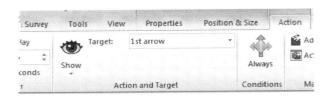

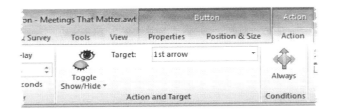

## BRIGHT IDEA

For the **Show** action to do anything, the target must not be already visible. It can either be hidden by a previous action or because the **Initially Hidden** check box has been checked on the target's **Properties** tab.

## CAUTION

Flashing objects can not only be distracting but can also be harmful to people with certain disabilities. Per Section 508, avoid flashing faster than 2 hz (twice per second) and slower than 55 hz.

## Objects: Move Action

The **Move** action moves an object to a different point on the screen. For example, you might want to move a graphic for emphasis or move a game piece along a path.

There are three parts to a **Move** action.

- **Target**: From the drop-down menu, select the item that you want to be moved.

- **Move To**: Click the pencil icon to enter the X position (# of pixels from the left side of the page) and Y position (# of pixels from the top of the page) where you want the object to appear.

- **Speed**: Use the slider to indicate how fast you want the object to move.

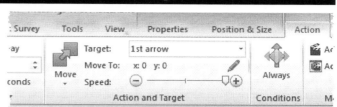

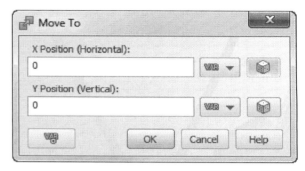

### POWER TIP

You can base the X/Y destination coordinates on the value of a variable. In the **Move To** dialog box, click the **VAR** drop-down button to select an existing variable or click the dice button to enter minimum and maximum values for a random variable.

### BRIGHT IDEA

- Remember that you can also use transitions to move an item when it first appears or disappears.

- If you aren't sure what X/Y coordinates you want, position the object where you want it to move and write down the coordinates that show in the **Status Bar**.

# Objects: Resize Action

The **Resize** action resizes an object to be smaller or larger than it initially appears. For example, you may want to enlarge an object while it is being discussed or when the student rolls the mouse over a trigger. You can resize the object to a specific pixel dimension or to a percentage of the current on-screen size.

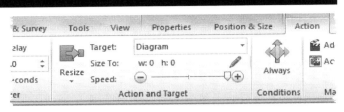

There are three parts to a **Resize** action.

- **Target**: From the drop-down menu, select the item that you want to resize.

- **Size To**: Click the pencil icon to enter the new width and height of the object, in pixels.

- **Speed**: Use the slider to indicate how fast you want the object to change size.

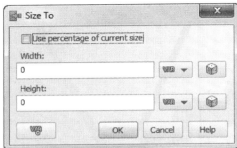

 **CAUTION**

- Be careful about enlarging an object so much that it loses quality.

- When you enter the width and height, you'll need to calculate the numbers yourself to make sure your image doesn't get stretched in either direction.

- If you use the percentage option, the object will grow or shrink that much each time the student activates the action. A few clicks can make for a very large or very small object.

 **POWER TIP**

Just as with the **Move** action, you can click the pencil icon for a **Resize** action to use a variable to determine your width and height. In addition, you can check the box at the top to change the size based on a percentage of the current size rather than a fixed value.

# Objects: Set Character Pose

If you use one of the characters in the Lectora Stock Library, you can create actions to change the pose of that character. For example, you could change a character to have a happy expression if the student gets a question right and a sad expression if the student gets a question wrong.

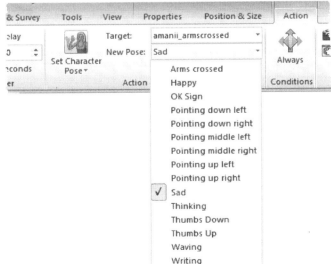

# Commands: Display Message Action

The **Display Message action** displays a text message to the student in a small pop-up window. Simply enter your text in the field provided.

If you check the lightbox option when publishing, the main page is grayed out, giving emphasis to the pop-up window. If you deselect the lightbox option, the window appears as a system message.

 Publishing Options, p. 259

 ## DESIGN TIP

The **Display Message** option is very quick and easy to set up. However, it doesn't give you any formatting options. For more choices, use the **Display Page in Popup** option on the next page.

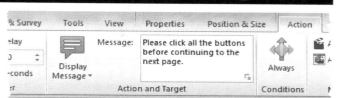

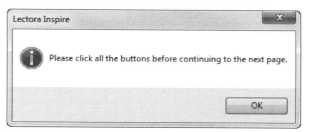

*Message with lightbox effect*

*Message without lightbox effect*

 ## POWER TIP

If you click the arrow in the message entry box, a larger window appears that includes the option to insert variables (including a random value) into the message.

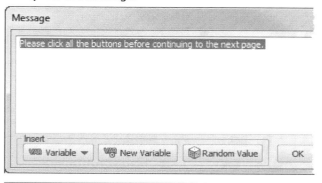

# Commands: Display in Popup Page Action

With this action, you can display any page in your title as a pop-up page. For example, you might have a link at the top of your course to a help page. When the student clicks the link, a small page appears in a pop-up window with contact information for who to contact with questions or problems.

In the **Target** field, select the page from the title you want to have in the pop-up window. In the **Scroll To** field, you can choose to have the page jump to a specific object, which is especially useful on long, scrolling pages.

As with the **Display Message** action, the new page either appears with the lightbox effect or in a standard system window, based on your publishing preferences.

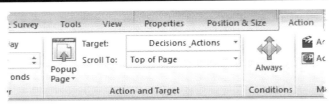

 **BRIGHT IDEA**

This action is not new to version 11. However, it is now a standalone action. Before it was part of the **Go to** action.

 **DESIGN TIPS**

- Make pop-up windows smaller than the main title pages so students can still see the main course page underneath and won't get "lost."

- Avoid bringing up a pop-up page with full navigational elements. If there are two instances of the course open, the student (and the LMS) may get confused.

- Create a separate chapter for pop-up pages that doesn't have standard navigation, isn't included in a table of contents, and uses a smaller page size.

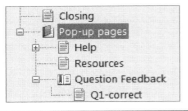

## Commands: Print Current Page Action

The **Print Current Page** action brings up the **Print** dialog box in the user's browser so he or she can print the current page. The student will still need to configure any print settings and click the **Print** button in the pop-up window.

 **CAUTION**

If you plan to have students print a page, you might want to first try it yourself to make sure it looks good. For example, if you have hidden objects, rollovers, or a very wide interface, the page may not look good when printed.

## Commands: Send Email Action

The **Send Email** action opens the user's e-mail program (such as Outlook) and creates a blank e-mail message using the address you type in the field provided. You might use this button for an "Ask the Expert" feature.

 **CAUTION**

- Your student's browser settings determine what e-mail application is used to generate the e-mail. You may want the corporate Outlook account, but the student's browser might launch Gmail.

- Strict security settings might keep this action from working properly.

 **TIME SAVER**

The **Lectora Stock Library** has a print button and an email button that have appropriate icons and actions already attached.

## Documents: Launch a Program/Document Action

This action opens a document or starts a program/application based on the location you enter in the **File** field.  For example, you can launch a PDF from your intranet site or launch another published Lectora title.

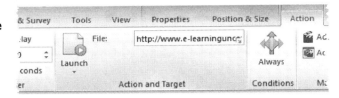

## Documents: Open Attachment

This action opens a document such as a policy document, reference guide, template, or a transcript.  The attached document is then stored in the title's **extern** folder.  For the student, the document opens in a new window.

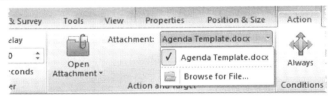

From the drop-down menu, either select a file that has been previously attached, or select **Browse for File** to find and select the document you want.

 **BRIGHT IDEAS**

- The attachment "lives" with the course files. If the document ever needs to be updated, you can either copy over the document in the **Extern** folder (if the new document has the same name), or open the title, attach the new document, and republish (if it has a different name).

- You can also link to a document via the **Go to Web Address** action.  For example, you can use this action to link to a document stored on your intranet site.

# Media Actions

The following actions work with audio, video, and animation files.

## Play Action

The **Play** action causes the media to play, if it is not already playing. For example, you can use this when you have a video that should play once the audio is done, or when you want a certain sound to play when the student performs a certain task. If the object is set to auto start on the **Properties** tab, this action is not necessary.

## Pause Action

The **Pause** action pauses the media, keeping track of where it was paused. A subsequent **Play** action plays the media from where it left off. For example, you may pause the audio if the student clicks an object on the page that also has audio. The pause point is lost when the student navigates off the page.

## Stop Action

The **Stop** action stops the object completely. A **Play** action following a **Stop** action plays the object from the beginning.

## Toggle Play Mode

This action switches back and forth between the **Play** and **Pause** commands with each successive click.

## Mute FLV Media

This action mutes the audio portion of any FLV audio or video in the entire title. This is useful for a global audio on/off button as it carries over from page to page. The media still downloads and plays – the student just can't hear it.

## Unmute FLV Media

This action unmutes the audio portion of any FLV audio or video in the entire title. It could be used as part of a global audio on/off button. This action does not start a media file. Instead, it unmutes the audio of a clip that has some other trigger to start it playing.

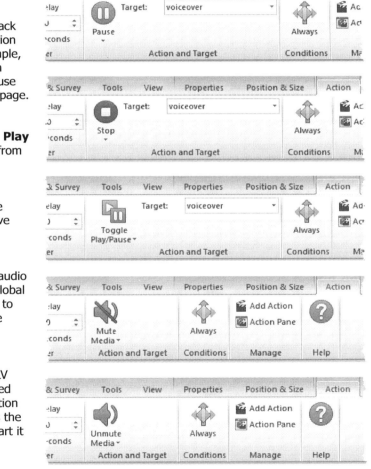

 **BRIGHT IDEA**

Remember, you can include a controller with media elements that includes play, pause, and stop controls, in which case, you wouldn't need to set up any of these actions.

**DESIGN TIP**

### Creating Rollover and Pop-up Interactions

In a pop-up, the student clicks an object (trigger) and something appears (target). The item(s) that appears might show up on the page or might appear in a pop-up window.

In a rollover, the student hovers the mouse over the trigger to see the target, which usually disappears when the mouse leaves the trigger. Typically, the items appear directly on the page and not in a pop-up window.

### Create a Pop-Up (target on the page)

1. Create the trigger object that the student interacts with.
2. Create the target object that will appear.
3. Go to the target object's **Properties** tab and make it initially hidden.
4. Add an action to the trigger object.
   - Trigger: On Click
   - Action: Show
   - Target: Your target object

### Create a Pop-Up (in a new window)

See page 106.

### Create a Rollover

1. Create the trigger object that the student interacts with.
2. Create the target object that will appear.
3. Go to the target object's **Properties** tab and make it initially hidden.
4. Add two actions to the trigger object.

   Show Action
   - Trigger: Mouse Enter
   - Action: Show
   - Target: Your target object

   Hide Action
   - Trigger: Mouse Exit
   - Action: Hide
   - Target: Your target object

When setting up your trigger and target objects, name them logically so it's easier to set up the actions, i.e., **Trigger 1** and **Pop-Up 1**.

Set up the first pair completely, and then copy and paste additional pairs. That way, the actions and properties are already set up.

If you want more than one object (such as text and an image) to appear at once, group the target objects together and show/hide the group.

 **POWER TIP**

### Adding Multiple Actions

- You can attach more than one action to an object.
- The actions "fire" in the order they appear in the **Title Explorer**. With some interactions, the order is very important. As with any objects in the **Title Explorer**, you can drag and drop the actions to put them in the order you want or even change what object they are attached to.
- If you have multiple actions, you can use the green forward and back arrows on the **Action** tab to move quickly between the different actions.
- It's easy to view all the actions on an object with the new **Action Pane**. Click the **Action Pane** button on the **Action** tab to view the pane. Click an action to view its properties on the **Action** tab. Click and drag the three dots on the left of an action to change the order.

 **CAUTION**

If the rollover or pop-up doesn't work when you first set it up, ask yourself:

- Is the target object set to be initially hidden? (The **Show** action has no impact if the item is already showing.)
- Did you attach the action to the *trigger* object? (It's easy to add it to the *target* object by mistake.)
- Did you select the right *target* object in the action's dialog box? (It's easy to select the *trigger* object by mistake.)

# Adding Buttons and Hyperlinks

Buttons and hyperlinks are two great ways to work with **On Click** actions.

There are four ways to make buttons:

- Add a pre-made button from the Lectora Stock Library.
- Create a text button using a wizard.
- Create a transparent button that the student can't see (which is usually layered on top of something the student can see).
- Import a button—either a static button or a 3-phase animated gif.

Hyperlinks can be added to any selection of text and are especially useful for glossary terms.

## Add a Stock Button

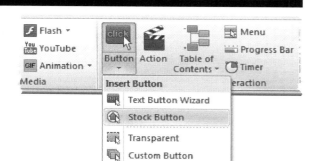

**To add a pre-made button from the Lectora Stock Library:**

1. Go to the **Insert** tab.
2. Click the **Button** drop-down menu.
3. Select **Stock Button**.
4. Double-click the folder for the type of button you want.
5. Double-click the button you want.

### ⏱ TIME SAVERS

- Many of the stock buttons already have actions attached, such as next, back, print, home, and close.
- Rather than go to the **Insert** tab, you can also navigate to the button options by clicking the **Stock Library** tab.

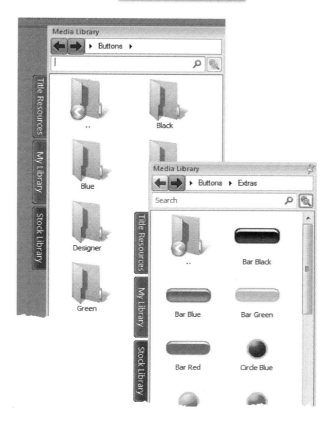

# Create a Custom Text Button

**To create a custom text button:**

1. Go to the **Insert** tab.
2. Click the **Button** drop-down menu.
3. Select **Text Button Wizard**.
4. Select the button shape you want.
5. Click the **Next** button.
6. Enter the number of buttons you want.
7. If more than one, enter details about the alignment and spacing of the buttons.
8. Click the **Next** button.
9. Type the text that will go on the button.
10. Select the formatting options you want.
11. Click the **Finish** button.

   *If you are creating multiple buttons, click **Next** instead of **Finish** to set up the other buttons.*

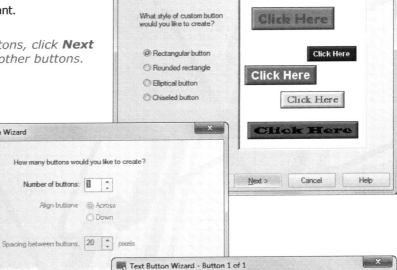

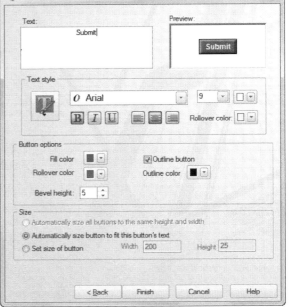

## Button Formatting Options

**Text Style:** Here you can either select a pre-made text style or set up the individual formatting elements.

 Text Styles, p. 40

**Button Colors:** Here you can choose the standard fill color, the color that it changes to when the student rolls over it, and an outline color. In this section, you can add more or less depth to the button by changing the height of the bevel.

 Selecting Colors, p. 64

**Size:** If you are making more than one button, you have the option of setting all the buttons to be the same size. The default option is for Lectora to determine the size of the button based on the size of the text. Select the last option if you want to enter your own width and height.

## Create a Custom Text Button (cont'd)

### Adding Actions

Buttons already have an **Action** tab. Go to that tab to set up your action(s).

### Editing Buttons

Once your button is created, go to its **Properties** tab to change the formatting and to the **Action** tab to add actions to the button.

 **DESIGN TIP**

You can use graphics fonts, such as Webdings, to create custom graphic buttons out of text.

## Create a Transparent Button

A transparent button shows up light blue while you are working with it in edit mode, but is invisible to the student when the course is published.

**To create a transparent button.**

1. Go to the **Insert** menu.
2. Click the **Button** drop-down menu.
3. Select **Transparent**.

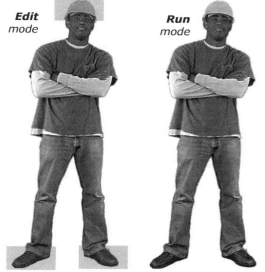

*Edit* mode          *Run* mode

# Add a Custom Button

In addition to the buttons that come with Lectora, you can add your own buttons. You can either design them yourself or find them on a clip art site. In most web applications, buttons have three different states that make them "highlight" when the user hovers the mouse over them and "indent" when the student clicks them.

| Normal State | What they look like when nothing is happening | |
| Down State | What they look like when they are clicked | |
| Over State | What they look like when the user's mouse is over them | |

**To add a custom button:**

1. Go to the **Insert** tab.
2. Click the **Button** drop-down menu.
3. Select **Custom Button**.
4. In the **Normal** field, select the image you want for the normal state.
5. If you want a down state and an over state, select an image from the respective drop-down menus.
6. Click the **OK** button.

If you want to change any of the three state images later, you can do that on the button's **Properties** tab.

## Add a Hyperlink

**To add a hyperlink:**
1. Select the text you want to use for the hyperlink.
2. On the **Home** tab, click the **Hyperlink** button.
3. Set up your action on the dialog box that appears.
4. Click OK.

**DESIGN TIP**

To change the color of a single hyperlink, use the **Text Color** drop-down menu as with any other text. To change the default color for all hyperlinks in your title, go to the **Design** tab, and use the **Hyperlink Color** drop-down menu.

## Edit/Remove a Hyperlink

**To edit a hyperlink:**
1. Double-click the text box to go into text edit mode.
2. Double-click the hyperlinked text.
3. Make your changes in the **Add Hyperlink** dialog box.
4. Click **OK**.

**To remove a hyperlink:**
1. Double-click the text box to go into text edit mode.
2. Right-click the hyperlinked text.
3. Select **Remove Hyperlink**.

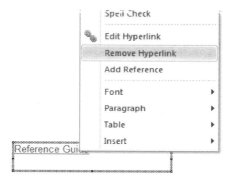

# Notes

# Advanced Actions and Variables

## Introduction

In the previous chapter, you learned what actions are, how to add one to an object, and how to use the simple action types. In this chapter, you'll learn how to work with action groups, events timed to audio, conditions, variables, and advanced action types.

# Notes

# Action Groups

When working with multiple actions, you can use action groups to organize them. Group actions together just to keep them visually organized or to make it easy to use them over and over again. For example, the same show message, play sound, and add point actions may apply to every question in a game. You can create a single action group and then trigger it with each question. That way, you don't have to set up all three actions on each and every question.

Action groups do not run on their own. Any action put in an action group loses its trigger function. Instead, the group is run by using a separate action, **Run Action Group**.

## Create and Run an Action Group

**To group actions together:**

1. Select the actions you want to group.
2. Go to the **Home** tab.
3. Click the **Group Selection** button.

——— or ———

1. Select the actions in the **Title Explorer**.
2. Right-click any of the items.
3. Select **Group**.

——— or ———

1. Go to the **Insert** tab.
2. Click the **Group** button to create an empty group.
3. Add actions to the group by dragging an existing action there in the **Title Explorer** or selecting the group and then adding a new action.

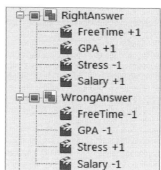

**To add items to an existing group:**

1. In the **Title Explorer**, drag the action(s) into the group.

**To ungroup the entire group:**

1. Right-click the **Group** icon in the **Title Explorer**.
2. Select **Ungroup**.

**To remove a single action from a group:**

1. Right-click that action in the **Title Explorer**.
2. Select Ungroup.

——— or ———

1. Drag the item out of the group.

**To run an action group:**

1. Add an action to the trigger object.
2. Select **Run Action Group** as the action type.
3. In the **Target** field, select the action group you want to run.

# Using Events to Time Actions to Audio and Video

If you want to time actions based on a certain point in an audio or video file, you can do that with events. For example, if you'd like individual text boxes to appear as they are discussed in the audio, you can time them to events. You would:

- Make each bullet point its own text box.
- Make them initially invisible.
- Create an audio event at each point where you want a text box to appear.
- Add an action to each event to show the corresponding text box.

 **CAUTION**

It might seem easier to time elements to your audio by using delayed actions (show text box 1 after 10 seconds, show text box 2 after 23 seconds, etc.). This may work when publishing to CD or EXE, but it is likely to cause trouble if the course will be viewed over a network. If the audio or video has any delays across a network, then your timing will be off. It is safer to use events when you want elements timed exactly.

## Add Events to Your Media Files with Lectora Inspire

To add events to your media file:

1. Go to the media file's **Properties** tab.
2. Click the **Edit** button.
3. Position the playhead **(A)** where you want the event.
4. Click the **Event** button.
5. Enter a name for the event.
6. Click the **OK** button.
7. Repeat steps 3 to 6 for additional events.
8. Click the **Save** button.
9. Close the editor.

If you want to later remove or reposition any of the events, click the **Event** drop-down button and select **View Event** List.

 Inspire Audio Editor, p. 79
Inspire Video Editor, p. 82

 **BRIGHT IDEA**

If you don't have the full Lectora Inspire license, you don't have the audio editor shown. However, you can still add events (called script commands) to your audio with Windows Media File Editor. It comes with the free download of Windows Media Encoder.

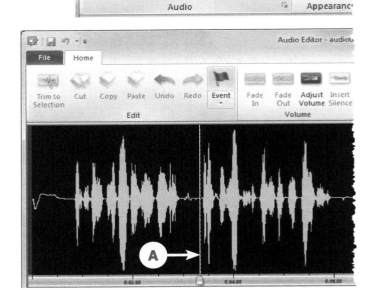

# Assign Actions to Events

**To assign an action to an event:**

1. Go to the media object's **Properties** tab.
2. Click the **Sync Events** button.
3. In the table, select the event you want to work with.
4. In the panel at the bottom, set up your action.
5. Repeat steps 3 and 4 for additional events.
6. Click the **OK** button.

 **BRIGHT IDEAS**

- Click the **Set Event Timings** button to go back to the media editor and adjust your events (if you have Lectora Inspire).

- If you want to attach more than one action to an event, use an action group.

 Action Groups, p. 119

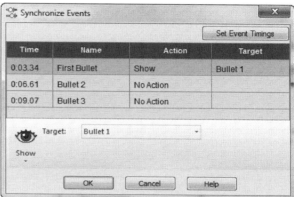

# Set Actions to a Timer

Rather than timing actions to a media file, you can also set them to a new timer object. For example, in a game, you can have the submit button disappear when time is up.

**To add a timer object:**

1. Go to the **Insert** tab.
2. Click the **Timer** button.
3. Go to the **Properties** tab.
4. In the **Type** menu, select either **Count Down** or **Count Up**.
5. In the **Time** fields, enter the duration for the timer.
6. Check or uncheck the **Auto Start** based on whether or not you want the timer to start as soon as it appears.
7. Configure any of the other properties you want.

**To set an action to trigger when the timer finishes:**

1. Select the timer object.
2. Go to the **Action** tab already on the timer.
3. Set the action you want.

 **BRIGHT IDEAS**

- You can add a timer to show to the student even if you don't have an action attached to it.

- If you uncheck **Auto Start**, you'll have to add a **Play** action to start the timer.

- The **Action** tab for the timer is already set with the **Done** Playing trigger.

# Other Advanced Actions

## Commands: Flash Command

If you have a Flash file (.swf) file on your page, you can control it from within Lectora. For example, you can jump to a specific frame in the Flash file or receive or set variable values. Select the command you want from the drop-down menu, and then enter any settings asked for.

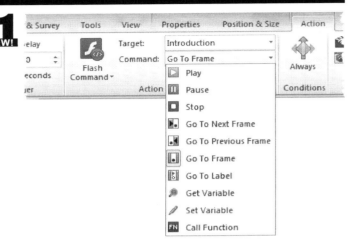

## Commands: Run JavaScript

With this action, you can add custom JavaScript code to your title to extend the capabilities of Lectora. Add your script to the **JavaScript** field.

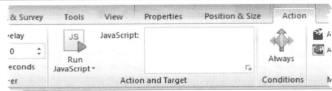

# Commands: Tin Can Statement

Tin Can, often referred to as "the next generation of SCORM" tracks course completion and test scores much like SCORM does. In addition, Tin Can can also receive information about individual learning activities within a course, such as answering a question or sharing content. With this action, you can send such details to a Tin Can learning record store (LRS).

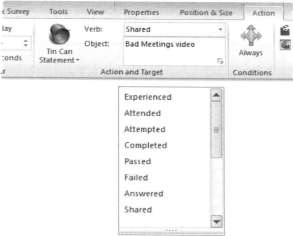

To create a **Tin Can Statement** action, select the verb you want from the Verb menu. Then enter the name of the object for that verb in the **Object** field. For example, if you want to write a statement that the student shared a video, the name of the video would go in the **Object** field.

By default, the **Object** field is populated with the name of the object that the action is attached to. However, you can change the text to whatever you want. As with many actions, you can also click the small arrow in the bottom corner of the field for a dialog box with more options, such as including variable values.

# Working With Variables

A variable is a stored piece of information within the title that you can use to set up if/then logic and create dynamic content.

Variables come from many places:

### Pre-Defined

Lectora keeps track of course and user information automatically, such as the name of the current chapter, section, and page; the current date; and the student's name (if pulling from an LMS). These are read-only variables that you cannot change. Many of them only appear if you are publishing to AICC/SCORM.

### Student-Modified

If you have any form elements, such as a text entry box, you can capture information from the users as they take the course.

### Question-Based

Anytime you add a question (test question or survey question), the answer is automatically kept, along with whether they got it right or wrong. The test's overall score and pass/fail status is stored as well.

### Action-Driven

You can create any variable you want and use actions to change the value.

You might use variables to keep track of:

- Number of points received in a game.
- Number of turns a user has taken in a game.
- Whether everything has been clicked on a page.
- Preferences about having the audio on or off.
- Whether the user is manager/front-line, hourly/salaried, etc.

There are any number of things you can do with that information:

- Display the user's score.
- Turn a feature off/on once something has been accessed.
- Create a certificate with the student's name and date of completion.
- Create a branching scenario where the path changes based on the student's answers.

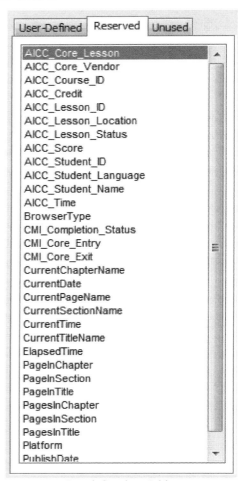

*Pre-defined variables*

*User-defined variables*

# Create a New Variable

**To create a new variable:**

1. Go to the **Tools** tab.
2. Click the **Variables** button.
3. Click the **Add** button.
4. In the **Variable Name** field, enter the name for the variable.
5. Enter the settings you want for your variable.
6. Click the **OK** button.
7. Click the **Close** button.

## Variable Settings

### Initial Value

By default, all variables start with a value of 0. If you want something different, enter it here. You can use a different number, or even words. For example, you might want the value to be on or off.

### Retain Variable Value Between Sessions

When unchecked (the default), all variable values are reset back to the initial value when the student leaves the course. Check this box if you want the values to stay in place for the next time the student returns.

### Random Initial Value

If you check this box, you get **Min Value** and **Max Value** fields instead of the **Initial Value** field. This generates a random initial value between and including the minimum and maximum numbers you enter. For example, if you had a scenario with dice, you could have a random value between 1 and 6, used to determine which picture to display (which side of the die).

 **CAUTION**

- When naming your variable, it must be a unique name (can't be the same as any other in the title) and cannot use spaces or special characters except underscore.

- When retaining values, the information is stored with the LMS (if publishing to an LMS) or with cookies on the user's computer (if publishing to HTML).

  With HTML, the variables reset if the user clears his or her cookies. Only one set of variables can be stored per user profile.

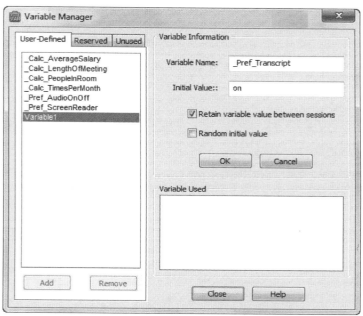

 **BRIGHT IDEAS**

- Unlike actions, variables are not found in the **Title Explorer**. To remove or edit the settings of a variable, go back to the **Tools** tab and click **Variables**. Select the **variable** you want and either click **Edit** or **Remove** at the bottom.

- If you will be using a question or form element to capture information, you do not need to set up a variable yourself. One will be created automatically when you add the object to your title.

- When using variables, you have to select them from a drop-down menu in alphabetical order. To help find your user-defined variables easily, start them with the underscore character (_) so they are alphabetized at the top. If you have several variables for the same interaction or purpose, put a "code" after the underscore so that related variables are alphabetized together.

# Change the Value of a Variable

Some variables are controlled fully by the course (such as **CurrentDate**).  Some are modified by the system but can also be modified by you (such as a test score).  Any variable you create yourself needs to be updated by you.

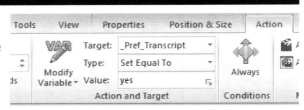

**To modify a variable:**

1. Add an action to the trigger object.
2. Select **Modify Variable** as the action type.
3. From the **Target** drop-down, select the variable you want to modify.
4. From the **Type** drop-down menu, select the type of modification you want.  (See below.)
5. In the **Value** field, enter the value to use for the modification. (See below.)

## Modification Types

**Set Equal To**: Replaces the current variable value with what is in the **Value** field.  (May be text or a number.)

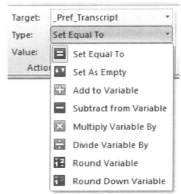

**Set As Empty**: Deletes the current variable value.

**Add to Variable**: Adds the value in the **Value** field to the current variable value.  If the variable or the value is text, the new value is put at the end of the existing variable. (**3** added to **Attempt** becomes **Attempt 3**.)  If both are numbers, the two are added.  (**3** added to **4** becomes **7**.)

**Subtract from Variable**: Subtracts the current variable by the number in the **Value** field.  (Both must be numbers.)

**Multiply Variable By**: Multiplies the variable by the number in the **Value** field.  (Both must be numbers.)

**Divide Variable By**: Divides the variable by the number in the **Value** field.  (Both must be numbers.)

**Round Variable**: Rounds the variable to the nearest whole number.  Numbers with .5 and higher are rounded up; numbers below that are rounded down.  (For numbers only; no value is needed.)

**Round Down Variable**: Truncates the variable, rounding it down to the next lower whole number.  (For numbers only; no value is needed.)

## Advanced Value Options

If you click the small arrow in the **Value** field, a dialog box with more options appears.

Use the **Variable** drop-down menu to use another variable as your value.  For example, if calculating the monthly cost of a meeting, you might multiply the cost of one meeting by the number of meetings per month, which is stored in another variable.

Use the **Random Value** button to set a minimum and maximum value for a random number as your value.  For example, you might want to set the variable to be a random number between 1 and 100.

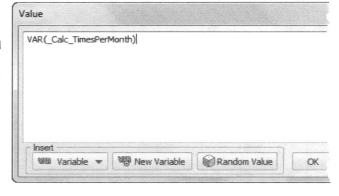

## Reset All Variables

This action resets all variable values to their initial value, including author-defined variables, tests, surveys, forms, and completion status.  For example, you can attach this action to a button so the student can reset them or use an automatic action (**Show** trigger) based on certain conditions.

 **BRIGHT IDEA**

Remember that when you set up a variable, you can set it so that the values are not retained between sessions.  With tests and surveys, you can make the same choice in the test chapter or survey chapter properties.

## Submit Variable Values

This action lets you submit the values for all variables in the title to an e-mail address or to an online database (CGI program).

### E-Mail Address

In the **Address** field, use the following format: mailto:<emailaddress>. The user needs to have an e-mail program on his or her computer, and configuration settings need to allow for communication between the course and the user's software.

### CGI Program

You can submit the variable values to an online application such as a database.  In the **Address** field, enter the full or relative Web address to send the information to.

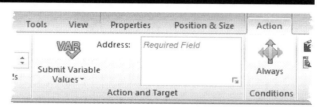

# Conditional Actions

You can build if/then logic by placing conditions on your actions.  For example, you could:

- Add one point to a score if the student answered a certain question correctly.
- Subtract one point if the student answered a question incorrectly.
- Show a table of contents to allow free navigation if the student has completed the course.
- Play the audio file if the audio preference is set to "on."
- Skip the next chapter if the student is not a supervisor.

Conditions are set up on the **Condition** button on the action's **Properties** tab and are based on the value of a variable.  If you don't add any conditions, then the action fires whenever the trigger occurs (mouse click, etc.).  If conditions are added, the action only fires when the trigger happens and the conditions are met.  Conditions are one way to create a branching scenario.

## Add a Condition to an Action

**To add a condition to an action:**

1. Go to the **Action** tab for the action you want to modify.
2. Click the **Conditions** button.
3. In the **Variable** column, use the drop-down menu to select the variable you want to use for the condition.
4. In the **Relationship** field, enter the type of condition you want. (See table below.)
5. In the **Value** field, enter the value for the relationship, if needed.
6. Repeat steps 3 through 6 if you want more than one condition.
7. Click **OK**.

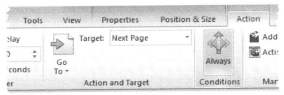

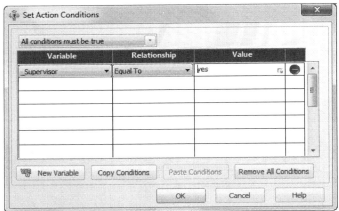

| Relationship Type | Typical Use | Comments |
|---|---|---|
| **Contains/Does Not Contain** | Go to a certain page if a form entry has a certain prefix. | The **Value** field needs to match the variable value's spelling and capitalization exactly. |
| **Equal To/Not Equal To** | Display information based on the student's choice in a menu, form, etc. | |
| **Greater Than/Less Than** | Show a message after the student has made three attempts. | Can also be used with number-based or time/date-based variables. |
| **Greater Than or Equal To/ Less Than or Equal To** | Show a message if a student has gotten above 80%. | |
| **Is Correct/Is Not Correct** | Go to a certain page if the answer is correct. | Only available when the variable is a question.  No value needed. |
| **Is Empty/Is Not Empty** | Display a warning message if the student leaves a field blank. | No value needed. |
| **Is Passed/Is Not Passed** | Only show a certificate if the test has been passed. | Only available when the variable is a test. No value needed. |

## Add a Condition to an Action (cont'd)

Here are some additional tips for working with conditions.

- To delete a condition, click the red delete button at the end of the row.

- If you'd like to use another variable or a random number as the value for the condition, click the small arrow in the Value column to bring up a dialog box with those options.

- If you have more than one condition, use the drop-down menu at the top to indicate if all of the conditions have to be met in order for the action to fire or if only one of them has to be met. For example, would someone have to be hourly AND part-time for the action to fire, or could it be someone who was either hourly OR part-time?

- If you have several actions using the same conditions, use the **Copy Conditions** button to copy them, and then go to the other actions and use the **Paste Conditions** button to paste them. Even if you have to change the variable or the value, it can still save you a lot of time and reduce errors.

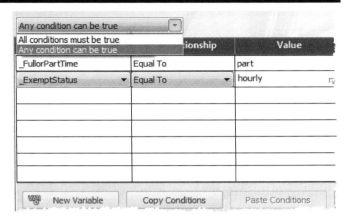

## Add an Alternate Action

When you add a condition, an **Else Action** section is added to the **Action** tab. If the conditions are not met, you can set up an alternate action to run instead. For example, if students go to the next page if they are a supervisor, then anyone who is not a supervisor would go to a different page.

If you need to run multiple actions if the condition is not met, create an action group and use this panel to run that action group.

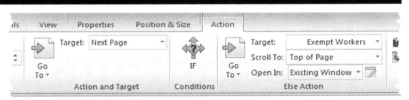

# DESIGN TIP

This design gallery shows how to set up the conditional actions described on page 128.

*Add one point to the score if the student answers the question correctly, and subtract one point if the student gets it wrong.*

*Show a table of contents to allow free navigation if the student has completed the course.*

*Play the audio file if the audio preference is set to "on."*

*Skip the next chapter if the student is not a supervisor.*

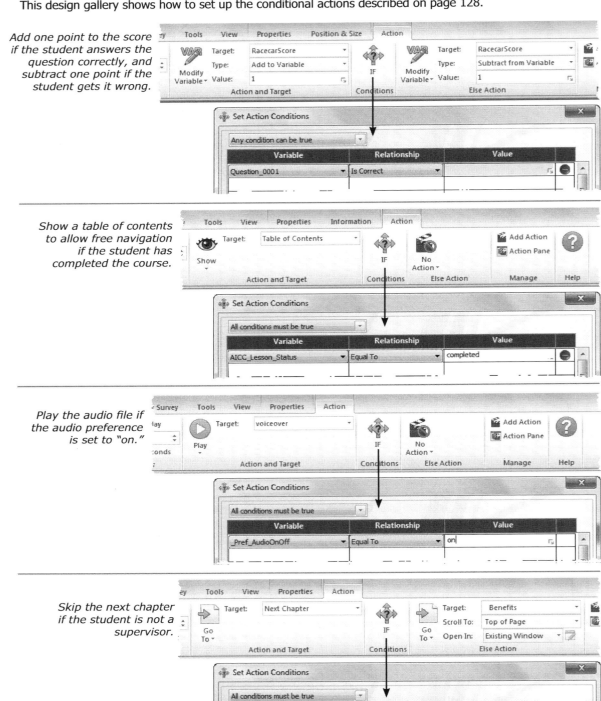

# Additional Variable-Related Features

The **Change Contents** action lets you swap out the contents of a graphic, media clip, text box, or question. This lets content get dynamically updated based on the student's actions. For example:

- Change the contents of a graphic in a game based on a certain score: A stack of money could become higher, a runner on a racetrack could be in a different place, or the needle on a meter could be further to the right.

- Change the contents of an audio clip based on what the student answered in a previous question.

- Change the contents of a text box to show the value of a variable, such as the current score, current date, or answer to a question.

Image and media clips can be swapped out for any other image or media clip. Text boxes can be swapped out to display text you enter or the value of any variable.

**To change the contents of an image or media clip:**

1. Attach an action to the trigger object.
2. Select **Change Contents** as the action type.
3. In the **Target** field, select the object you want to change the contents of.
4. In the **Resource** field, find and select the image or media clip you want to use.

**To change the contents of a text box to text you enter:**

1. Attach an action to the trigger object.
2. Select **Change Contents** as the action type.
3. In the **Target** field, select the text box that you want to change.
4. In the **Value** field, select **Set Text**.
5. In the **Text** field, enter the text you want to display.

**To change the contents of a text box to the value of a variable:**

1. Attach an action to the trigger object.
2. Select **Change Contents** as the action type.
3. In the **Target** field, select the text box that will display the variable value.
4. In the **Value** field, find and select the variable whose value you want to display.

**CAUTION**

If you are using a **Change Contents** action to show the student the value of a variable, realize that when the variable changes, the display does not automatically update. Every time you modify the variable, you'll need to run another **Change Contents** action to update the display.

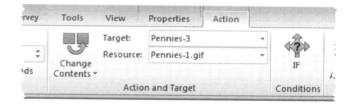

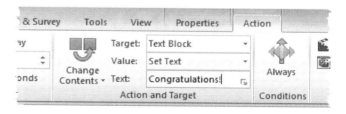

# The Variable Manager

The **Variable Manager** (found on the **Tools** tab) is where you can set up and edit your variables. However, you can use it for other things, as well.

- If you select a variable, the pane in the bottom-right shows you where that variable is being used.

- If you click the **Unused** tab, you can see which variables are not being used and remove them if you want to.

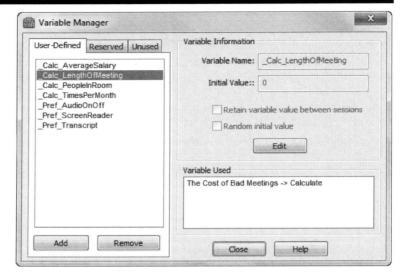

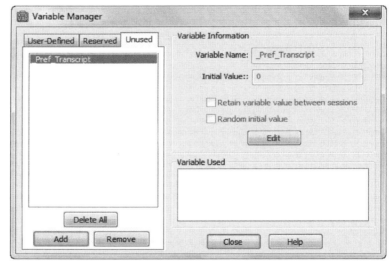

# Debug Mode

When you are testing and troubleshooting your actions, preview them in **Debug** mode.  When you do this, a small window appears in the corner as you run the course.  Each time an action is fired, it shows you what is happening and what variables are being used.  This can help you spot possible problems.

**To run debug mode:**

1. Go to the **View** tab.
2. Click the **Debug** button.

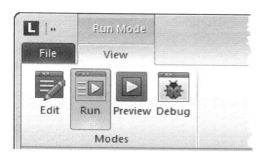

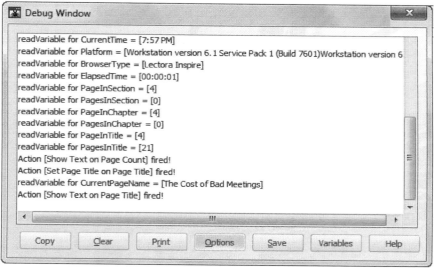

# Notes

# Custom Interface Design

CHAPTER
**10**

## Introduction

When creating a title, you have several choices that give you maximum flexibility in terms of course functionality, navigation, as well as look and feel. You can:

- Use a pre-existing template as-is.
- Use a pre-existing template and make changes and modifications.
- Use a template you saved based on another title.
- Start with a blank title and build it yourself.

Many of the tools and features already covered in this book can help you create a custom interface design, such as:

- Changing title properties
- Adding shapes and lines
- Adding buttons

- Adding images
- Adding text boxes
- Adding actions

In this chapter, you'll learn about other useful tools such as:

- Tables of contents
- The page numbering tool
- Breadcrumbs and page titles

- Custom menus
- Progress bars

### In This Chapter

- Sample Custom Interface Design
- Placement of Interface Elements
- Tables of Contents
- Custom Menus
- Smart Text Objects
- Location Indicators

# Notes

# Sample Custom Interface Design

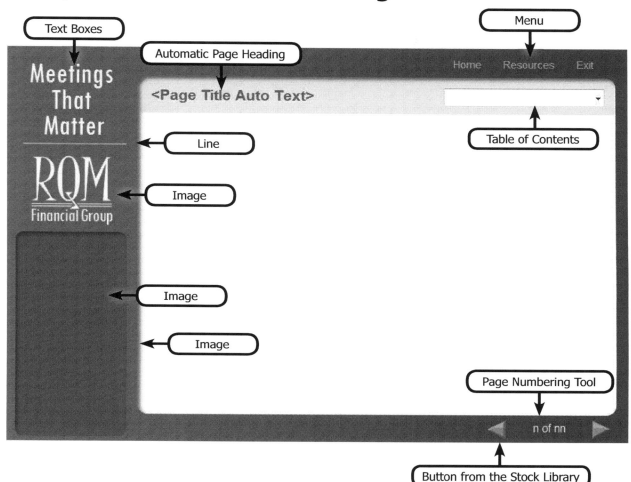

# Placement of Interface Elements

If you want to have an element appear throughout the entire title, first select the title icon before you add the element (or the AU object for an AICC/SCORM/Tin Can course).

You can also have interface elements appear on just a given chapter, section, or title, if that's what you have selected when you add the object.

 **CAUTION**

Be careful about what object you have selected when you add these objects. If you accidentally add an object to a page when you meant to add it at the title level, you'll wonder why it isn't showing up on every page.

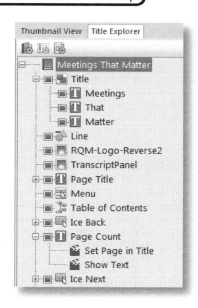

# Tables of Contents

You can include a table of contents (TOC) with your title to let students navigate around the course. Each of the three format options (shown below) are automatically populated and updated based on the structure and names in the **Title Explorer**. All items in the TOC are hyperlinks that take the student to that page.

## Table of Contents Types

### Drop-Down List

A menu appears showing the name of the current page. Students click the menu, scroll through the pages (shown in outline form), and select the one they want to go to.

- This format is the most space-efficient.
- This format usually resides at the title/AU level.

### Indented List

A scrolling text box appears showing all the pages in outline form. Students scroll to find what they want and click on it to go there.

- The list can be set up to show or hide the chapter/section/page icons.
- This format is one of the least space efficient. It works well on its own page (such as a home page) instead of always being available in the interface.

### Tree View

A scrolling text box appears showing the course elements in a tree view. Students can expand/collapse the chapters and sections to find and select the page they want to go to.

- The list can be set up to show or hide the chapter/section/page icons.
- It can be sized small and put in the interface, or sized large and put on a Home page.
- When in the interface, this format serves as a visual indicator of where the student is in the course at any given time, as the current page is highlighted.

### 🕐 TIME SAVER

Even if you don't want your students to have a table of contents, you may want to temporarily include a drop-down TOC for the review cycles, making it easier for reviewers and developers to move around the course. When it comes time to publish the final course, simply remove it.

# Add a Table of Contents

**To add a Table of Contents:**

1. Select the location where you want the TOC (title, chapter, section, or page).
2. Go to the **Insert** tab.
3. Click the **Table of Contents** drop-down arrow.
4. Select the type you want.

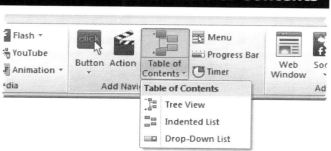

# Table of Contents Properties

Here are properties unique to a TOC.

### Scope

If your table of contents is somewhere other than the title level, you can indicate what part of the title to include. For example, a chapter-level TOC might only display the pages in that chapter.

### Frame

If you are using frames in your title, you can put the TOC in one frame to navigate the pages in another frame. Use this drop-down list to select which frame the TOC should refer to.

### Included Pages

Click this button for a dialog box to designate any pages that you don't want to have appear in the TOC, such as a final quiz or pages used for pop-up windows. Click the gray box next to a page to leave it out of the TOC. Click it again to put it back in.

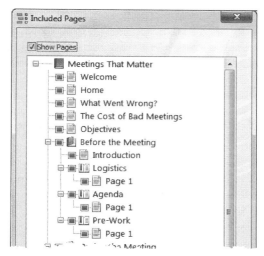

#### Show Pages

For drop-down or indented TOC styles, you can uncheck this box if you only want chapter and section levels to appear. Individual pages will not be shown.

### Type

From this menu, you can change the type of TOC.

### Frameless in HTML

If you are publishing to the Web, you can check this box to have a transparent background on the TOC.

### Use Icons

For indented and tree TOC types, you can uncheck this box if you don't want to show the icons for chapters, sections, and pages and just want to show the names.

##  TIME SAVER

In earlier versions of Lectora, the ability to exclude chapters, sections, and pages from the TOC was found in the chapter, section, or page properties. Having it all in one place makes it easier to manage.

# Custom Menus

Custom menus are a great way to add streamlined navigational options to your titles. Many title templates (like the one shown below) use a vertical menu to provide navigation to the different chapters. Horizontal menus are useful for special course features and utilities, such as Help, FAQs, and Resources. Both horizontal and vertical menus can have separator lines as well as submenus that appear when the student clicks the associated main menu item.

Submenus can have their own submenus as well. Each menu item can have its own action, such as going to a chapter or page, bringing up a pop-up window, launching a document, etc.

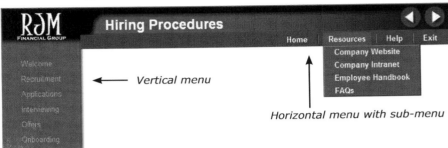

## Add a Custom Menu

### To add a custom menu:

1. Go to the **Insert** tab.
2. Click the **Menu** button.
3. Click one of the menu items in the list on the left.
4. In the **Name** field at the top, name the menu item.
5. In the **Menu Item Action** section, set up the action for that menu item.
6. Repeat steps 3 to 5 for the additional menu items.
7. Format the menu and submenus on the two style tabs. (See next page.)
8. Click the **OK** button.

### Menu Configuration Options

- For more than three menu items, click the **Add Item** button.
- Delete a menu item by selecting it from the list and clicking the **Delete** button.
- Click the **Add Separator** button to put a line between menu items.
- Use the up and down arrow buttons to change the order of the menu items.
- Use the left and right arrow buttons to indent items, which creates submenus.
- Check the **Create Menu from Table of Contents** check box to create menus and submenus out of the chapters and sections in your course.

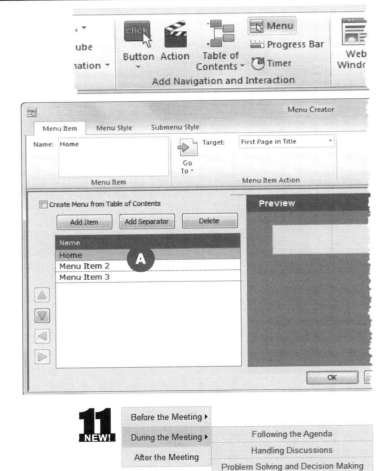

*Menu created from the table of contents*

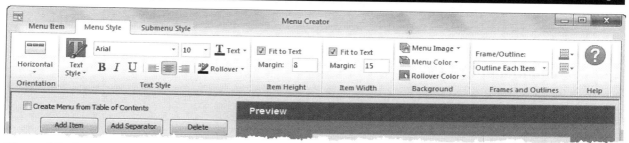

## Menu/Submenu Style

The menu can be formatted from the **Menu Style** and **Submenu Style** tabs in the **Menu Creator** or later from the same tabs in the main interface.

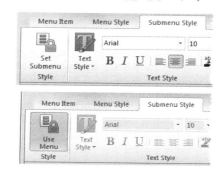

The options are the same on both menus, with one exception: the first button.

- **Orientation**: On the **Menu Style** tab, use the first button to indicate if you want a horizontal or vertical menu.

- **Set Submenu Style**: On the **Submenu Style** tab, the first button, by default, is **Set Submenu Style**, which means that the submenu can have different formatting. If you click this button, it becomes **Use Menu**, meaning that the submenu will use the same formatting as the main menu. When this option is chosen, the formatting options on this tab are locked. Click the button again to unlock the submenu and give it its own formatting.

Many of the formatting options you'll see on the style tabs are the same options you've seen before, such as text formatting. Here are some of the options unique to menus.

**Text Rollover Color**: Select a different color for the text when the student's mouse hovers over that menu item.

**Fit to Text**: Adjust the size of the menu based on the amount of text you have.

**Margin**: Indicate how much extra space you want around the text of the individual menu items.

**Menu Image**: Use this drop-down menu to select an image to serve as the background for the menu.

**Menu Color**: Change the color of the menu background.

**Rollover Color**: Change the color of the menu background when the student's mouse rolls over it.

**Frame/Outline**: Select an outline style for the menu items.

**Separator Color**: Select a color for any separators you added between menu items.

**Outline Color**: Select a color for the outline, if you added an outline.

# Smart Text Objects

## Add Breadcrumbs and a Page Title

If you've taken the time to name all of your chapters, sections, and pages in the Title Explorer, you don't need to re-type all of that information on the page for the student's benefit. Instead, you can add automated text boxes at the title level that automatically populate each page with that information.

Breadcrumbs tell your students where they are in the course, showing the chapter, section, and page name. The page title option shows just the page name. Note that both options are display-only and are not live hyperlinks.

**To add breadcrumbs:**
1. Go to the **Insert** tab.
2. Click the **Breadcrumb** button.

**To add an automatic page heading:**
1. Go to the **Insert** tab.
2. Click the **Page Title** button.

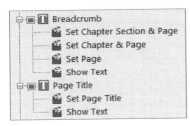

Breadcrumbs and page title in Edit mode

Breadcrumbs and page title in Run mode

 **BRIGHT IDEA**

These text boxes are set to be initially hidden. They come with actions that set the contents of the text box, followed by an action that then shows the text box. This is so the student doesn't see the placeholder text for a split second when the page is loading.

Breadcrumbs and page title in the Title Explorer

## Add Date and Time

Whether part of your interface or on a content page, you can add a dynamic text box that automatically updates with the current date and time, based on the student's system date and time.

**To add the date and time:**
1. Go to the **Insert** tab.
2. Click the **Date/Time** button.

**To add the date or the time:**
1. Go to the **Insert** tab.
2. Click the **Date/Time drop-down arrow**.
3. Select **Date** or **Time**.

**Planning Committee Agenda**
March 03, 2013

*Automated date/time*

# Add Page Numbers

The page numbering tool lets you add page numbers to your course without having to do it manually. You can set it up to number the entire title, start over at every chapter, start over at every section, etc.

**To add page numbers:**

1. Go to the **Insert** menu.

2. Click the **Page Number** button.

3. From the **Scope** drop-down menu, indicate if you want to number all pages in the title sequentially or if you want to start the numbering over with each chapter or each section.

4. Check or uncheck the box to indicate if you want to include the total number of pages (n of nn).

5. From the **Page** drop-down menu, select the text you want at the beginning of the text string: **Page**, **#** or nothing.

6. In the **of** drop-down menu, select **of** or **/** to delineate the page number from the total number of pages (if you selected that option).

7. In the **Font and Color** section, select either a text style to use or set your formatting with the individual formatting options.

8. Click the **OK** button.

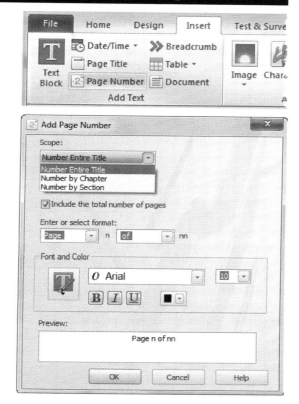

*Page counter as it appears in the Title Explorer*

---

 **BRIGHT IDEAS**

- Make sure your text box has enough room for your largest page number. A text box that can handle **1 of 11** may not be big enough for one that needs to hold **39 of 39**.

- Remember you can use inheritance with any interface element if you have certain chapters and pages where you don't want to include them. For example, if you have a chapter of pop-up pages at the end of your title, you probably don't want them numbered.

 Inheritance, p. 27

 **POWER TIP**

You can further customize the page numbering by going into the advanced action used to create it.

One common need is to change the total number of pages in your title. For example, you might have a chapter with pop-up pages that shouldn't be included in the page count. You can go into the action and change **VAR (PagesInTitle)** to the exact number you want, such as **35**. (You'll need to manually update this if your number of pages changes.

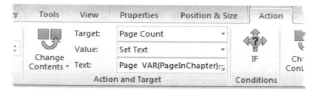

# Location Indicators

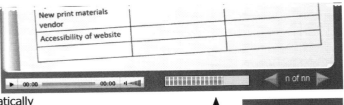

You can pick from three types of progress bars that have a variety of uses.  Two of them work automatically, and the third progresses based on actions you set up.

- **Timer** progress bars count down or up automatically based on the amount of time you set and can be used to add a "beat-the-clock" element to games and quizzes.

- **Table of Contents** progress bars automatically show students their progress through a given course, chapter, or section, based on how many pages they've completed.

- **Custom** progress bars move forward based on actions that you set up.  For example, you could set up a progress bar to move based on how many points the student scores in a game.

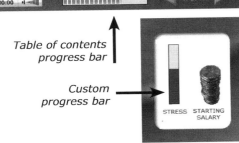

*Table of contents progress bar*

*Custom progress bar*

## Add a Progress Bar

**To add a progress bar:**

1. Go to the **Insert** tab.
2. Click the **Progress Bar** button.
3. Go to the **Properties** tab for the progress bar.
4. From the **Orientation** menu, select **Horizontal** or **Vertical.**
5. In the **Type** section, select the type of progress bar you want.
6. Configure the rest of the settings as described next.

### Properties for All Progress Bar Types

**Default Image (A):** By default, a progress bar is filled with small, green rectangles.  You can use this field to select a different image to fill the bar, or you can select **No Image.** When you do this, the **Fill** color button activates so you can pick a solid color to fill the progress bar.

**Tick Marks (B):** Check this box if you want to include tick marks along the bar.

**Empty Bar (C):** By default, the bar starts empty and fills up as the progress bar continues.  Check this box if you want the bar to start full and then empty as the bar progresses.

Additional options for color, border, position, etc. are the same as for any object.

*Progress bar with custom image*

*Progress bar with tick marks*

# Progress Bars (cont'd)

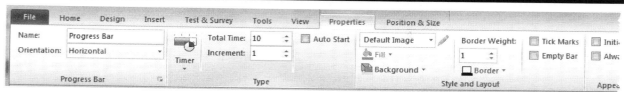

## Properties Specific to a Timer Progress Bar

**Total Time:** Indicate the number of seconds for the timer.

**Increment:** Indicate how often (in seconds) the timer updates.

**Auto Start:** By default, the timer does not start when it first loads (meaning you'll need a **Start** action to start it). Check this box if you want it to start automatically.

## Properties Specific to a Table of Contents Progress Bar

**Scope:** Use the drop-down menu to indicate if you want to include the entire title, just a given chapter, etc. The options on the menu vary based on what object (title, chapter, page) the progress bar is attached to.

**Frame:** If you are using frames, indicate which frame's content you want to use for the table of content's progress.

**Included Pages:** Click the button to indicate which pages from the title should be included in the progress calculations.

## Properties Specific to a Custom Progress Bar

**Range:** In this field, indicate how many increments you want in the progress bar. For example, if it is for a game with 8 points, your range might be 8.

**Step Size:** Indicate how many increments the bar will move each time you have the bar move a step up or down. For example, in the game, it might move 2 points up or down per question.

**Variable:** If you want, you can select a variable where you store the value of the progress bar.

**Initial Value:** Set the starting increment for the progress bar.

**Retain Value:** Check this box if you want to save the position of the progress bar between the student's sessions.

## Actions for Moving a Custom Progress Bar

Remember that custom progress bars don't move on their own like the other two types. Therefore, you need to create the actions to move it up or down. There are two choices.

**Step Progress Bar Position:** When you run this action, the progress bar moves by the increment you entered in the **Step Size** field.

**Set Progress Bar Position:** With this action, you set the value of the bar to a specific number.

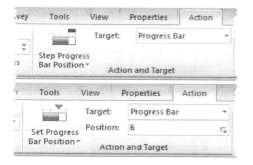

# Notes

# Special Object Types

## Introduction

- **Equations**: Create visuals for complex mathematical and scientific equations.
- **Charts**: Create several different types of charts with a simple spreadsheet tool.
- **Web Windows**: Embed a live website into the course.
- **Social Objects**: Quickly insert widgets that let you incorporate Twitter, Facebook, and Google+.
- **RSS Feeds**: Embed live, syndicated content to your course, such as from a new site or a blog.
- **HTML Extensions**: Include your own custom HTML code to add your own capabilities to Lectora.
- **Attachments**: Add files or folders to your title that the student can open.
- **Certificates**: Create an automatic certificate of completion with the date and the student's name.
- **Reference Lists**: Compile a list of all the references used throughout the course.
- **QR Codes**: Automatically create a QR code that links to other content.

## In This Chapter

- Equation Editor
- Chart Wizard
- Web Windows
- Social Objects
- RSS Feeds
- HTML Extensions
- Attachments
- Certificate Wizard
- Reference Lists
- QR Codes

# Notes

# Equation Editor

If you are teaching mathematical or scientific concepts that require complex equations, you can use the built-in **Equation Editor** to help you display the equations properly on your page.

The **Equation Editor** is made by Design Science. From the **Help** menu in the editor, you can go to their website for more details on how to use this tool.

**To create an equation:**
1. Go to the **Insert** tab.
2. Click the **Equation** button.
3. Create your equation in the editor.
4. Click the **File** menu.
5. Select **Close and Return to Lectora Inspire**.

**To edit an equation.**
1. Go to the equation's **Properties** tab.
2. Click the **Edit** button. **(A)**
3. Make the changes in the editor.
4. Click the **File** menu.
5. Select **Close and Return to Lectora Inspire**.

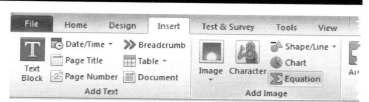

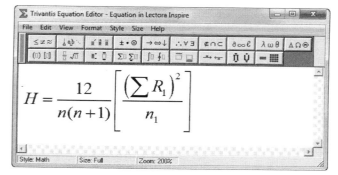

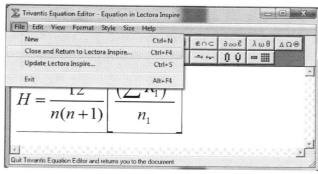

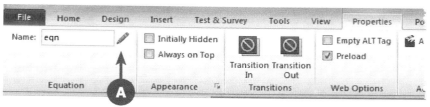

# Chart Wizard

Lectora's chart wizard lets you create four types of charts in several different formats based on data you enter in a spreadsheet-like panel.  Once the chart is added, you can treat it like any other image (move, resize, etc.).

To edit a chart once you've created it, simply go to its **Properties** tab and click the **Edit** button.

## Create a Chart

**To create a chart:**

1. Go to the **Insert** tab.
2. Click the **Chart** button.
3. In the **Chart Type** drop-down menu, select the type of chart you want.
4. In the spreadsheet section, enter the values you want.
5. Click the **Title & Legend** tab.
6. In the **Chart Title** field, enter the text you want to have appear in the image above the chart.
7. Click the **Font** button and change the font settings for the title, if needed.
8. Check or uncheck the **Show Legend** box to show or hide the legend in the image.
9. Click the drop-down arrow and select the position for the legend.
10. Click the **Font** button and change the font settings for the legend, if needed.
11. Click **OK**.

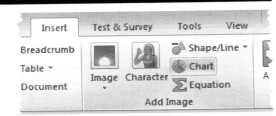

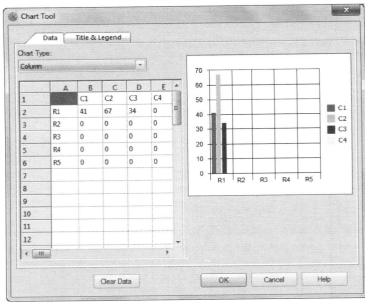

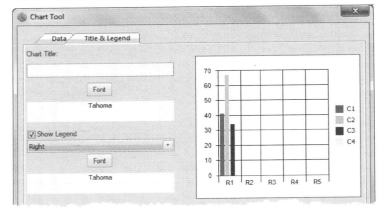

# Chart Types

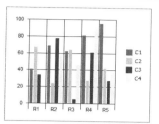

Column

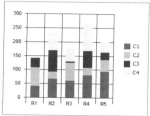

Column (Stacked)

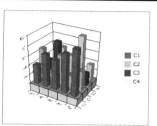

Column (3D)

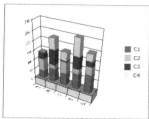

Column (3D Stacked)

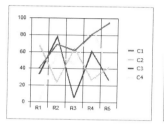

Line

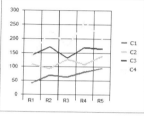

Line (Stacked)

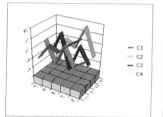

Line (3D)

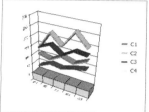

Line (3D Stacked)

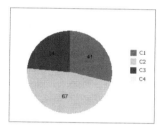

Pie Chart

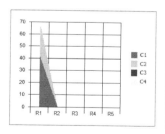

Area

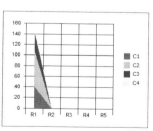

Area (Stacked)

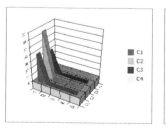

Area (3D)

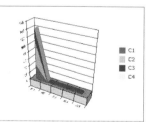

Area (3D Stacked)

# Web Windows

Web windows let you incorporate live web content into your title. Whereas a hyperlink to a website opens in its own browser window, a web window is embedded right into the course without the browser toolbars. This can help keep your students focused on the course content even though they are viewing a live web page.

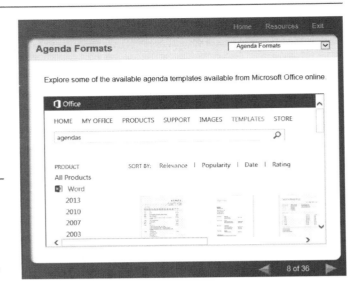

## ! CAUTION

- For most of the web window options, the student must have internet access to be able to view the content.

- Web windows do not work in **Preview** mode. You need to either preview in a browser or publish your title to view them.

- Web windows do not work when publishing to CD or to .EXE.

## Add a Web Window

**To add a web window:**

1. Go to the **Insert** menu.
2. Click the **Web Window** button.
3. From the **Window Source** drop-down menu, select the type of content you want to add.
4. Enter source information in the next field(s) based on the source you chose. (The name of the field varies based on the source you chose.)
5. Click the **OK** button.
6. Resize and position the web window frame on the page.

### Window Sources

- **Web Address**: Embed a live webpage from the internet by entering a URL.

- **Local Web-based content**: Load HTML content that is stored on your computer or network location. When you do this, all the associated files are included with your published title.

- **Page in Title**: Embed a fully functioning page from elsewhere in your title.

- **Google Maps Location: Enter an address to embed a** Google map on the page.

- **Wikipedia Entry**: Enter a term to embed the Wikipedia entry for that term.

- **Google Document**: Enter the topic to embed a *public* Google document.

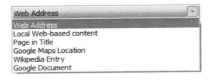

# Social Objects

The **Social** menu lets you add live feeds and streams from popular social media sites such as Twitter, Facebook, and Google+.

**To add a social object:**

1. Go to the **Insert** tab.
2. Click the **Social** drop-down arrow.
3. Select the object type you want.
4. Configure any settings that appear.

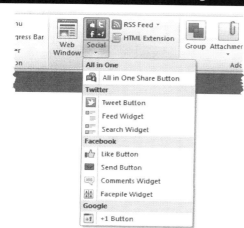

 **CAUTION**

- These objects require an internet connection and, in most cases, an account with these social media sites.
- Some objects will only work once the published files are hosted on a web server.
- Make sure you understand the privacy issues with these objects. For example, a student's friend can comment on a Facebook post, which would appear in your course.

## Social Object Types

| Description | Sample |
|---|---|
| **All in One Share Button**: This widget includes a **Like** button (Facebook), **Tweet** button (Twitter), **+1** button (Google+), and a **Share** button that has a drop-down menu with additional social media sites. | 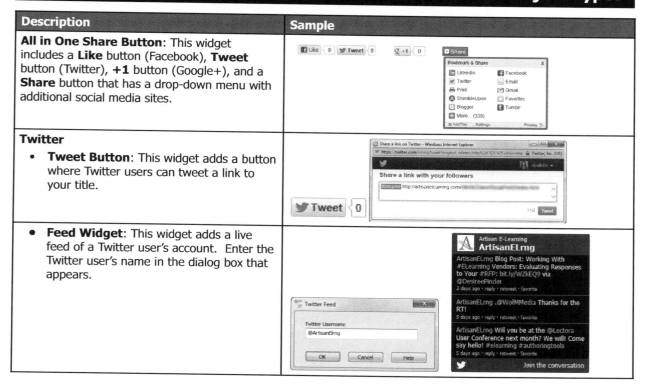 |
| **Twitter**<br><br>• **Tweet Button**: This widget adds a button where Twitter users can tweet a link to your title. | |
| • **Feed Widget**: This widget adds a live feed of a Twitter user's account. Enter the Twitter user's name in the dialog box that appears. | |

# Social Object Types (cont'd)

| Description | Sample |
|---|---|
| **Twitter**<br>• **Search Widget**: This widget shows a feed for a particular search, such as a term or a hash tag.  Enter the search term and a caption to appear at the top of the feed. | 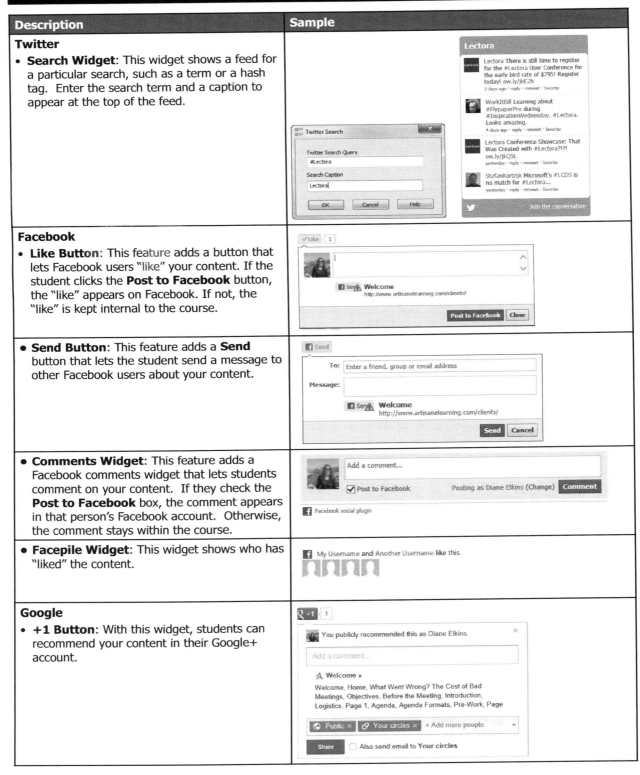 |
| **Facebook**<br>• **Like Button**: This feature adds a button that lets Facebook users "like" your content. If the student clicks the **Post to Facebook** button, the "like" appears on Facebook. If not, the "like" is kept internal to the course. | |
| • **Send Button**: This feature adds a **Send** button that lets the student send a message to other Facebook users about your content. | |
| • **Comments Widget**: This feature adds a Facebook comments widget that lets students comment on your content.  If they check the **Post to Facebook** box, the comment appears in that person's Facebook account.  Otherwise, the comment stays within the course. | |
| • **Facepile Widget**: This widget shows who has "liked" the content. | |
| **Google**<br>• **+1 Button**: With this widget, students can recommend your content in their Google+ account. | |

# RSS Feeds

Short for Really Simple Syndication, an RSS feed is a web feed of frequently updated web content, such as blog entries or news articles. By embedding an RSS feed in your course, you can include up-to-date content about a particular subject or from a particular source. You can select from a popular feed or set up your own feed.

**11 NEW!**

> **E-Learning Uncovered**
> Working With E-Learning Vendors: Evaluating Responses to You...
> by Desiree (Ward) Pinder - Mar 27, 2013
> In my last post, I gave some tips on what to include in the Request for Proposal (RFP). Now, let's look at some tips on how to ...
>
> ▶ Working With E-Learning Vendors: Evaluating Responses to Your RFP
> Special Thanks to the E-Learning Dream Teams
> Our Essential iOS Apps
> E-Learning Development – The Two-Computer Solution

---

## Add an RSS Feed

**To add a pre-defined feed:**

1. Go to the **Insert** tab.
2. Click the **RSS Feed** drop-down arrow.
3. Select the feed you want.

**To add a custom feed:**

1. Go to the **Insert** tab.
2. Click the **RSS Feed** drop-down arrow.
3. Select **Custom RSS Feed**.
4. Enter the address for the feed.
5. Click **OK**.

**Popular RSS Feeds**

- BBC News
- CNN Top Stories
- Dictionary.com Word of the Day
- Engadget
- ESPN
- New York Times
- Quote of the Day
- Slashdot
- Sport Illustrated
- Yahoo News

**Add your own RSS feed**
- Custom RSS Feed

**Add Custom RSS Feed**

RSS Feed
http://feeds.feedburner.com/e-learninguncove

OK    Cancel    Help

## 💡 BRIGHT IDEA

How do you find the address for an RSS feed? Most news and blog sites have a link for an RSS feed. Click that link to find the address to use for the feed. Different sites will be structured differently.

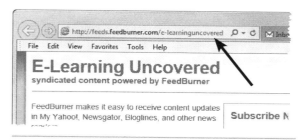

# HTML Extensions

When you publish your title to any of the Web-based formats (HTML, AICC, SCORM, etc.), Lectora automatically generates the HTML code needed for the course to work. However, you also have the ability to add some of your own HTML code to the course, letting you create custom features and functions. For example, you could:

- Add JavaScript to a pop-up window, controlling its size and position.
- Add HTML code to embed a calendar from Google calendars.
- Work with cascading style sheets, ASP .NET, or any number of other types of code supported by HTML.

In all cases, you will need to put together the code yourself, and then insert it into the appropriate place in your title.

 **CAUTION**

- If you don't understand HTML, JavaScript, or other programming languages, this procedure may not make a lot of sense. This feature is designed for those who understand how to work with the code and want to be able to customize the code that Lectora automatically generates.

- Any code you add only works if you are publishing to one of the HTML formats.

## Add an HTML Extension

**To add an HTML extension:**

1. Go to the **Insert** tab.
2. Click the **HTML Extension** button.
3. Go to the **HTML Extension Properties** tab.
4. In the **Type** menu, select the type of code you want to add. **(A)**
5. Enter your code in one of two ways.
   - Click the **File** drop-down menu to find and select the **.class** or **.jar** file you want to add. **(B)**
   - Click the **Edit** button and enter your code in the dialog box that appears. **(C)**

### Additional Settings

- **Additional Files**: If your code refers to other files, add them here. This makes sure those files get published with the rest of the files.

- **Required Variables**: If your code requires the use of Lectora variables, you can specify those variables here.

- **Java Applet Parameters**: If you are working with a Java Applet, you can use the **Parameters** tab to pass parameters from the page to the applet.

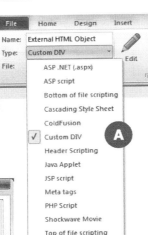

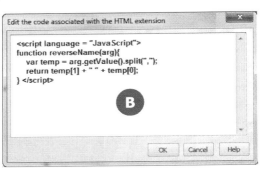

# Attachments

The **Attachment** button on the **Insert** menu lets you add files or folders to your title.  While it does add files/folders to your title, they are not automatically added to your page. You can then set up an **Open Attachment** action that launches that attachment.  You can view any of your attachments from the **Resource Manager**.

Open Attachment action, p. 108
Resource Manager, p. 222

## Add an Attachment

**To add an attachment to your title:**

1. Go to the **Insert** tab.
2. Click the **Attachment** drop-down arrow.
3. Select **File** or **Folder**.
4. Find and select the file or folder you want to attach.
5. Check one or both of the check boxes at the bottom, if desired.  (See below.)
6. Click the **Open** button.

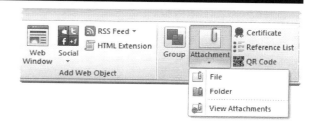

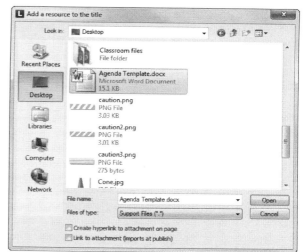

## Options

### Create Hyperlink to Attachment on Page

If you check this box, a hyperlinked text box is added to the page with an **Open Attachment** action already added.  If you do not check this box, you will manually need to add an **Open Attachment** action somewhere.

### Link to Attachment (Imports at Publish)

If you leave this option unchecked, a copy of the file or folder is added to the **Extern** file as part of your Lectora title files.  When you publish, the file/folder is also included in the published files.

If you check this box, the file is not added to the **Extern** folder.  Instead, Lectora links to the document in its current location.  When you publish the title, however, the file/folder will be added to the published folders.

## POWER TIP

If you have a text document (.txt or .rtf) that you want to include with your title, you can include it as an attachment as described here, or you can embed it in a scrolling panel on the page.  Either drag and drop the file on the page or go to the **Insert** tab and click the **Document** button.

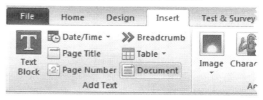

# Certificate Wizard

The certificate wizard automates the process of creating a customized, professionally designed certificate of completion at the end of your course.  The wizard walks through your choice of graphics, text, and logic that includes automatically populating the date and student's name.

## Create a Certificate

**To create a certificate:**

1. Select the page just before where you want the certificate.
2. Go to the **Insert** tab.
3. Click the **Certificate** button.
4. In the first drop-down menu, select the certificate style you want.
5. Click the first **Font** button to change the font style for the certificate text.
6. Click the second **Font** button to change the font style for the student name and date.
7. Click the **Next** button.
8. Enter the text you want to use as the header.
9. Click the **Next** button.

   *(continued)*

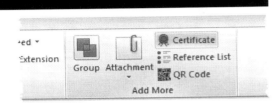

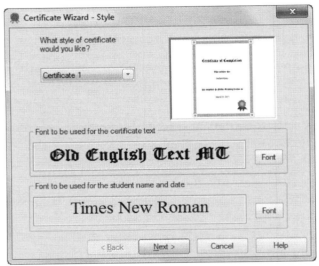

 **DESIGN TIPS**

- Be purposeful about where you put the certificate.  You may want it on a page the students can only access if they complete the course and/or pass the test.

- The student's name and date are populated by a **Change Contents** action.  This means you cannot use the Convert to Image feature that lets you use a non-standard font.  So be sure to use a system font for those two fields.

- If working with an LMS, you can pull the name from the LMS variables.  If not, use a text entry field where students can enter their names.

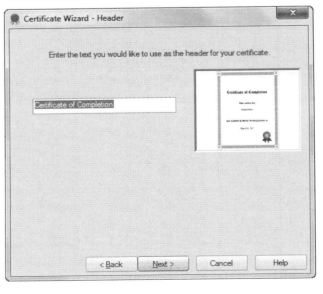

## Create a Certificate (cont'd)

10. Enter the text you want to use in the middle of the certificate.

11. Check the box if you want to use a variable to automatically populate the student's name.

12. From the drop-down list, select the variable to use, or click the **New Variable** button to create a new one.

13. Click the **Next** button.

14. Enter the text you want at the end of the certificate.

15. Check the first box if you want the date automatically included.

16. Check the second box if you want an automatic **Print Page** action to be added to the certificate page.

17. Click the **Finish** button at the bottom of the dialog box.

The certificate is added on its own page with all the text, graphics, and actions you set up in the wizard. Any of these elements can be changed directly on the page.

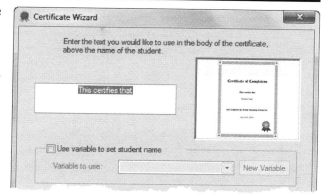

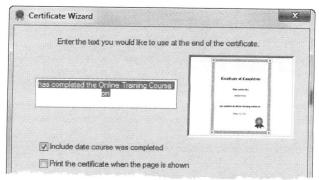

## Certificate Design Options

### Certificate 1
(gray)

### Certificate 2
(royal blue)

### Certificate 3
(blue and yellow)

### Certificate 4
(reddish brown)

### Certificate 5
(blk/wht w/red)

### Certificate 6
(gold and black)

### Certificate 7
(light blue)

### Certificate 8
(olive green)

### Certificate 9
(dark green)

### Certificate 10
(medium blue)

### Certificate 11
(red)

### Certificate 12
(green)

# Reference Lists

When you add an object such as an image or other media, you can add reference information from that object's **Properties** tab. You can then compile all of that information in a reference list, designed to be shown to the student either as part of the course, or put on a page the students never see, just for internal reference.

 Object Properties, p. 63

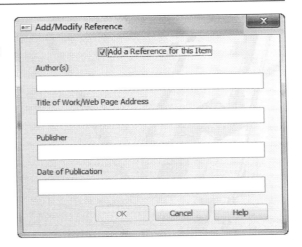

## Add a Reference List

**To add a reference list:**

1. Go to the **Insert** tab.
2. Click the **Reference List** button.
3. Go to the **Properties** tab for the list.
4. From the **Scope** drop-down menu, select what part of the course you want to include reference for.
5. Change any other settings you want.

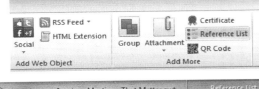

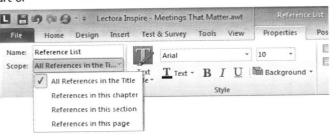

# QR Codes

Short for Quick Response Code, a QR code is a bar code that can be scanned by a special QR reader to provide additional information, such as link to a website.

## Add a QR Code

**To add a QR Code:**

1. Go to the **Insert** tab.
2. Click the **QR Code** button.
3. From the **Contents** drop-down menu, select the type of content you want.
4. Fill in the requested details based on the type of content you chose.
5. Click the **OK** button.

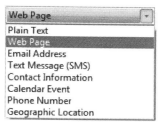

# Notes

# Tests and Quizzes

## Introduction

Questions can be put in a formal, graded test or assessment, bundled together in an informal quiz, or used individually throughout your title – sprinkled in for reinforcement and interactivity.

- If you want a single question that doesn't count towards any score, just add a question to a page.

- If you want an informal quiz where each question is graded but there is no overall score, then just put several question pages together in a row.

- If you want a more formal assessment that has a total score, pass/fail logic, and can send scores to a Learning Management System, an e-mail address, or an online database, then create a test chapter to put the questions in.

You can have a separate page for each question, or several questions on the same page.

You can choose to provide feedback on individual questions as they are answered, provide feedback only at the end of a test or quiz, or merely show the final score and whether the student passed or failed a formal assessment.

## In This Chapter

- Test Chapters
- Test Questions
- Special Question Options

# Notes

# Test Chapters

When you include questions in a test chapter, you can add pass/fail logic or send the scores through email or a database. The test chapter contains key properties that govern this logic as well as overall test settings. Once you create the chapter, you would add the individual questions.

## Add a Test Chapter

**To add a test chapter:**

1. Go to the **Test & Survey** tab.
2. Click the **Test** button.
3. Go to the test chapter's **Properties, Behavior,** and **Results** tabs.
4. Configure the settings.

The **Properties** tab is the same as for any chapter. The other two tabs are covered next.

 Chapter Properties p. 27

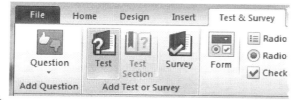

 **CAUTION**

Even though the **Properties** tab for a test chapter is the same as for a regular chapter, inheritance is set to inherit NO objects from parents. This includes all of your interface elements. Click the **Inherit** button to put any of those elements back.

 Inheritance, p. 27

## Test Chapter Structure

When you add a test chapter, the following objects are added.

- **Page Count**: The test chapter comes with its own page numbering. You can delete the page count text box if you don't want it.

- **Cancel, Next, and Back buttons**: These three buttons attached to the chapter appear on every page in the chapter (except the last page). **Cancel** cancels the test and initiates the action you designate for canceling the test (see next page). **Back** goes to the previous page. **Next** goes to the next page and also grades/processes the question.

- **Page 1**: The test chapter comes with one blank page for your questions. You can put all of your questions on that one page or add additional pages for additional questions.

- **Last test page**: The last page contains a **Done** button which includes an action to process the test/survey. It is this action that determines the grade and initiates any actions you have for when the student passes or fails. If you delete this button, be sure to add this action in another way.

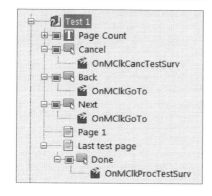

# Test Chapter Behavior Tab

## Show Feedback for Each Question

Each question can have its own correct/incorrect feedback. However, it will only show up if this check box is selected at the test chapter level.

## Student Must Answer Each Question

If you leave this box checked, students get an error message if they try to move forward without answering a question or try to navigate away using anything other than the test navigation buttons. This ensures they answer the questions and means they can't go back and look up the answers.

## Retain Answers Between Sessions

If you check this box, questions they've answered will still be there if they exit and re-enter the course. If you leave it unchecked, all questions will revert back to being blank.

## On Completed/Passed and On Canceled/Failed

You can set up separate **Go To** actions based on whether the student passes or fails the test. For example, you could have a "Congratulations" page and a "Sorry, you did not pass" page. Or, you could re-direct the student back to the beginning of a section if he or she didn't pass the test.

## Randomly Select Pages

If you check this option, you can specify how many of the available question pages you want to present to the student.

If you select the full number of question pages available (eight of eight, for example), then all students get all questions – in a random order.

If you select a smaller number than what is available (four of eight), students get a slightly different sub-set of question pages in a random order. If students take the test again, they are presented with a different set of questions.

If you don't have any questions yet, you can't activate the randomization option. It's best to wait until you are finished with all your questions, so that the **Pages From Test** menu has the full number of questions.

## Timed Test

If you check this option, a timer object is added to the test chapter that is set with an action to grade the test (Process Test/Survey) when the timer is done.

 Timer Objects, p. 121

 **CAUTION**

- If you are re-directing students back to the beginning of a section, it's a good idea to let them know what's happening. If they are simply "transported" back several pages, they may get confused. Instead, direct them first to a page that explains it, and then give that page the **Go To** action that takes them to the beginning of the section.

- Avoid using timed tests for formal assessments without a job-related need. Students with language difficulties, reading issues, etc. may suffer needlessly.

 **DESIGN TIPS**

- If you randomly present a sub-set of your questions, realize that all of your objectives may not be tested. To avoid this, set up a test section for each objective, and randomize each *section* instead of the test as a whole. Then you know each objective has questions presented.

- If you randomize a test, remove the **Done** button completely. Otherwise, it could end up in the middle of the test or not appear at all. The test will process when the student leaves the last test page.

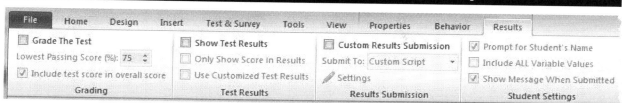

**Test Chapter Results Tab**

### Grade the Test

If you check this option, Lectora calculates a percentage score for the test. This box must be checked to send the score to your LMS.

### Lowest Passing Score

If you select **Grade the Test**, you can use this field to indicate the lowest passing score. This determines whether the test variable is set to pass or fail.

### Include Test Score in Overall Score

If you check this option, Lectora includes this test score in the overall score for the course. You can have more than one test contribute to the overall score.

### Show Test Results

Check this box if you'd like a summary pop-up window at the end of the test. It includes the questions, the student's responses, the questions' status (correct, incorrect, or not answered), and the correct answers.

### Only Show Score in Results

If you check this box, only the final score and the pass/fail status displays in the test results window. This is useful for certification-type exams in which it's extremely important that students don't share answers.

### Use Customized Test Results

If you are showing test results at the end of a test, check this box to turn the results page into a customizable page. A **Test Results** icon appears in the **Title Explorer**, where you can change page and results properties, edit and format text, etc. The page, by default, includes buttons that take the student back to the question.

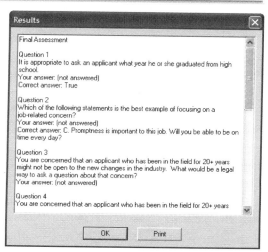

*Standard test results window*

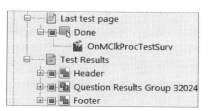

*Customized test results object in Title Explorer*

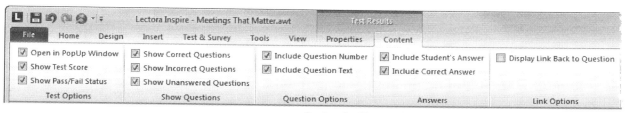

*Customization options for the customized test results page*

# Test Chapter Results Tab (cont'd)

| File | Home | Design | Insert | Test & Survey | Tools | View | Properties | Behavior | Results |
|------|------|--------|--------|---------------|-------|------|------------|----------|---------|

| | | |
|---|---|---|
| ☐ Grade The Test | ☐ Show Test Results | ☐ Custom Results Submission | ☑ Prompt for Student's Name |
| Lowest Passing Score (%): 75 ⬍ | ☐ Only Show Score in Results | Submit To: Custom Script ▾ | ☐ Include ALL Variable Values |
| ☑ Include test score in overall score | ☐ Use Customized Test Results | ✎ Settings | ☑ Show Message When Submitted |
| Grading | Test Results | Results Submission | Student Settings |

## Custom Results Submission

If you are not working with an LMS, you can transmit the test information in one of three other ways:

- **Custom Script**: This option sends the results to a CGI (Common Gateway Interface) application, such as an online database. This option requires the use of CGI or ASP scripting to send the data properly to the database.

- **Email**: Use this option to send an e-mail with the test results. The student must have an e-mail program installed on the computer they are using. You may also need to coordinate security settings where the course is hosted to make sure there aren't any restrictions blocking the communication.

- **Google Drive**: Use this option to submit the results to a *public* Google form. Simply enter the Web address for the form.

Check the box and then select the method you want from the **Submit To** drop-down menu. When you select an option, the rest of the tab changes accordingly.

## Options for All Methods

### Prompt for Student's Name

If you check this option, a dialog box appears at the beginning of the test so the students can enter their names. This information is submitted with the test results.

### Include All Variable Values

If you check this option, all variables will be sent – not just the ones related to the test. This includes ALL variables, including any created for games, activities, etc. (This option is not available for Google Drive submission.) This can be useful if you want to track other information.

### Show Message When Submitted

If you check this option, the student will be notified if the submission is successful.

## 💡 BRIGHT IDEAS

- If you are publishing your course to an AICC, SCORM, or Tin Can LMS, you don't need to do any of this. The communication to the LMS is handled through the publishing process.

 Publishing to an LMS, p. 264

## Options for Custom Script

**Settings**: Click this button for a dialog box with the following options.

- **Submit To**: Enter the Web address where you want the results sent.

- **Method**: Use **GET** if there are fewer than 256 characters of data. Use **POST** if you have something larger.

**Receive Response**: Check this box if you want to store the response from the custom script in a variable. After checking the box, select the variable you want to use from the drop-down menu.

## Options for Email

**Settings**: Click this button for a dialog box with the following options.

- **Send To**: Enter one or more e-mail addresses (separated by semicolons) to send the test results to.

- **Subject**: If you want an e-mail subject line other than "Test Results," enter it in this field.

- **Submit in XML Format**: Check this box to submit the results in XML format. Use this option if you plan to run a program to process the results.

## Options for Google Drive

**Settings**: Click this button for a dialog box with the following option.

- **Google Drive Form URL**: Enter the web address of the *public* Google form that will store the results.

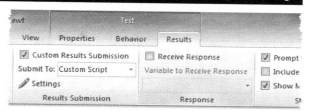

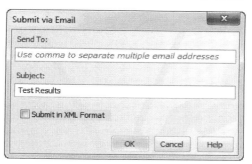

## POWER TIP

You can find templates on the Google Drive site for a form that accepts test results. Go to https://drive.google.com/templates, click the **Public Templates** tab, and search with the term "Lectora."

# Test Sections

Just as you can organize a regular chapter into sections, you can also organize your test chapter into sections. You might want to organize your tests into sections for a number of reasons.

- You want to visually organize your questions in the Title Explorer for your own benefit.
- You'd like to track the score for the section separately, or use the section score or pass/fail status for some special navigation or logic.
- You want to create sections for each content area to help you make sure all of your information is covered adequately.
- You want to randomize the test in sections so you know that you are pulling pages from every part of the test.
- You want to use different properties, such as page size, formatting, or inheritance for each section.

Test sections can only be added to test chapters.  Test sections cannot have sub-sections.

## Add a Test Section

**To add a test section:**

1. Click the test chapter in the **Title Explorer**.
2. Go to the **Test & Survey** tab.
3. Click the **Test Section** button.
4. Go to the test chapter's **Properties** and **Behavior** tabs.
5. Configure the settings.

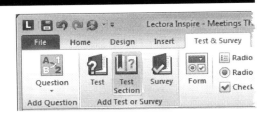

The test section's **Properties** tab is identical to the test chapter's **Properties** tab.  If you want to use the same properties for the section as for the chapter, then you don't have to do anything.  If you want different properties, you can change them here to override what is set at the chapter level.

The test section's **Behavior** tab has only one option: randomization.  All other **Behavior** options are set at the test chapter level.

*Behavior tab for a text section*

 Randomization, p. 166

# Test Questions

Questions can be added to a test chapter, a test section, or on any page within your title. You can have one page for each question or a single, long, scrolling page that has many questions. The procedure for adding each type of question is extremely similar. In this section, you'll learn the set-up steps that are common across all question types. Then in the next section, you'll learn about the steps unique to each individual question type.

## Add a Question

**To add a question:**

1. Go to the **Test & Survey** tab.
2. Click the **Question** drop-down button.
3. Select the question type you want.
4. Enter question parameters on the **Question**, **Feedback**, and **Attempts** tabs. (See the following sections).
5. Click the **OK** button.

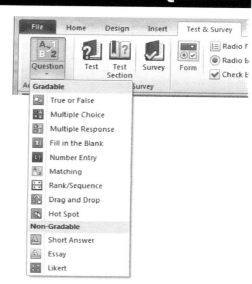

 **DESIGN TIP**

In earlier versions of Lectora, the question wizard gave you the option of either putting the question on the existing page or of creating a new page for the question. In version 11, the question is always added to the page you have selected at the time.

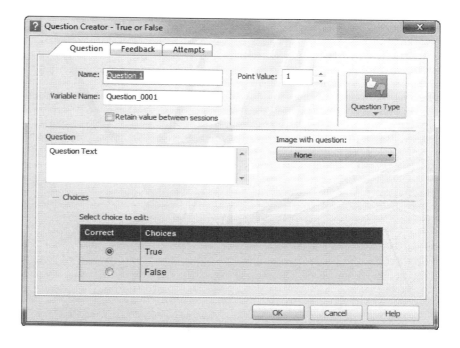

# Question Creator: Question Tab

Much of the information on the **Question** tab varies based on the type of question you chose. Here are the properties that are the same for most question types. Details on properties for individual question types start on page 178.

### Name

This is the name of the question as it appears in the **Title Explorer**.

### Variable Name

The student's answer for every question is stored automatically in a variable. The name of the variable is auto-generated. Change it in this field if you want a different name for the variable.

 Variables, p. 124

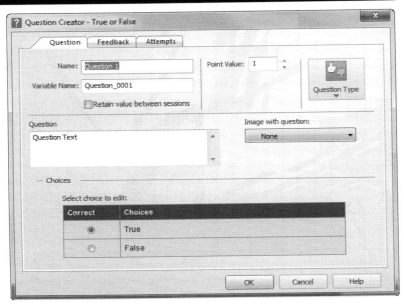

### Retain value between sessions

If you check this box, the student's answer will be saved when exiting the course. If you leave it unchecked, the answer will be cleared when the student exits.

### Point Value

Type the number of points you want to assign to the question.

### Question Type

Here you can change your mind about what question type you want.

### Question

In this field, type the question and/or question instructions.

### Image with question

If you want to include an image with the question (such as a diagram used to answer the question), you can add it from the drop-down list. Some question types manage questions differently.

 **DESIGN TIPS**

- You can also add an image directly to the page instead of through the wizard. The advantage of adding it through the wizard is that the image stays with the question if you ever copy/paste or import it somewhere else.

- Naming the question variables is useful if you plan to use that information later. You may have trouble remembering what **Question_0001** is, but a variable named **Scen1_Q2** or **Obj_3b** might be easier to figure out.

- Changing the weight of questions only matters in a scored test. By default, all questions are set to 1 point. But if one question is particularly important, you can give it more weight. In addition to assigning points for the question being right versus wrong, some question types let you assign points for each individual answer option.

## Question Creator: Feedback Tab

The **Question Creator** provides a number of options for what happens when the student gets a question right or wrong. For example, you can display a message, branch to a different page, or even run an action group that runs a number of actions. For most questions, you get one action for the correct answer and one for the incorrect answer. For multiple-choice questions, you can have separate actions for each individual answer option.

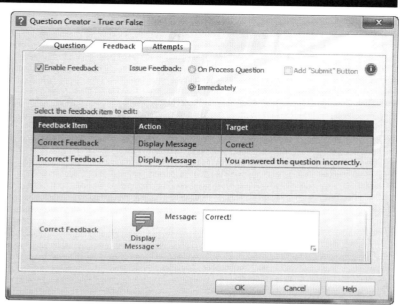

### Enable Feedback

By default, the feedback option is turned off. Check this box to set up feedback for the student.

### Issue Feedback

Once you turn on the feedback, you can indicate when you want the feedback action to be performed.

- **On Process Question**: When you select this option, the feedback action is triggered when the student clicks the **Next** button or when a **Process Question** action is initiated.

- **Add Submit Button**: If you choose the **On Process Question** option, you can choose to add a **Submit** button that has the **Process Question** action attached to it.

- **Immediately**: By default, the feedback action is triggered as soon as the student answers the question.

### Feedback Action Table

Use this table to set up separate actions for the correct and incorrect feedback. Select the feedback option in the table at the top to configure it in the  table at the bottom. In that pane, you can select and configure an action just like you would on the **Action** pane for a regular action.

 Actions, ch. 8

###  DESIGN TIP

What's the advantage of using the **Next** button vs. a **Submit** button? Here are some factors to consider.

- Students may find the **Submit** button clearer, as they may not realize the **Next** button grades the question.

- If you are using **Go To** actions to create branching feedback, you may not want to use the **Next** button, as the students aren't necessarily going to the next page.

- If you are using standard feedback actions (such as displaying a message or showing a page in a pop-up window), grading the question with the **Next** button takes the students to the next page when they close the pop-up window. If you use a **Submit** button with a **Process Question** action, the students stay on the page after the feedback window is closed.

# Question Creator: Attempts Tab

New in version 11, you can set a maximum number of attempts for an individual question. By default, the student can attempt a question an unlimited number of times (if navigation allows the student to stay on or return to the question page).

You can also limit the number of attempts a student can have.

To limit the number of attempts, check the box at the top of the **Attempts** tab and set the various parameters.

## Maximum Attempts Allowed

Set the number of attempts that you want to give the student. When the maximum number of attempts is reached, the question will be locked and the student cannot make another attempt to answer the question.

## Count Attempts

Use these radio buttons to indicate what counts as an attempt. For example, if set to **Immediately** and the student clicks **A** and then **C** on a multiple-choice question, it counts as two attempts. But if it is set to **On Process Question**, the student can click on all the different options, but it does not count as an attempt until the student clicks the **Next** or **Submit** button. The choice here is the same as on the **Feedback** tab—if you change it here it changes on the **Feedback** tab and vice-versa.

## Enable Feedback for Maximum Attempts

Check this box and enter a message if you want to display a message to the students if they reach the maximum number of attempts.

## Question Structure

The question appears as its own object in the **Title Explorer**. All of the related text boxes, check boxes, radio buttons, etc. are attached to the question object.

You can select individual objects in the **Title Explorer** or on the page. Or you can select the question object to select all of the question's objects at once.

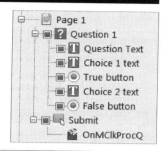

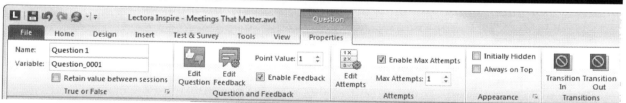

## Edit a Question

**To edit a question:**

1. Select the question icon in the **Title Explorer**.
2. Go to the **Properties** menu.
3. Make your changes.

A question's **Properties** tab has all of the same options as the **Question Creator**, just in a different format. Some options can be changed right on the tab. Other options are accessed by clicking the **Edit Question** button or **Edit Feedback** button, both of which take you back to the **Question Creator**.

 **BRIGHT IDEAS**

- Simple text edits to the question can be made right on the screen without going back into the **Question Creator**.

- If you'd like the text of the questions to be larger, you can do so with the page or chapter level properties. It is best to do this before adding your questions so that the text boxes can be sized appropriately.

 Default Text Properties, p. 22

# Gradable Question Types

| | |
|---|---|
| **True or False**<br>Student decides between two options.<br><br>• Can change labels to anything you want:<br>  yes/no, allowed/not allowed, agree/disagree, etc. | The primary purpose of a team meeting is for the team leader to get an update on what all of the team members are working on.<br><br>○  True<br>○  False |
| **Multiple Choice**<br>Student selects one choice from a list of options.<br><br>• Can be displayed as radio buttons or a drop-down list<br>• Can use text, images, or both as the question choices<br>• Can have separate feedback for each choice | Which of the following is the best reason to have an in-person meeting?<br><br>○  Receive status updates from team members<br>○  Discuss and resolve issues<br>○  Catch up on the latest gossip<br><br>Which of the following is the best reason to have an in-person meeting?<br><br>[ ▼ ]<br>Receive status updates from team members<br>Discuss and resolve issues<br>Catch up on the latest gossip |
| **Multiple Response**<br>Student selects more than one choice from a list of options.<br><br>• Can be displayed as check boxes or a list box<br>• Can use text, images, or both as the question choices<br>• Can award partial credit | Which of the following are good reasons to have an in-person meeting?  Select all that apply.<br><br>☐  Receive status updates from team members<br>☐  Discuss and resolve issues<br>☐  Catch up on the latest gossip<br>☐  Brainstorm ideas<br><br>Which of the following are good reasons to have an in-person meeting?  Select all that apply.<br><br>Receive status updates from team members<br>Discuss and resolve issues<br>Catch up on the latest gossip<br>Brainstorm ideas |
| **Fill in the Blank**<br>Student types an answer in the blank.<br><br>• Can set up multiple answers to be correct<br>• Can use OR logic or AND logic with multiple answers | The best way to get people to come to a meeting on time is to [        ] on time. |
| **Number Entry**<br>Student types a numeric entry in the blank.<br><br>• Can set up multiple answers to be correct<br>• Can use OR logic or AND logic with multiple answers<br>• Can evaluate answers mathematically, such as greater than, in between, etc. | The ideal length for a daily scrum meeting is [      ] minutes. |

# Gradable Question Types (cont'd)

## Matching

Student selects an item on the left and then its matched pair on the right.

- Can have unused options on either side (distractors)
- Can be text-to-text, text-to-image, image-to-text, or image-to-image

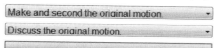

*Match each meeting challenge with the parliamentary procedure used to manage it. First click the challenge on the left and then the corresponding procedure on the right.*

Discussion has gone on too long and is unproductive. ———— Call the question

You don't have enough information to make a decision.

You want to change the details of what you are voting on.        Motion to table

You need to consider a different motion other than the one currently being discussed.        Motion to amend

There has been a lively and useful debate that has gone past the allotted time.        Motion to postpone

## Rank/Sequence

Students put items in the proper sequence.

- Can pick a number from a list or pick the items from a list.

Put the steps for amending a motion into the proper order.

| 7 ▾ | Discuss the amended motion. |
| 5 ▾ | Discuss the motion to amend the motion. |
| 1 ▾ | Make and second the original motion. |

Put the steps for amending a motion into the proper order.

| Make and second the original motion. ▾ |
| Discuss the original motion. ▾ |
| ▾ |

Vote on the amended motion.
Second the motion to amend the motion.

## Drag and Drop

Student drags items to the appropriate place on a graphic/diagram.

- Can drag text boxes or images
- Can have unused dragging items or unused drop zones (distractors)

*Determine which items belong in the meeting minutes. Drag each item to either the meeting minutes document or the trash.*

Mary doesn't think we should move up the deadline.

Marc will follow up with the vendor.

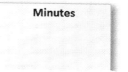

**Minutes**

**Trash**

## Hot Spot

Student selects a designated point(s) in a graphic.

- Can have one spot correct or multiple spots correct
- Can use radio buttons and check boxes or transparent rectangles for the hot spots
- For single-correct questions, can have separate feedback for each choice

Which of these items do not belong in the minutes? Select all that apply.

| Agenda Item | Decisions | Actions |
|---|---|---|
| Updating content on website more frequently | ☐ Change blog frequency once a month. | ☐ Danielle to create new blog schedule by end of week. |
| | ☐ Research syndicated content options. | ☐ Terrell to research syndication options and report back at 9/23 meeting. |
| | ☑ Some people thought we should require a log-in to access the resources. | |

Which of these items do not belong in the minutes? Select all that apply.

| Agenda Item | Decisions | Actions |
|---|---|---|
| Updating content on website more frequently | • Change blog frequency once a month. | • Danielle to create new blog schedule by end of week. |
| | • Research syndicated content options. | • Terrell to research syndication options and report back at 9/23 meeting. |
| | • Some people thought we should require a log-in to access the resources. | |

# True or False Questions

Here are some of the extra options for a true or false question.

In the table at the bottom, select the correct choice by clicking the radio button next to that choice.

To change the choice label (**Yes/No**, **Allowed/Not Allowed**, etc.), click in the row and then click the text to edit it.

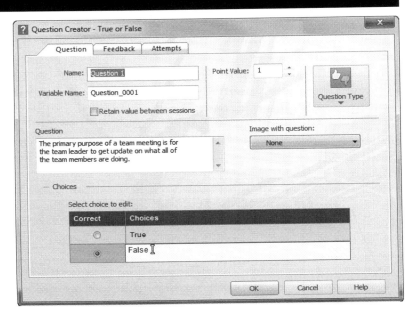

 **CAUTION**

Remember that a true/false question asks the student to evaluate a *statement*. Be careful not to accidentally put a question mark at the end of it!

# Multiple-Choice Questions

Here are some of the extra options unique to a multiple-choice question.

## Question Tab

### Randomize Choices

If you check this box, the choices will appear in a random order for each student.

### Show Choices as DropList

Check this box to show the choices in a dropd-down menu instead of as a series of radio buttons.

### Choices

- To enter text for each choice, select the row for that choice, and then click the text to edit it.
- To rearrange the choices, click and drag the four dots on the left side of the row.
- To delete a choice, click the gray **Delete** icon **(A)** for that row.
- To add another choice, click in the empty row at the bottom.
- To indicate the correct choice, click the radio button for that choice.

### Choice Images

As with most question types, you can add an image that is associated with the question as a whole. But you can also associate an image with each individual choice—either in addition to or in place of the text. To add an image, click in the row, and then click the drop-down menu to find and select the image you want.

## Feedback Tab

Rather than have one feedback action for correct feedback and one for incorrect feedback, you can select **Individual Feedback by Choice** from the drop-down menu at the top. When you do this, the feedback grid changes to show each option. Click an option in the table and then configure the action in the pane at the bottom.

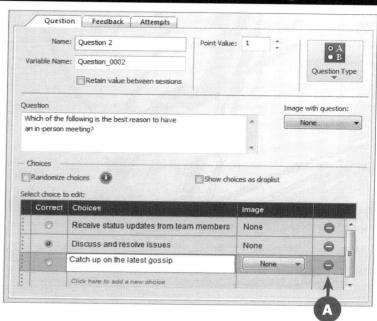

## ⓘ CAUTION

If you randomize the choices, be careful about using language that is position-specific, such as an option that says "All of the above." That option might be randomized to the top of the list.

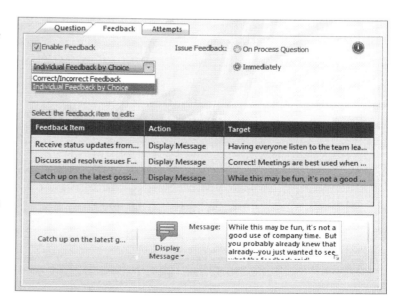

# Multiple-Response Question

A multiple-response question is different than a multiple-choice question in that the student can select more than one answer. In previous versions of Lectora, the two question types were combined.

Most of the options are the same as for a multiple-choice question, with the following exceptions.

## Question Tab

### Grade Each Choice

Check this box if you want each option to be worth the given number of points, instead of the whole question being worth that many points. This allows for partial credit if the student answers some correctly but not all.

### Show Choices as Listbox

Just as with a multiple-choice question you can have the choices displayed in a drop-down list. The difference is that the student can select more than one option from the listbox using the **Shift** or **Ctrl** keys.

### Correct Options:

Since more than one option may be correct, the choices have check boxes instead of radio buttons. Check the boxes for all the options that are correct.

## Feedback Tab

The feedback options are the same as for most other questions—you can set one action for the correct response and one for the incorrect response. (You cannot set feedback for each individual option with this question type.)

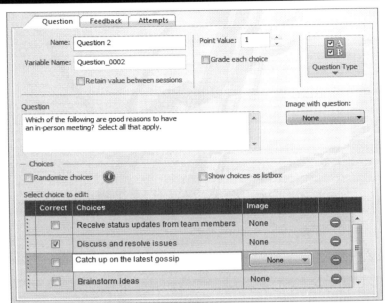

 **CAUTION**

If more than one option is correct, be sure to let the students know. If you are using a listbox, be sure to indicate *how* to select more than one option.

 **TIME SAVER**

After you've created a multiple-choice or multiple-response question, you can come back to the **Question Creator** and switch back and forth between the two question types.

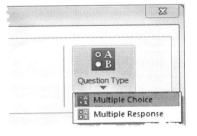

# Fill in the Blank and Number Entry Questions

Fill-in-the-blank and number entry questions are similar with two specific differences:

- Fill-in-the-blank accepts letters, numbers, and special characters, while number entry only accepts numbers.

- With number entry, you can evaluate the answer mathematically, such as a range of numbers.

Feedback options for these question types are the same as covered on page 173. Here are options unique to these question types.

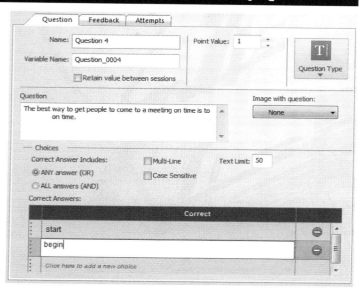

## Question

Lectora creates a text-entry box that needs to be manually placed in the proper position. So if the blank is in the middle of the sentence, you'll need to leave room for it.

## Choices

If there is more than one correct answer possible, select **OR** if the student needs to answer only one of them. Select **AND** if the student needs to include all of the terms in the answer. (For number entry questions, these options appear in a drop-down menu.)

## Multi-Line

For fill-in-the-blank, check this box for the text-entry box to wrap to more than one line.

## Case Sensitive

For fill-in-the-blank, check this box if the student's entry needs to match the same capitalization as the correct answers listed.

## Text Limit

Here you can specify the maximum number of characters the student may type.

## Choices

- For fill-in-the-blank questions, click in a row in the table to type a correct answer.

- For number entry, select a relationship for how the answer is evaluated, such as **Equal To** or **Less Than**. Then enter the value(s) needed for that logic. For example, **Between Including** requires two values.

- Click in the blank row at the bottom to add more correct answers.

- Click the gray **Delete** icon to delete a correct answer.

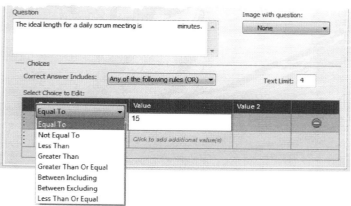

The best way to get people to come to a meeting on time is to _____ on time.

*Fill-in-the-blank question as it first appears on the slide—the text entry box needs to be placed in the statement.*

## DESIGN TIPS

- Only use fill-in-the-blank questions when you have cut-and-dry answers. Avoid answers that are conceptual and may have many synonyms or those that have many formatting or spelling options (such as a time or date).

- Decide if you want to accept misspellings. If so, enter likely misspellings as possible correct answers.

# Matching Questions

With matching questions, students match up items (text and/or images) from two columns. An item cannot be matched with more than one other item.

Here are the elements that are unique for matching questions.

## Question Tab

### Grade Each Choice

Check this box if you want each pairing to be worth the given number of points, instead of the whole question being worth that many points.

### Line Color and Width

When the student clicks an item in the left and then the right column, the items are connected by a blue line, by default. Use these fields to change the color and width of those lines.

### Matching Pairs

Set up each pair correctly in its own row. When the question is displayed to the student, the items in the left column stay in the same order, and the items in the right column get rearranged.

### Name

When a student answers a question, the answer is stored as a variable. You can use that variable for if/then logic or display it to the student in the **Test Results** window. With matching, the answer shows using the values in the **Name** column (**1L-1R**, **2L-2R**, etc., by default), which isn't very useful feedback for the student. You can change the values in the **Name** column to make the feedback more useful to the student.

### Text and Image

Enter the text for each column. If you would like to have an image for either column, use the drop-down menu in the **Image** field to find and select it.

### Managing Choices

- Rearrange the order of the pairs (how the left column appears on screen) by clicking and dragging the four dots on the left side of the row.
- Delete a choice by clicking the gray **Delete** icon on the right side of the row.

### Distractors

If you want to have an option in one of the columns that doesn't have a match, enter it here. Indicate if you want it to appear in the left column or the right column.

---

Question 6
Match each meeting challenge with the parliamentary procedure used to manage it. First click the challenge on the left and then the corresponding procedure on the right.
Your answer: 1L-1R,2L-2R,3L-3R,4L-4R,(not answered)

*Test results using default names*

Question 6
Match each meeting challenge with the parliamentary procedure used to manage it. First click the challenge on the left and then the corresponding procedure on the right.
Your answer: Discussion too long-Call the question,Not enough info-Postpone,Change the details-Amend,Consider different motion-Table,(not answered)

*Test results after changing names*

# Rank/Sequence Question

With this question type, students put items, such as steps in a process, into the correct order.

Here are the elements that are unique to this question type.

## Question Tab

### Grade Each Choice

Check this box to give the student points for having a given item in the correct place. (For example, step 3 was correctly identified, but step 2 was not.)

### Randomize Choices and Correct Order

For this question to be effective, the choices must not start in the correct order. There are two ways to do this.

One option is to put them in the correct order in the **Choices** column and then check **Randomize Choices**. When you do this, the choices will appear in a random order for each student.

The other option is for you to put them in a certain, incorrect order in the **Choices** column. Then, in the **Correct Order** column, indicate the correct position for each choice.

### Show Choices in Droplist

By default, each choice appears on screen with a drop-down menu where the student selects the number for that step. If you check this box, only drop-down menus appear, and the student selects which step goes in each position from the drop-down menus.

### Choices and Image

- For each choice, type text into a row and/or use the drop-down menu in the Image column to find and select an image.
- Rearrange the order of the pairs (how the left column appears on screen) by clicking and dragging the four dots on the left side of the row.
- Click in the blank row at the bottom to add more correct answers.
- Click the gray **Delete** icon to delete a correct answer.

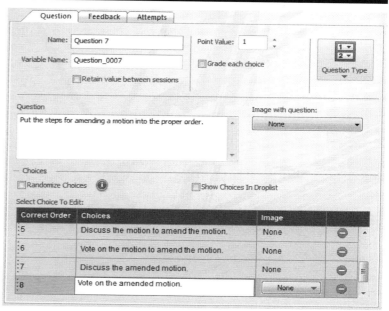

*Default question format where students select a number position for each choice.*

*Droplist format where students select the choice for each position in the list.*

# Drag-and-Drop Questions

Drag-and-drop questions have three components:

- Drop items: the text boxes or images that are dragged and dropped onto the drop zones.
- Drop zones: the areas of the image where items can be dropped.
- Drop image: the image upon which the drop zones are placed.

Here are the elements that are unique to this question type.

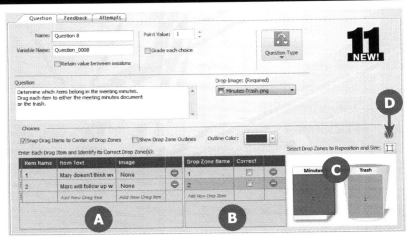

## Question Tab

### Grade Each Choice

If you check this box, the student gets points for each individual drag item that is dropped in the proper drop zone.

### Drop Image

Unlike other question types, the drop image is required.

### Snap Drag Items to Center of Drop Zones

Check this box if you want the drag item to snap to the center of the drop zone when the student drops the item. Otherwise, the item will stay exactly where the student dropped it.

### Show Drop Zone Outlines

If you want the student to see the edges of the drop zones, check this box and select the color you want for the outline.

## Drag Item/Drop Zone Table (A/B)

### Item Name/Drop Zone Name

When a student answers a question, the answer is stored as a variable. You can change the values in these columns to make this information more useful (instead of **1-1**, **2-2**, etc.).

### Item Text and Image (A)

Enter the text and/or image you want to use for the drag item.

### Drop Zones (B)

By default, the question comes with three drop zones. Add more zones by clicking in the blank row. Delete drop zones by clicking the gray **Delete** icon for that zone.

In the preview pane **(C)**, drag the drop zones to the proper position on the image. Click the button above the preview **(D)** for a pop-up window **(E)** with more precise controls.

### Specifying the Correct Answer

Select a drag item in section **(A)** of the table. Then in section **(B)**, check the box(es) for the drop zone(s) that are correct for that drag item. Then repeat the process for each additional drag item.

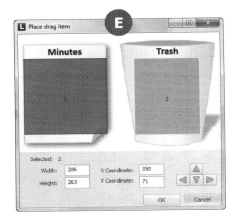

 **DESIGN TIPS**

- Version 11 gives you more flexibility when designing your questions. Your drop zones can now be bigger than your drag items. Plus, you can have more than one drag item go to the same drop zone.

- Create distractors by having drag items with not drop zones marked as correct or by having drop zones that no drag items have marked as correct.

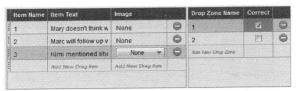

*Item 3 belongs in drop zone 1*

# Hot Spot Question

In a hot spot question, students select one or more areas of an image. You can use check boxes and radio buttons or transparent rectangles to indicate the correct and incorrect spots.

Here are the elements that are unique to this question type.

## Question Tab

### Hot Spot Image

As with drag-and-drop, you must include an image for this question type—otherwise, there is nothing for the student to click on.

### Hotspot

Indicate whether you want radio buttons (if only one choice is correct) and check boxes (if more than one choice is correct) or transparent rectangles as the hot spot.

### Correct Answer Includes More Than One Choice

If more than one hot spot is correct, check this box.

### Outline Color

If you are using transparent hot spots, the hot spots are outlined in blue when the students click them. Here you can change the color of the outline.

### Correct

Check the box(es) for which hot spots are considered correct.

### Name

When a student answers a question, the answer is stored as a variable that can use for if/then logic or to display to the student. You can change the values in this column to make that information more useful.

### Hot Spot Placement

In the preview pane **(A)**, drag the drop zones to be in the proper position on the image. Click the button above the preview **(B)** for a pop-up window **(C)** with more precise controls.

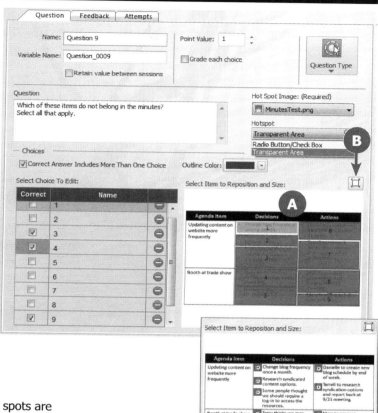

*Hot spot placement when using radio buttons and check boxes*

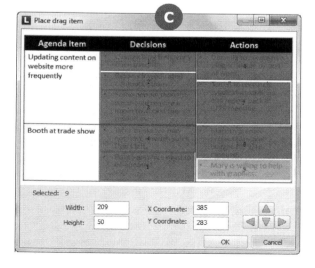

# Special Question Options

## Change Radio Button and Check Box Style

You can easily change the look of all radio buttons and check boxes in the course.

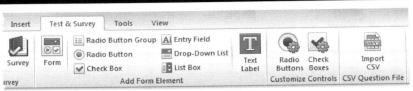

**To change the style:**

1. Go to the **Test & Survey** tab.
2. Click **Radio Buttons** or **Check Boxes**.
3. In the dialog box, select the option you want for both the selected and non-selected version of the button/box.
4. Click **OK**.

 **CAUTION**

When you make this change, realize that it changes all of the radio buttons or check boxes for the entire course.

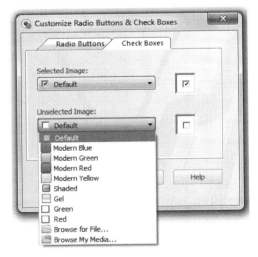

# Import Questions From a CSV File

Rather than build your questions directly in Lectora, you also have the option of importing certain question types from a CSV (comma-separated value) file. A CSV file is a text file that can come from a number of sources, such as Excel or Wordpad. You can import the following question types:

- True/False
- Multiple Choice
- Essay
- Short Answer

## To import questions:

1. Prepare your CSV file in accordance with Lectora specifications. (Use the **File Format Instructions** link for guidance.)
2. Go to the **Test & Survey** tab.
3. Click the **Import CSV** button.
4. Click the **Browse** button to find and select your file.
5. Check the **Create as Test** box if you want the questions to be added to a new test chapter.
6. Indicate how far from the top and left margins you want the questions to appear.
7. Select the font attributes for the question text.
8. Click the **OK** button.

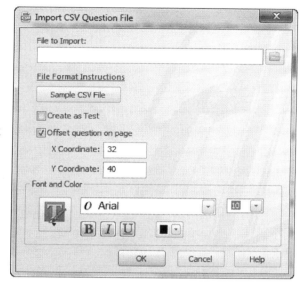

## BRIGHT IDEA

You can also import a QTI (Question and Test Interoperability) file. Go to the **File** tab, select **Import**, and then **QTI**.

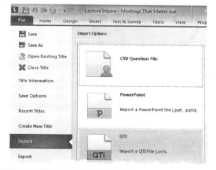

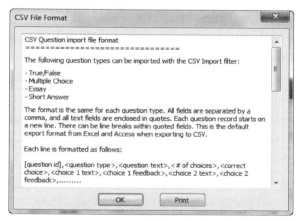

*Instructions*

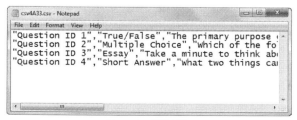

*Sample CSV file*

# Question-Related Actions

There are several actions that specifically relate to questions and surveys. Many of them are included automatically in different test/survey features. But you can manually add them if you want custom functionality.

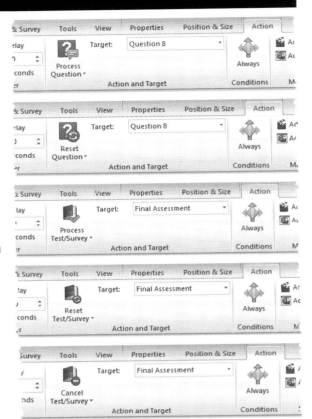

### Process Question Action

This action is added behind the scenes to the **Next** button on any page with a test or survey question. If, in the **Question Creator**, you choose to add a **Submit** button, that button contains this action.

### Reset Question Action

Use this action when you want to clear out the student's answers to a single question.

### Process Test/Survey Action

This action grades the test and initiates pass/fail actions you set up on the test chapter's **Behavior** tab. When you add a test or survey chapter, the last page in the chapter has a Done button that contains this action.

### Reset Test/Survey Action

Use this action when you want to clear out the student's answers to all the questions in a test or survey.

### Cancel Test/Survey Action

This action cancels the logic on a test and initiates the **On Canceled/Failed** action you set up on the test chapter's **Behavior** tab. When you add a test or survey chapter, the pages have a **Cancel** button that contains this action.

## DESIGN TIPS

- A text description in a message window may not be the best for a matching, drag-and-drop, or hot spot question. Consider taking a screen capture of the question answered correctly and pasting that image on a pop-up page.

- Here are some options for providing hints to your students in a question.
    - Bring up a special page in a pop-up window with key information on it.
    - Link to a Website that can help them with the answer.
    - Show/hide a text box hidden on that page with the hint.
    - Launch a document to serve as a job aid.

    Be careful about linking the student back to the main course page where they first learned the information. This may cause the student to get "lost" in the course or end up with multiple instances of the course open at the same time.

- It's a good idea to include instructions on HOW to use the question. You wouldn't want students to get the question wrong when they know the right answer, just because they aren't sure what they are supposed to do. Sample wording:
    - True/False: "Decide if the following statement is true or false."
    - Multiple Choice: "Select the best answer." or "Select the best answer from the list.'
    - Multiple Response: "Select all that apply." or "Select all that apply. Press CTRL to select more than one."
    - Fill in the Blank/Short Answer/Essay: "Type your answer in the space provided."
    - Matching: "Click first on the xxx in the left column and then on the corresponding xxx in the right column."
    - Rank/Sequence: "For each item, select a number for which step it is in the process." or "Select the first step from the first drop-down list, the second step from the second drop-down list, etc."
    - Drag and Drop: "Drag each item to the appropriate place in the diagram."
    - Hot Spot: "Click on the appropriate spot(s) in the diagram."
    - Questions with distractors: "Some of the options will not be used."

## POWER TIP

The **Change Contents** action can be applied to questions. It doesn't change the question itself, but rather changes the answer captured for the question. Use this when you want to design a question using features other than what's found in the question wizard.

For example, you might be creating a game using buttons, form elements, or images with actions instead of a question from the standard question types. However, you need the student's answer to be included in an overall grade. What you can do is set up a "fake" question that the student doesn't see and then change the contents of that question based on how the student answers the question you made yourself in the game.

To do this, first set up a question that will be hidden from the student's view. (For example, make it initially hidden and then never show it.) Then, set up a **Change Contents** action to trigger when the student answers the question (clicks the image, for example). With this action, you can set the question's variable to be a text value or the value of another variable. The question is populated with that answer, just as if the student had answered the question in the traditional way. The student gets the feedback, and the answer is tracked as with any other question.

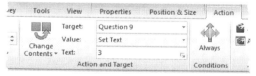

Change Contents Action, p. 131

# Notes

# Creating Surveys

## Introduction

Surveys and survey questions are very much like tests and test questions. You can put individual questions anywhere in your course or organize them in a survey chapter. The main difference is that survey questions are not graded or scored, don't provide any feedback, and don't allow multiple attempts.

You can use any gradable question as a survey question. If it is a standalone question, just disable the feedback on the **Feedback** tab. If you are adding a gradable question to a survey chapter, the feedback is disabled for you. In addition to the gradable questions, there are three non-gradable question types: short answer, essay, and Likert.

If you are integrating with an LMS, survey results will be included with other interaction data. If you want to send the results via e-mail, to a CGI program, or to a Google form, then the questions need to be put in a survey chapter. Survey questions that don't need to be sent anywhere can just live on a page by themselves.

Note: This chapter will make the most sense if you have already read chapter 12 on tests and test questions.

## In This Chapter

- Survey Chapters
- Survey Questions

# Notes

# Survey Chapters

When you include questions in a survey chapter, you can send the results through email, to a CGI program, or to a public Google form. The survey chapter contains key properties that govern this logic. Once you have the chapter, you would add the individual questions.

## Add a Survey Chapter

**To add a survey chapter:**

1. Go to the **Test & Survey** tab.
2. Click the **Survey** button.
3. Go to the test chapter's **Properties** and **Behavior & Results** tabs.
4. Configure the settings.

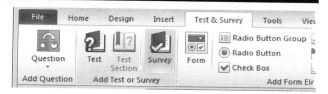

The **Properties** tab is the same as for any chapter. The **Behavior & Results** tab is similar to a test chapter. The differences will be covered on the next page.

 **BRIGHT IDEA**

Even though there isn't a survey section option, you can organize your survey chapter into sections. Just use a regular section within the survey chapter.

 Chapter Properties, p. 25
Test Chapter Properties, p. 166

## Survey Chapter Structure

When you add a survey chapter, the following objects are added (much like a test chapter).

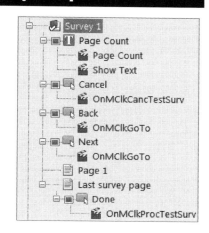

- **Page Count**: The survey chapter comes with its own page numbering. You can delete the page count text box if you don't want it.

- **Cancel, Back, and Next buttons**: These three buttons attached to the chapter appear on every page in the chapter (except the last page). **Cancel** cancels the survey and initiates the action you designate for canceling the survey (see next page). **Back** goes to the previous page. **Next** goes to the next page.

- **Page 1**: The test chapter comes with one blank page for your questions. You can put all of your questions on that one page or add additional pages for additional questions.

- **Last survey page**: The last page contains a **Done** button which includes an action to process the test/survey. This is the action that sends the results—if you have set up the survey to do that. If you delete this button, be sure to add this action in another way.

# Behavior & Results Tab

The **Behavior & Results** tab has about half the features of the **Behavior** tab and **Results** tab for a test chapter—eliminating the features that don't apply to an ungraded survey.

With a survey, you do NOT have the following options:

- Showing feedback
- Branching based on pass/fail (you can branch based on completed/canceled)
- Randomization of questions
- Time limits
- Grading and test results

All other features work the same way as for a test chapter.

    Test Chapter Properties, p. 166-167

# Survey Questions

Survey questions can be added to a survey chapter or to any page within your title. You can have one page for each question or a single, long, scrolling page that has many questions. Remember that any question can be made into a survey question if you don't enable the feedback. If you place the question in a survey chapter, the feedback is automatically disabled.

The procedure for adding survey questions is extremely similar for all question types, including the gradable questions. The basic process is covered in chapter 12. In this section, you'll learn about the elements that are unique to non-gradable survey questions.

 **BRIGHT IDEA**

Non-gradable questions can be added to a graded test. Those questions, however, will not be graded and will not count towards the overall score of the test.

## Add a Survey Question

**To add a survey question:**

1. Go to the **Test & Survey** tab.
2. Click the **Question** drop-down button.
3. Select the question type you want.
4. Enter question parameters on the various question properties tabs.
5. Click the **OK** button.

 **BRIGHT IDEA**

The non-gradable question types only have a **Question** and a **Feedback** tab. Gradable question types put in a survey chapter also have the **Attempts** tab, but the options are disabled.

# Non-Gradable Question Types

| | |
|---|---|
| **Short Answer**<br>Student types an answer to an open-ended question.<br><br>• Can't be graded by the system<br>• Useful for "reflection" questions or self-graded questions<br>• Can accept up to 2048 characters for the answer | What is one thing you can do for your very next staff meeting that can make it more productive? |
| **Essay**<br>Student types an answer to an open-ended question.<br><br>• Scrolling answer box for longer answers<br>• Can't be graded by the system<br>• Useful for "reflection" questions or self-graded questions<br>• Can accept up to 2048 characters for the answer | If you were able to spend one less hour per week in unproductive meetings, what would you be able to accomplish that you can't do now? |
| **Likert**<br>Students rate items on a scale such as "agree to disagree" or "always to never."<br><br>• Can have students evaluate one or more statements using the same scale<br>• Can have up to 5 points on the scale<br>• Can pick from several scale choices or create your own. | Strongly Agree / Agree / Disagree / Strongly Disagree<br>Meetings start on time.<br>Relevant materials are distributed before the meeting.<br>People come prepared for meetings.<br>Discussions focus on decisions and actions. |

# Short Answer and Essay Questions

Short answer and essay questions are almost identical. The main difference is the text entry box for the question. With short answer questions, the student can only enter one line of text for the answer. With essay questions, the student can enter multiple lines of text.

Here are the elements that are unique to this question type.

## Question Tab

### Maximum Answer Length

You can designate how many characters you want to accept, with a maximum of 2048. If the student tries to type more than that, the course will not allow any more.

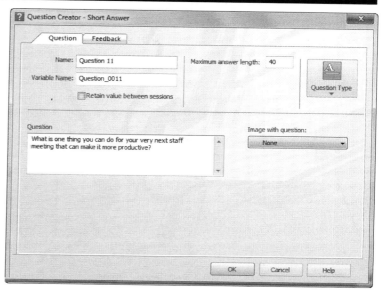

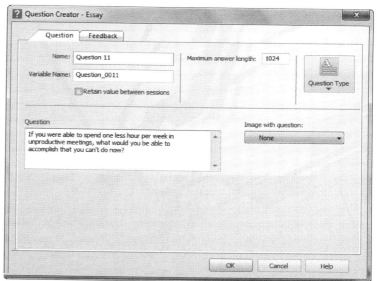

# Likert Question

With a Likert question, students rate statements on a scale. You can have one or more statements evaluated at once, select different types of scales, and select what the connecting bar looks like.

Here are the elements that are unique to this question type.

## Question Tab

### Statement(s)

Enter each of the statements to be evaluated by the student. As with other questions, you can rearrange the statements by dragging the four dots on the left and can delete statements by clicking the gray **Delete** icon.

### Scale

Select from 12 pre-made scale options (such as agree to disagree or important to not important) or select **Custom Labels** to create your own scale.

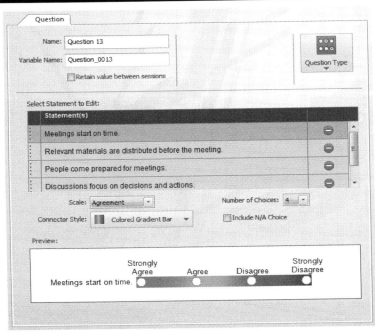

### Number of Choices

Indicate how many points you want on the scale, up to 5.

### Connector Style

From the drop-down menu, select the visual appearance you want for the connector bar.

### Include N/A Choice

Check this box if you want the last option to be **N/A**, meaning not applicable. This option is only available if you don't already have five points on the scale.

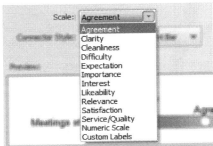

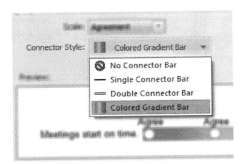

# Forms and Form Elements

## Introduction

Forms and form elements let you capture information from the student in the finished course and do a number of different things with that information:

- Send the information somewhere, such as capturing contact information and sending it to an e-mail address or online database.

- Use the information for conditional logic, such as special navigation based on whether the student is a manager or a supervisor.

- Display the information back to the student, such as placing the student's name in a game or on a certificate.

- Create custom interactions, such as creating a game using form elements (instead of the Question Creator) when you want more customization options. For example, if you want to ask a question in a game in which the answer triggers several actions, it might be easier to do this with a form drop-down list than with a multiple-choice question with the Question Creator.

### In This Chapter

- Understanding Forms and Form Elements
- Form-Related Actions

# Notes

# Understanding Forms and Form Elements

Form elements are the individual interactive objects, such as a radio button or a drop-down list. The form object is a "container" that holds them. If you want to use the information just within the course and don't need to send it anywhere, then you can just place the individual form elements directly on any page. But if you do want to send the information anywhere, those elements must live in a form object. The form object controls the logic about where to send the information.

 **DESIGN TIP**

Your students can use the **Tab** key to move from field to field in your form. The tab order is set by the order of your form elements in the **Title Explorer**. So when you are laying your elements out logically on the page, also think about the best way to arrange them in the **Title Explorer** for maximum usability.

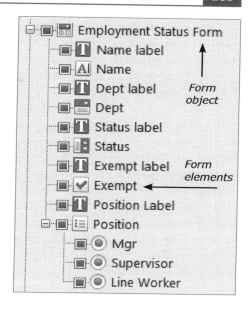

## Form Element Choices

| | | |
|---|---|---|
| Name: | [text entry field] | *Text entry field* |
| Department: | [drop-down] | *Drop-down list* |
| Employment Status: | Full-Time<br>Part-Time<br>Temporary<br>Temp-to-Perm<br>Seasonal | *List box* |
| Exempt? | ☐ | *Check box* |
| Position: | ○ Manager<br>○ Supervisor<br>○ Line Worker | *Radio buttons in a radio button group* |

Test & Survey  Tools  View  Properties

Form

Radio Button Group  Entry Field
Radio Button  Drop-Down List
Check Box  List Box

Add Form Element

# Add a Form Object

## To add a form object:

1. Go to the **Test & Survey** tab.
2. Click the **Form** button.
3. Go to the form object's **Properties** tab.
4. Configure the properties. (See below.)

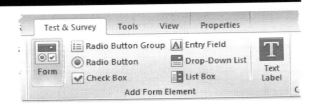

## Form Properties

Many of the properties are the same as for a test chapter. For example, you can choose to save or clear answers between sessions or send the answers to an email address, custom database, or public Google form. Refer to pages 166–167 for details on the properties that are similar. There is one button that is unique to a form object.

## Additional Values

In addition to the information the students fill out in the form, you can also send other information along with it. Simply set up the information: **Name** is the name of the piece of information (similar to a variable name), and **Value** is the actual value.

## To add additional values:

1. Click the **Additional Values** button.
2. In the **Name** field, type the name you want to give the parameter.
3. In the **Value** field, type the value you want to give to the parameter.
4. Click the **Add parameter** button.
5. Repeat steps 2–4 for additional values.
6. Click the **OK** button.

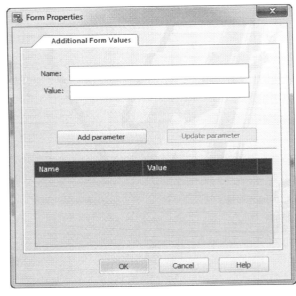

# Add a Radio Button Group

A radio button group is an organizing object that groups radio buttons together. If you merely put four radio buttons on a page by themselves, each one can be selected independently of the others. But if you put them in a radio button group, then only one can be selected at a time.

When you add a radio button group, it includes three radio buttons.

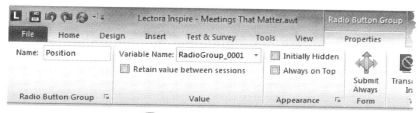

### To add a radio button group:

1. Go to the **Test & Survey** tab.
2. Click the **Radio Button Group** button.
3. Go to the group's **Properties** tab.
4. Configure the properties. (See below.)

## Radio Button Group Properties

### Name

Enter the name for the radio button group.

### Variable Name

This is the name of the variable used to store the radio button group's value. Whatever choice the student selects is stored as the value for that variable.

### Retain Value Between Sessions

If you check this box, the value for this group will be kept if the students exit and return to the course. If you leave it unchecked, the value reverts back to being blank when they re-enter the course.

### Submit Always/Submit If

This button lets you set up conditions that have to be met for this object's values to be submitted. You can use this feature to set up data validation.

For example, you make certain fields required by adding a condition that the object's variable not be empty or that an text entry field for an e-mail address contain the @ character.

This button is only available if the form elements is in a form object.

 Conditions, p. 128

### Else Message

If you set up a condition, a text field appears where you can type a message that is displayed to the student if the condition is not met.

## BRIGHT IDEAS

- If you are just adding form elements to the page, select the page before going to the **Insert** tab. If you are adding them to a form object, be sure to select the form object before going to the **Insert** tab. If you forget, you can always drag them to the form object later.

- Remember that you can change the appearance of the check boxes and radio buttons from the **Tests & Surveys** tab.

 Customize Controls p. 186

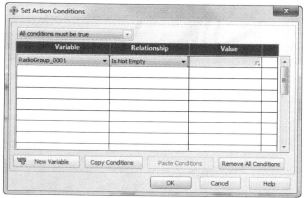

# Add a Radio Button

Remember that you can add a radio button individually or in a group. If you add one individually, its selection is not linked to the selection of any other radio button, and it is stored as its own variable. To add one individually, select the page or form object before going to the **Insert** menu. To add one to a radio button group, select the group before going to the **Insert** menu.

**To add a radio button:**

1. Go to the **Test & Survey** tab.
2. Click the **Radio Button** button.
3. Go to the radio button's **Properties** tab.
4. Configure the properties. (See below.)

## Radio Button Properties

Many of the properties are the same as described on the previous page. Here are a few that are different.

### Label

Type the text you want to have appear on the page with the radio button, telling the student what the radio button designates. The label and the radio button appear as a single object on the page.

### Label on Left

By default, the text label appears on the right side of the radio button. Check this box if you want it on the left instead.

### Variable

Just as with a radio button group, this is the name of the variable that stores the student's answer. If the radio button is in a radio button group, then this option is grayed out, and the variable is managed on the radio button group's properties tab.

### Initially Selected (On)

With a radio button or group, all buttons are in the deselected state when the student gets to the page. If you check this box, you can have the button pre-selected. (The student can still select something else.)

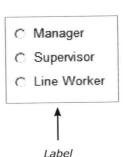

Label

 **BRIGHT IDEA**

Looking for the **On Select/Change** tab? This feature, which lets you assign an action when the form element is selected or changed by the student, is now a trigger on the **Action** tab as opposed to a tab on the form object.

 Triggers, p. 99

# Add a Check Box

Check boxes can be used by themselves or with other check boxes. Unlike radio buttons, if you are using more than one check box, they do not need to be grouped together. That's because the student can check more than one; so, no special logic is needed to link them together. Each check box's value is stored as an individual variable.

**To add a check box:**

1. Go to the **Test & Survey** tab.
2. Click the **Check Box** button.
3. Go to the check box's **Properties** tab.
4. Configure the properties.

The properties are the same as for a radio button, as described on pages 203 and 204.

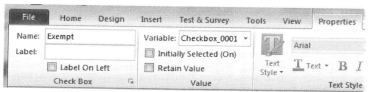

# Add a Text Entry Box

A text entry box lets the student type in the response.

**To add a text entry box:**

1. Go to the **Test & Survey** tab.
2. Click the **Entry Field** button.
3. Go to the radio button's **Properties** tab.
4. Configure the properties. (See below.)

## Text Entry Box Properties

Many of the properties are the same as for a radio button, as described on pages 203 and 204. Here are the properties that are unique to entry boxes.

### Initial

By default, the text entry box is blank when the student first sees it. If you want to have text pre-populated in the field (that the student can still change), enter it here.

### Max Characters

In this field, you can enter the maximum number of characters the student may enter in this field.

### Multi-Line

If you check this box, the student's response will flow to multiple lines, instead of staying on a single line.

### Number

If you check this box, only numbers can be entered.

### Password

If you check this box, the student's answer appears to them as asterisks. If the form values are submitted or displayed elsewhere in the course (via a **Change Contents** action, for example), the actual value is used, not the asterisks.

### Read Only

If you check this box, the students can only see the value of the field, not enter anything themselves. For example, you may be using form elements to simulate the look of certain software. You can make a form field read-only if you are showing a field that is read-only (unavailable) in that software.

## DESIGN TIP

Entry fields, drop-down lists, and list boxes do not have a **Label** option in their properties. That means you'll need to add a text box on the page explaining what the student should do with those fields.

If making your course Section 508 compliant to be accessible to someone using a screen reader, you'll need to link the text box to the form element on the text box's **Properties** tab so that the screen reader knows which text box is describing which form element.

# Add a Drop-Down List or List Box

A drop-down list lets the student select one option from a drop-down list.

A list box displays all of the items and the student can select more than one using the **Ctrl** or **Shift** key (if that option is enabled).

**To add a drop-down list or list box:**

1. Go to the **Test & Survey** tab.
2. Click the **Drop-Down List** or **List Box** button.
3. In the **Edit List** dialog box that appears, enter the values (separated with a hard return) that will appear on the list.
4. Click the **OK** button.
5. Go to the list's **Properties** tab.
6. Configure the properties. (See below.)

## Drop-Down List and List Box Properties

Many of the properties are the same as for a radio button, as described on pages 203 and 204. Here are the two properties that are unique to these form objects.

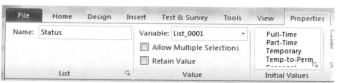

### Allow Multiple Selections

Available only for a list box, check this option if you want the student to be able to select more than one option.

### Initial Values

Click in this field to re-open the **Edit List** dialog box to make changes to the list.

## Edit List Dialog Box Options

By default, nothing in the list is selected when it is first shown to the students. You can check any of the items if you want them to be pre-selected for your students.

Use the **Add**, **Remove**, **Move Up**, and **Move Down** buttons to manage the items on the list.

 **DESIGN TIP**

Your students may not automatically know that they can select more than one option using the **Shift** or **Ctrl** keys, so be sure to provide clear instructions.

# Form-Related Actions

## Submit Form Values

If your form elements are in a form object, you have the option of submitting your form values to an e-mail address or a CGI program. The specifications for doing this are set up on the form's **Properties** tab.

To actually send the values, however, you must create an action that submits the values. Set up a button or other trigger and attach a **Submit Form** action to it. Then select the form you want in the **Target** field.

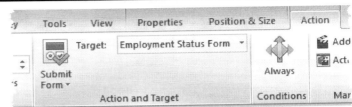

## Reset Form Values

You can also add an action that resets the form's values, either at the student's request or automatically. For example, if you are using the form elements for a game or to simulate a paper form the students might fill out on the job, it might be nice if they had a restart button to let them start over at the beginning.

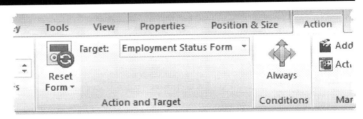

Just add a **Reset Form** action to your course, and select the form object from the **Target** drop-down menu.

Remember that all form values will be reset when the student exits and returns to the course, unless you have the option checked in the form object or form elements to retain the variable values.

# Special Tools and Wizards

## Introduction

In this chapter, you are introduced to a number of tools that span every aspect of production: from design to project management; from saving time to getting more organized.

- **Spell check:** Just as with most software, you can check the spelling for a single page or the entire title.
- **Notes**: Add production notes for you and your development team.
- **Error Checker**: Let Lectora review your title for issues, such as missing resources or incomplete actions.
- **Accessibility Checker**: Check your course for compatibility for those with disabilities who are using assistive technology, such as a screen reader.
- **Media Libraries**: Organize your media assets and take advantage of a stock library of media assets.
- **Resource Manager**: Find where images and other media are used and clean out unused files.
- **Library Objects**: Save and reuse course elements to save development time.
- **Translation**: Export your text to a file that can be translated and re-imported.
- **Import/Export Options**: Import and export content to reuse it, back it up, etc.
- **Printing**: Print screens or an outline to help with review processes.
- **ReviewLink:** Post your title online with a free online tool that captures and manages reviewer comments.
- **Templates**: Save a file's title-level settings as a template to help create new courses more quickly.
- **Author Control**: Password protect your title (down to the object level) to prevent other authors from changing content they should not.

### In This Chapter

- Spell Checker
- Notes
- Error Checker
- Accessibility Checker
- Media Libraries
- Library Objects
- Resource Manager
- Translation
- Importing and Exporting
- Printing
- ReviewLink
- Title Templates
- Author Control

# Notes

# Spell Checker

**Run Spell Check**

**To run spell check:**

1. Go to the **Tools** tab.
2. Click the **Spell Check** button.

As with spell check in most other software, you can:

- Choose to ignore a word found or ignore all instances of that word.
- Add that word to the dictionary so that it is recognized in the future.
- Select an item from the suggestions and change that occurrence or change all occurrences.
- Type the correction yourself and change that occurrence or all occurrences.

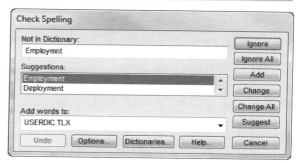

 **TIME SAVER**

If you just want to check a single page, click the **Spell Check** drop-down arrow and select **Current Page**.

 **POWER TIPS**

- While running spell check, click the **Dictionaries** button to create and manage custom dictionaries, which are especially useful if you have industry-specific terminology or are localizing a course.
- Click the **Options** button to change the logic regarding what types of errors to look for.

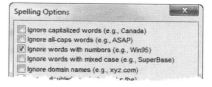

# Notes

Lectora notes are a great way to document important development information for you and your team. They can be added at any level of the course and appear only in **Edit** mode – not in preview mode or the published course. Notes can be viewed either on your course pages or in a report that can be sorted and printed.

 **BRIGHT IDEA**

Use notes for:

- Development standards such as color and font usage.
- RGB values of key design colors.
- Size or placement of design elements.
- Comments about open questions or work to be done.

## Add a Note

**To add a note:**

1. Select the level of the course (title, chapter, page, etc.) where you want to add the note.
2. Go to the **Tools** tab.
3. Click the **Add Note** drop-down button.
4. Select the note color you want.
5. Type the text for your note.
6. Click the **X** button in the top corner to close it.

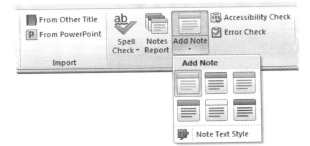

 **BRIGHT IDEA**

Any chapter, page, etc. with a note appears in bold italics in the **Title Explorer**. If a page has a note, the section or chapter it is in is also bolded.

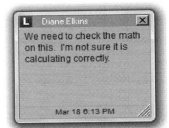

## Read a Note

**To read a note:**

1. Go to the level of the course (title, chapter, page, etc.) with the note.
2. Double-click the note icon.
3. Click the **X** button in the note to close it.

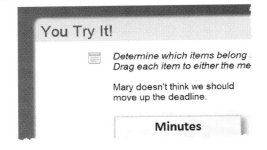

## Run a Notes Report

**To run a notes report:**

1. Go to **Tools** tab.
2. Click the **Notes Report** button.

In the dialog box, you can click any of the column headings to sort by that heading. Click the **Print** button to print the report. The sorting and printing options are especially useful if you use notes to track open tasks and issues for the project.

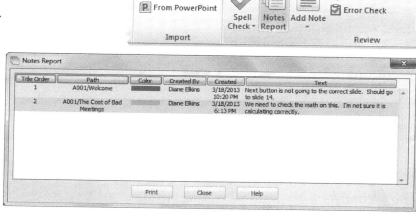

## Managing Notes

Here are a few options for managing notes.

- You can move both the notes icon and the note itself by clicking and dragging them to where you want them.
- If you need more room for your text, click and drag the bottom-right corner of the note to enlarge it.
- From the **Add Note** drop-down menu, select **Note Text Style** to change the font attributes for notes.
- Use the different colors for different uses, such as one color for instructions, one for open issues, etc.
- Right-click a note for additional options, including deleting the note.

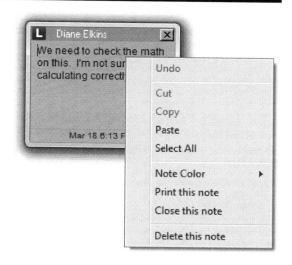

# Error Checker

The error checker looks for problems with your title such as resources that are missing, actions that are not complete, and LMS conflicts. It runs automatically when you publish your title, and you can run it at any time from the **Tools** menu.

## Run Error Check

**To run error check:**
1. Go to the **Tools** tab.
2. Click the **Error Check** button.

The error checker notes warnings in blue and errors in red.

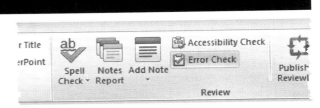

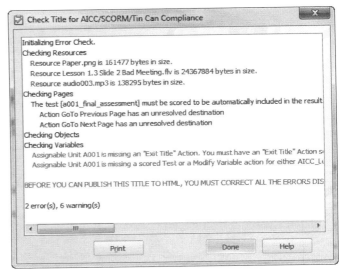

### Blue Warning Messages

These messages are about potential issues you might want to know about but won't prevent you from publishing the course. Some of the most common warning messages are:

- Resources such as images or audio that are included in the title, but not used. (See the next page for more information.)

- Media files such as audio or video that are large.

- Variables that have been created but are not being used.

- **Go To** actions with an unresolved destination. This usually means the action goes to a page that has been deleted. Either delete the action or edit it to point to the proper page.

You can address or ignore these messages.

### Red Error Messages

These messages involve a specific error that will keep your course from functioning properly. These issues should be fixed before the course is published.

Some of the most common error messages are:

- An action acts upon an object that is no longer available. An example of this is a **Show** action on an image that has been deleted or a **Play** action on an audio file that is no longer on the page. To resolve these issues, either delete the action, or edit the action and establish the target again.

- AICC/SCORM-related messages.

 Publishing for an LMS, p. 264

**TIME SAVER**

Double-click a warning or error message to go right to it in the **Title Explorer**.

# Accessibility Checker

The **Accessibility Checker** reviews your title for issues that would affect accessibility for those with disabilities who are using assistive technology. The checker looks for issues regarding Section 508 of the Rehabilitation Act and WCAG 2.0.

Accessibility guidelines focus on three main areas: people with impaired vision (who often use screen readers to determine what is on screen), people with impaired hearing, and people with impaired mobility (who may have difficulty using a mouse).

Making a course accessible involves certain design decisions and certain technical features. To make your course accessible to people with disabilities, you will need to become familiar with the requirements and determine how you best want to implement them in Lectora.

For more detailed information about Lectora and Section 508 compliance, visit the Screen Readers Forum in the Lectora Lounge, read the "Creating Web-based, accessible content" chapter in the Lectora user's guide, and search Lectora University for their self-paced course on 508 compliance.

## CAUTION

- Compliance with Section 508 and WCAG 2.0 is subject to interpretation and has legal ramifications. Use the checker as a guide to help you in your development process, but not as the final decision-maker as to whether or not your course is compliant.

- Just because your course passes the checker doesn't make it compliant. The checker can look for programmatic elements, but it can't check for design elements. For example, it doesn't know if you are using color to convey meaning or whether or not your ALT text is descriptive.

## BRIGHT IDEA

Even if you are not required by law to comply with Section 508 or WCAG 2.0, you may still want to implement the guidelines. Ask yourself (and your HR department and your legal team) the best way to make sure your training is accessible to those with disabilities.

## Run the Accessibility Checker

**To run the accessibility checker:**

1. Go to the **Tools** tab.
2. Click the **Accessibility Check** button.

Warning messages are displayed in blue and error messages in red. You can double-click an issue to be taken to the page/object with the issue. Once you've identified the issues and dealt with what you could, re-run the checker to see if they are resolved.

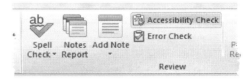

DESIGN TIPS: Lectora and Section 508

## Working With Actions

### Mouse Enter vs. On Click Actions

Someone using a screen reader can perform an on-click action (buttons, hyperlinks, actions). Because screen readers do not recognize mouse enter/mouse exit actions, do not use them in a 508-compliant course.

### Showing Objects After the Screen Loads

If you have an action that shows something on the screen after the page loads, a screen reader will not pick it up. For example, if you have an on-click event to show a hidden text box, a person with a screen reader will not get that information.

Any action that runs when the page initially loads will be caught by the screen reader.

One common workaround is to have "pop-ups" appear in their own window. Screen readers pick up information (text, video clip, image, etc.) that appears in its own window.

### Actions That Are Not Compatible

The following actions should not be used after the page loads initially:

- Change Contents
- Hide
- Move To
- Set Progress
- Show
- Size To
- Step Progress
- Toggle Visibility State

Also, it is best not to use keystroke actions since they may interfere with screen readers.

### Lightbox Style Pop-Ups

Screen readers do not recognize lightbox style pop-ups since the information does not really appear in its own window, but rather as an overlay on the existing page. Be sure to disable this option in the publishing dialog box for 508-compliant courses.

### Using Buttons, Hyperlinks, and Menus

- Screen readers can execute a hyperlink.
- Starting with Lectora X version, screen readers can execute Lectora buttons. With previous versions of Lectora, you should not use buttons on a 508-compliant course.
- Menus are not 508-compatible and should not be used.

### Layering Order

Screen readers read objects as they appear from top to bottom in the **Title Explorer**, so it is best to arrange your objects in a logical order. For example, you'd want the page heading to appear before the screen text. Items flagged as **Always on Top** will be read first by the screen reader. Inherited objects are read before page-level objects.

### Skip Navigation

Screen readers read every object on the page, including items inherited from the title, chapter, and section. That means students have to listen to all of those objects on every page. Provide a link to skip repetitive navigation, which lets them go straight to the main content.

1. Add a hyperlink or button to the very top of your title called **Skip Navigation** or **Skip to Main**. (It can be transparent since only screen readers need it.)

2. Organize your title-level objects so that **Skip to Main** is first and any objects that are not repetitive are last (such as a Page Heading text box). If you don't have such an object, create an object just for this purpose.

3. Add an action to the first object (step 1) that, on mouse click, goes to the current page, scrolled to the first of the objects that are not repetitive (step 2).

### Test and Survey Questions

Someone using assistive technology can successfully complete form elements and form-based question types. They cannot use question types that require a mouse or vision. Therefore, do not use matching, drag and drop, or hot spot questions.

## ALT Text

ALT text is a caption used on visual elements, such as photos, videos, and buttons to describe the object for people who cannot see them. Lectora uses the object name as the ALT text, which is read to the student by screen readers.

Here are some tips on ALT text:

- Name your objects in a logical, descriptive way.  Think about what information needs to be conveyed to someone who cannot see it.  Lectora allows up to 128 characters for the object name.

    Bad example: "Diagram of recruiting process"

    Good example: "Diagram showing 6 steps in the recruiting process: job description, pay analysis, job posting, screening, interviews, and offer."

- If 128 characters is not enough to adequately describe an object, you have several options.  You can add an on-screen caption that's visible to everyone.  You can include a separate text box that the students wouldn't see (behind an object, same text color as the background, etc.) but that screen readers would recognize, or you could add a **Display Message** action to the image with the information.

- For items that are purely decorative, use an empty ALT tag.  (Although some organizations have chosen not to use this option and use ALT tags for all images, in an abundance of caution.)

- If you have a non-text object (image, button, etc.) that links to something, use the ALT text to also describe what the link does.  For example: "Image of the request form. Click to go to a .pdf of that form."

- When you publish, enable the ALT tag option and disable short ID-based names.

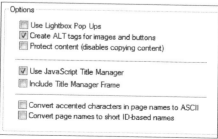

## Design Strategies

There are a number of design issues for 508-compliant courses that are not related to specific Lectora features:

- Include links to any players or plug-ins needed to view course content (such as Flash player or Adobe Reader).

- Make sure you don't use color as the only way to convey meaning.  For example, it is OK to have a green header at the top of a page with correct answer feedback and a red header at the top of incorrect feedback, as long as it also says **Correct** and **Incorrect**.

- Avoid having audio and video auto-start, as it would conflict with the audio from a screen reader.  Instead, provide separate controls for the audio and video.

## Object Types to Avoid

Other items to avoid in a 508-compliant course:

- Frames

- Document objects

- Custom style sheets added as an external HTML object

- Timed tests and any other timed interactions in which the student doesn't have the option to increase the amount of time available

- Flashing or flickering objects

## Other Accessibility Strategies

Several 508-related features are covered elsewhere in this book.

Form elements and text labels, p. 207
Closed-captioning video, p. 81
Header rows for tables, p. 47

# Media Libraries

There are three different libraries that help you manage the assets in your course, such as audio, video, and image files.

- **Title Resources**: This is a listing of all the assets that you've added to your title so far.
- **My Library**: This library is where you can store objects that you want to have available for all of your Lectora projects.
- **Stock Library**: This library contains ready-to-use elements such as images, buttons, and Flash elements.

Each of these libraries lets you browse and search for elements and then quickly add them to your title. You can access them by clicking one of the three tabs on the right side of the interface.

## Title Resources Library

From **Title Resources**, you can:

- Browse for course assets. Click the expand or collapse icons to show or hide panels for the different types of assets.
- Reuse an item in your title. Click and drag an item to the work area.
- Manage the item. Right-click the item for these options:

    **Edit**: If you have an editor assigned for that type of option, you can open it in the editor to make changes. For example, you can crop an image in SnagIt or edit an audio file in the audio editor.

    **Show in Resource Manager**: The Resource Manager gives you more options for managing resources.

     Resource Manager, p. 222

    **Show in Title**: If you select this option, you are taken to the page where that object lives.

    **Show in Windows Explorer**: This option opens up the folder where the resources file is stored, usually the **Media** or **Images** folder stored with the Lectora title.

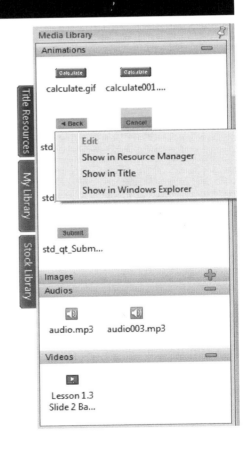

# My Library

The objects on the **My Library** are available in any title. With **My Library**, you can:

- Add an object from a file to the library. Click the **Add File** button at the top of the library panel to find and select a file to add.

- Add an object from your current title to the library. Right-click a media object, and select **Copy to My Library**.

- Organize your assets. Click the **Category** button to make a new folder to put assets in.

- Add assets to your current title.  Click and drag an item to the work area.

- Search for assets. Use the search field at the top of the panel.

- Share assets with the online community. Click the **Share** button.

- Open the folder with the underlying image.  Right-click the object in the library, and select **Show in Windows Explorer**.

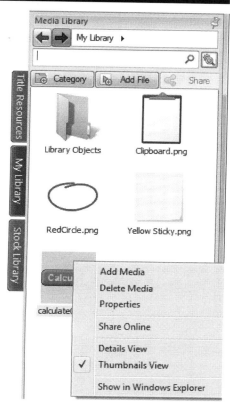

## BRIGHT IDEA

You can change where the library is stored in the Preferences dialog box.  For example, you might want a whole team to work from a common library on a shared drive.

  Preferences, p. 244

## POWER TIP

If you right-click an object in **My Library** and select **Properties**, you can add keywords to make the object easy to search for.  You can also add metadata and Flash parameters.  That way, you only have to do it once and those properties will stay with the object whenever you add it to a title.

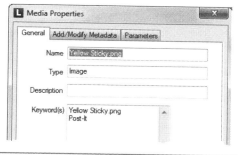

# Stock Library

The **Stock Library** contains a number of different types of assets that you can add to your title. You have already learned about most of these, which can also be added from the Insert menu. Going directly to the objects from the Stock Library tab might be more convenient for you.

You can use the search field at the top or browse through the folder structure to find what you want. To add an item to your title, simply click and drag it to the work area.

The Stock Library contains the following types of assets:

- **Buttons:** Here you can find the same stock button choices you get when you go to **Insert** > **Button** > **Stock Button**.
- **Character Poses**: These are the same options you get when you go to **Insert** > **Character**.
- **ClipArt**: These are the options you get when you go to **Insert** > **Image** > **ClipArt**.
- **Flash Activities**: These are the same choices as when you go to **Insert** > **Flash** > **Flash** Activity
- **Media Online**: This folder contains an expanded collection of assets, many provided by other Lectora users.
- **Music**: This folder contains music tracks, such as something you might want to use on a title slide.

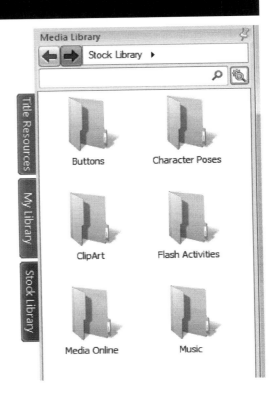

## DESIGN TIP

If you use the **Character Poses** folder, characters are organized based on pose. But if you go to the **Media Online** folder and then **Live Model Gallery**, you can browse by type (medical, industrial, etc.), gender, and character.

# Library Objects

Library objects make it easy to share and reuse elements from your courses.  For example, if you create a rollover interaction, you can save the entire interaction as a library object.  Then when you want to use something similar later, you can bring it into that course or any other course.  A library object might be:

- An individual object (such as a text box with instructions you use over and over).
- A group of objects and actions (such as the text and image that you use on each objectives page).
- An entire page (such as the instructions page at the beginning of a test or a standard page layout).
- A series of pages (such as a multi-page game or branching simulation).
- A chapter (such as a pop-up chapter for test feedback or a glossary).

## Create a Library Object

**To create a library object:**

1. Select the item(s) you want to save as a single library object.
2. Right-click any of the selected objects.
3. Select **Save as Library Object**.

## POWER TIPS

- Go to the **Preferences** dialog box to change where your library objects are stored on your computer.
- Library objects are saved as a single file with an extension of **.awo**.  If you go to the folder where they are stored on your computer, you can easily e-mail them to someone else to save and use.

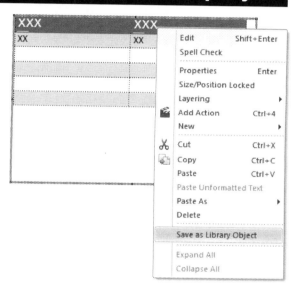

## Insert a Library Object

**To insert a library object into your title:**

1. Click the **My Library** tab.
2. Double-click the **Library Object** folder.
3. Click and drag the object to the work area.

## DESIGN TIP

You can share library objects with other Lectora users.  To share your object, select it in **My Library** and then click the **Share** button at the top of the panel.  To use objects that other people have shared, go to **Stock Library**, then **Media Online**, and then **Library Objects**.

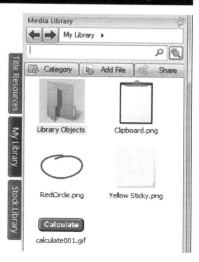

# Resource Manager

The **Resource Manager** helps you organize and manage all the media elements and documents used in your title. Go to the **Resource Manager** when you want to see where certain resources are used, clean out and delete resources that are no longer being used, search for a certain resource, or make a copy of a resource in case you want to modify a second version without changing the original.

## View Resource Usage

**To view resource usage:**

1. Go to the **Tools** tab.
2. Click the **Resources** button.
3. Perform the tasks you want to.
4. Click the **Close** button.

Once in the **Resource Manager**, you have several options for viewing the usage.

- Click the plus or minus sign next to the different categories to expand or collapse that category.
- Determine whether a resource is used or not by the "Used by" text next to the resource name.
- Select a resource to see a preview of it, as well as the location in the title where it is being used (if applicable) in the **Resource Used** pane.
- Click the **Search** tab to search for a specific resource.
- Click the **Unused** tab to see only the resources that are not being used.

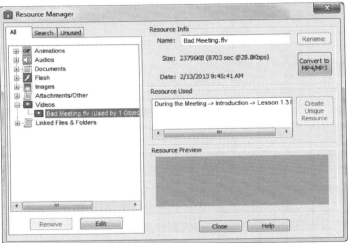

## Delete Unneeded Resources

If you add a media element and then delete it from the page, the file still lives in the **Images** or **Media** folder. When you publish the course, you have the option of deleting unused resources, but that is an all-or-nothing solution. If you'd like to go in and look at each resource and decide individually if you want to keep it or not, then the **Resource Manager** is the best approach.

**To delete unneeded resources:**

1. Go to the **Tools** tab.
2. Click the **Resources** button.
3. Click the **Unused** tab.
4. Find and select the resource you want to delete.
5. Click the **Remove** button.
6. Click the **Close** button.

You can also click the **Remove All** button to delete all the resources on the **Unused** tab.

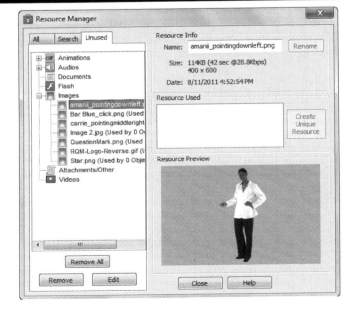

# Create a Unique Resource

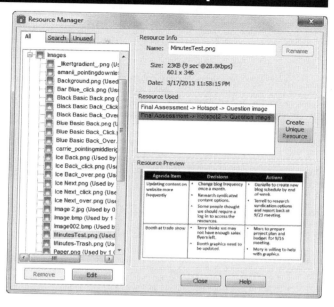

You can use a single resource, such as an image, shape, button, etc., many times in a course. Each instance of that object can have its own size, position, and actions. Each instance draws from the same file in the **Images** or **Media** folder. So if you want to edit that underlying file, it affects all instances of that object.

For example, if you have a graphic that is used twice in the course and you want to crop it on one page, you can't do that if both pages are calling the same exact image file.

Fortunately, the **Resource Manager** lets you make a copy of that object, so you can edit it independently and not affect the other places that object appears.

**To create a unique copy of a resource:**

1. Go to the **Tools** tab.
2. Click the **Resources** button.
3. Select the object you want to work with.
4. In the **Resource Used** pane, select the instance of that object you want to separate from the rest.
5. Click the **Create Unique Resource** button.
6. Click the Close button.

A new object is added with **_1** at the end of it, which can be edited independently from the original. For example, you can now go into the **_1** version of the image and crop it, leaving the other instance full size.

The **Create Unique Resource** button is only available with resources that are used more than once in a title.

## BRIGHT IDEAS

- If you select the item in the **Resource Used** pane, you will be taken to the page with that resource.

- With certain audio and video files, you can convert them to MP4/MP3 format. Select the audio or video file, and then click the **Convert to MP4/MP3** button in the top-right corner. (See previous page.)

# Translation

Lectora's Translation Tool makes the translation process a little bit easier. It exports all the text in any text box (even if you have it set to render as an image), text button, or **Display Message** action into a rich text file (.rtf). That text can then be translated and then imported back into the title.

When you publish your course, you can publish multiple languages at once.

 Publishing Languages, p. 262

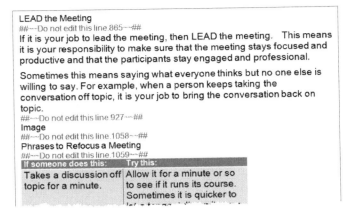

---

## Import and Export Text for Translation

**To export text for translation:**

1. Go to the **Tools** tab.
2. Click the **Translations** button.
3. Select **Export text to a translation file**.
4. Check the boxes for the items you want to include.
5. Select the option for the amount of the text you want to export.
6. Click the **Browse** button to select a location for the file.
7. Click the **OK** button.

**To import the translated text:**

1. Go to the **Tools** tab.
2. Click the **Translations** button.
3. Select **Import text from a translation file**.
4. Check the box if you want to increase text box sizes, if necessary.
5. Select the option for the amount of the text you want to import.
6. Click the **Browse** button to find and select the translated file.
7. Click the **OK** button.

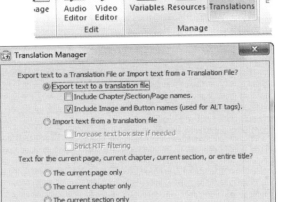

 **BRIGHT IDEA**

Since the translation tool creates a document with all your text, it can be used for other purposes as well, such as editing and reviews or for pasting into other documents, such as reference guides.

 **CAUTION**

- You'll want to check your page layouts carefully after re-importing the text. You may need to manually resize text boxes (unless you checked the automatic option for that), and you'll need to make sure text boxes don't overlap with other objects, get cut off, etc.

- The text file contains text in red that should not be changed or moved, as it is used to import the content back into your title.

  ##~~ Do not edit this line. 865~~##

# Importing and Exporting

There are a number of different reasons to import or export all or part of your title.

- You want to export to a ZIP file to back it up or archive it.
- You have elements in a different title that you want to use in the title you are currently working on.
- You have content created in another system that you were able to save in XML format and now want to bring into Lectora.
- You would like to create a new title from PowerPoint slides.
- You want to export all of your text to Microsoft Word.
- You want to move content back and forth between Lectora Inspire/Publisher and Lectora Online.

When you use the import and export options in Lectora, you are not publishing the course. You are importing and exporting the Lectora files only.

## Import and Export a ZIP File

The export to ZIP option exports the entire title. Importing a ZIP creates a new title.

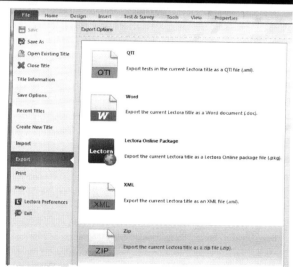

**To export to a ZIP file:**

1. Go to the **File** menu.
2. Select **Export**.
3. Select **Zip**.
4. Find and select the folder where you want to save the file.
5. Enter a name for the file.
6. Click the **Save** button.

**To import a ZIP file:**

1. Close any open Lectora files you have open.
2. Go to the **File** menu.
3. Select **Import**.
4. Select **Zip**.
5. Click the first **Browse** button to find and select the ZIP file you want to import.
6. Click the second **Browse** button to find and select the location where you want to save the imported file.
7. Click the **OK** button.

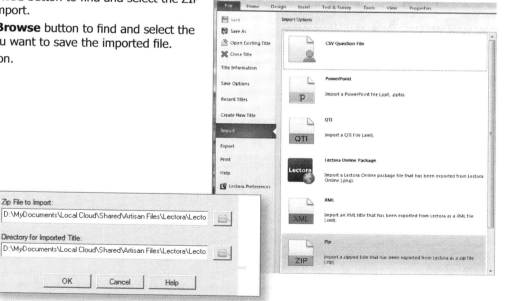

# Import and Export an XML File

The export to XML option exports the entire title. Importing an XML file creates a new title.

### To export to an XML file:
1. Go to the **File** menu.
2. Select **Export**.
3. Select **XML**.
4. Find and select the folder where you want to save the file.
5. Enter a name for the file.
6. Click the **Save** button.

### To import an XML file:
1. Close any Lectora files you have open.
2. Go to the **File** menu.
3. Select **Import**.
4. Select **XML**.
5. Find and select the **XML** file you want to import.
6. Click the **Open** button.
7. Click the **OK** button.

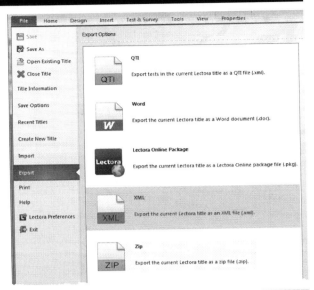

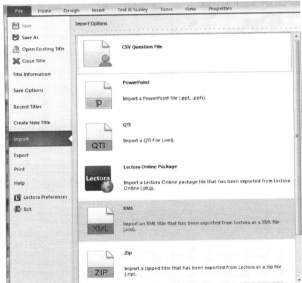

## POWER TIP

Titles saved in a newer version of Lectora cannot always be opened in older versions of Lectora. However, if you export the title to XML from the newer version, you can import the XML file in the older version.

You'll want to check the new title carefully, as the features in the newer software may not work properly in the older software.

# Import Content From Another File

If you have content in a Lectora title that you'd like to reuse in a different course, you can import all or part of it: an object, a page, a chapter, etc.

**To import content from another title:**

1. Select the chapter or page you want to import to.
2. Go to the **Tools** tab.
3. In the **Import** section, click **From Other Title**.
4. Find and select the Lectora file (.awt) you want to import.
5. Click the **Open** button.
6. Using the expanding menu, find and select the objects, pages, chapters, etc. you want to import.
7. Click the **Import** button.

If you import just individual objects, they appear on the page you are on when you import. If you select whole pages or chapters, they appear just after the page you are on at the time of the import.

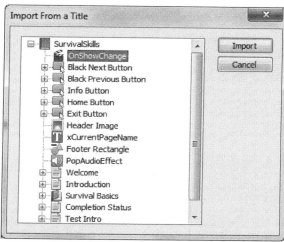

 **TIME SAVER**

If you are likely to use the same chunk of content over and over, consider saving it as a library object.

 Library Objects, p. 221

# Import PowerPoint Slides

You can create a new title by importing PowerPoint slides or import individual slides into an existing title.

**To create a new file from PowerPoint slides:**

1. Go to the **File** menu.
2. Select **PowerPoint**.
3. Find and select the PowerPoint file you want to use.
4. Click the **OK** button.

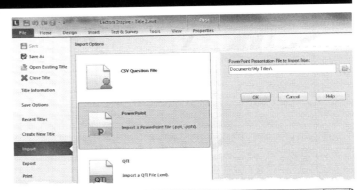

5. Enter a name for the new title.
6. Enter a location for saving the new title.
7. Click the **Next** button.

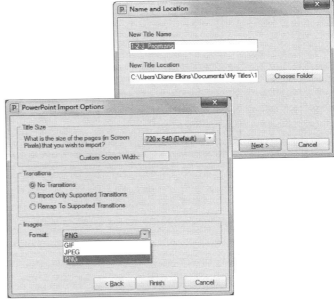

8. Enter the size, in pixels, that you want for the new title.  (Select from the drop-down list or enter your own width value.)
9. Indicate how you want to import the slide transitions.
10. Select the format you want to use for imported images.
11. Click the **Finish** button.

**To import individual slides into an existing title:**

1. Go to the **Tools** menu.
2. Click the **From PowerPoint** button.
3. Find and select the PowerPoint file you want.
4. Click the **Open** button.
5. Select the slides you want to import.
6. Click the **Next** button.
7. Select the import options you want.  (See steps 8–10 in the previous procedure.)
8. Click the **Finish** button.

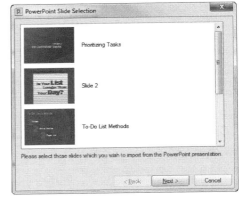

## Export to Microsoft Word

You can export the text in your title into a Microsoft Word document. This can be useful for reviews and proofreading. Each page in Lectora is exported as its own page in Word.

**To export text content to Word:**
1. Go to the **File** tab.
2. Select **Export**.
3. Select **Word**.
4. Find and select the location where you want to save the exported content.
5. Click the **OK** button.

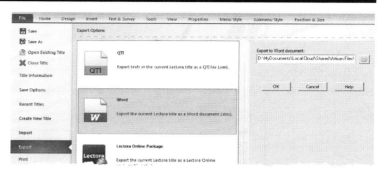

 **BRIGHT IDEA**

If you want to be able to re-import your content back into Lectora, then it would be better to use the translation feature.

 Translation, p. 224

## Import and Export to Lectora Online

Lectora Online is a cloud-based version of Lectora. You can move content back and forth between Lectora Inspire/Publisher and Lectora Online.

**To import content from Lectora Online:**
1. Close any open files.
2. Go to the **File** tab.
3. Select **Import**.
4. Select **Lectora Online Package**.
5. Find and select the package file you want to import.
6. Find and select the location where you want to save the imported content.
7. Click the **OK** button.

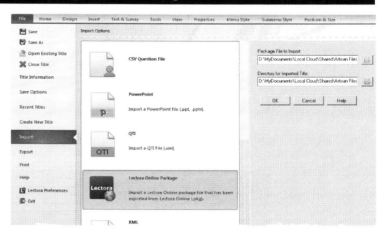

**To export content to Lectora Online:**
1. Go to the **File** tab.
2. Select **Export**.
3. Select **Lectora Online Package**.
4. Find and select where you want to save the file.
5. Click the **OK** button.

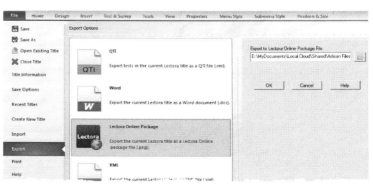

# Printing

You might want to print pages from your title to help with internal reviews, proofreading, or other reasons. Lectora gives several options for this.

## Print Pages From Your Title

**To print pages from your title:**

1. Go to the **File** menu.
2. Select **Print**.
3. In the **Layout** section, select the layout option you want.
4. At the bottom of the dialog box, check the boxes for any extra options you want to include.
5. Select other print settings based on your printer (properties, page range, number of copies, etc.).
6. Click **OK**.

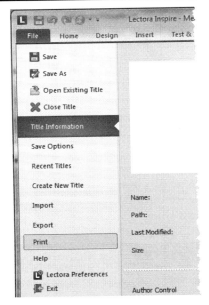

### Layout Formats

The first four layout options print a visual snapshot of each page, with 1, 2, 4, or 6 pages per sheet.

The **Storyboard** option places thumbnails of three pages on the left with blank lines next to each one, useful for taking notes during review meetings.

The **Outline** option includes all the text on each page. This is the best option if your goal is text proofreading or if you have a lot of pages with overlapping text that can't be read in a thumbnail.

### Layout Options

**Include Page Footer(s)**: If you leave this box checked, each page gets a footer with the title name and the page number.

**Include Notes**: Available with the Storyboard and Outline layouts, this option includes development notes in the printout.

**Include All Objects In Outline**: Available with the Outline layout, if you check this box, every object appears in addition to the full text.

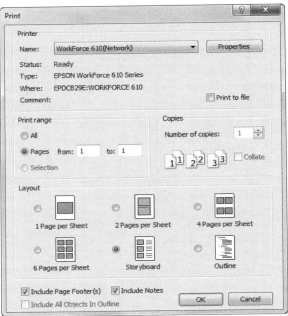

## Print Pages From Your Title (cont'd)

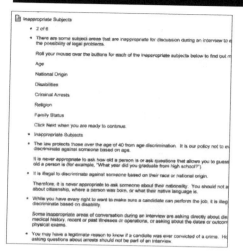

*Outline view*

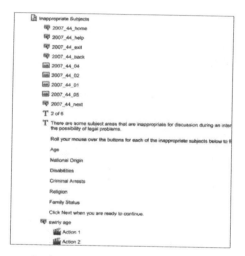

*Outline view with all objects included*

### ⏱ TIME SAVER

It can be difficult to figure out which page numbers you need to print if you are only trying to print a certain page or a certain section. Instead, right-click the level you want in the **Title Explorer** (chapter, section, page) and select **Print**. The **Print** dialog box opens with those pages already filled in for you.

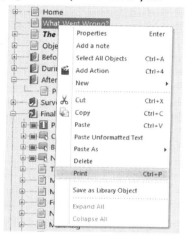

### ❗ CAUTION

If you have any overlapping objects on a page (as with a rollover or pop-up interaction), they will overlap on the printout as well.

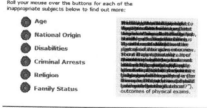

# ReviewLink

ReviewLink, which was new in version X.6, is a free online system where reviewers can view a course and make comments directly on the screen. Then the developers can view and manage the comments in a back-end database.

 Publishing, ch. 17

## Post a Course on ReviewLink

**To post a course on ReviewLink:**

1. Go to the **Tools** tab.
2. Click the **Publish to ReviewLink** button.

3. Manage any errors that may come up in the **Error Checker**.
4. Click the **Publish** button.

5. Sign in to or sign up for your ReviewLink account.
6. Click the **OK** button.

   *(continued)*

# Post a Course on ReviewLink (cont'd)

7. In the text field, enter the email addresses of the people you want to send a link to (separated by commas).
8. If you want to include a due date in the message, check the box and enter the date you want.
9. Configure any publish settings on the other two tabs.
10. Click the **OK** button.

 **BRIGHT IDEA**

If this isn't the first time you are publishing to ReviewLink, there are additional options for updating the content.

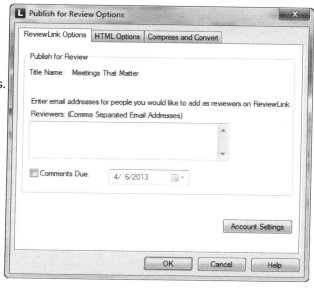

12. Click the **Upload Title** button.

13. Click the **OK** button in the confirmation dialog box.
14. Click the **Done** button in the publish dialog box.

An email with a link and a password will be sent to everyone whose email address you entered into the dialog box.

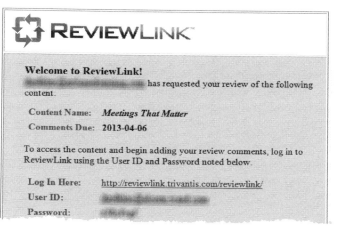

# View a Course in ReviewLink

**To open a course for review from an email:**

1. Click the link in the email.
2. Enter your email address.
3. Enter the password provided in the email.
4. Click the **Login** button.
5. Click the **Launch Content** button for the course you want to review.

**To open a course for review from Lectora:**

6. Go to the **Tools** tab.
7. Click the **Launch ReviewLink** button.
8. Click the **Launch Content** button for the course you want to review.

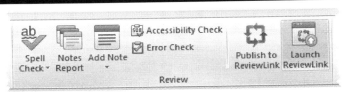

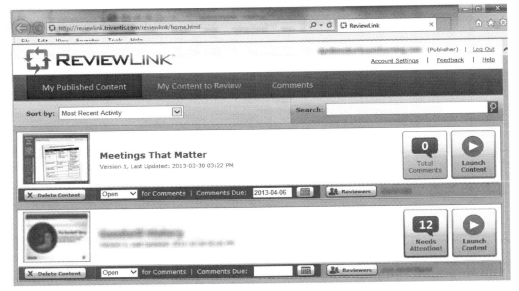

# Enter Comments Into ReviewLink

When reviewing the course in ReviewLink, you navigate through the course as you normally would. A bar at the bottom of the course provides the tools for making reviews.

**To make a comment on a page:**

1. Click the **New Comment** button.
2. In the **Comment Summary** field, enter a title for the comment.
3. In the **Comment Details** field, enter the comment.
4. If needed, click the **Add Attachment** button to add a file.
5. Click the **Submit Comment** button.

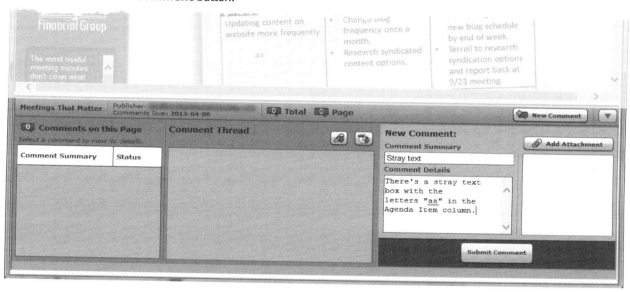

# Respond to Comments in ReviewLink

Reviewers can view other comments, respond to comments, approve comments, and download attachments and comment summaries.

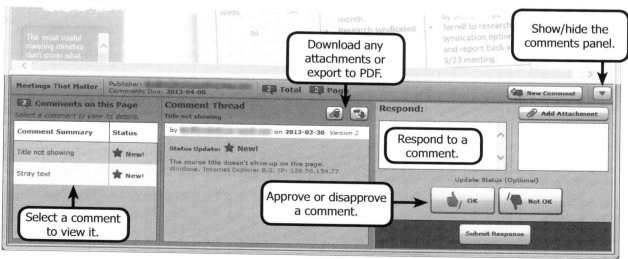

# Manage Comments in ReviewLink

As the publisher of the content, you have more options for managing individual comments via the **Comments** tab.

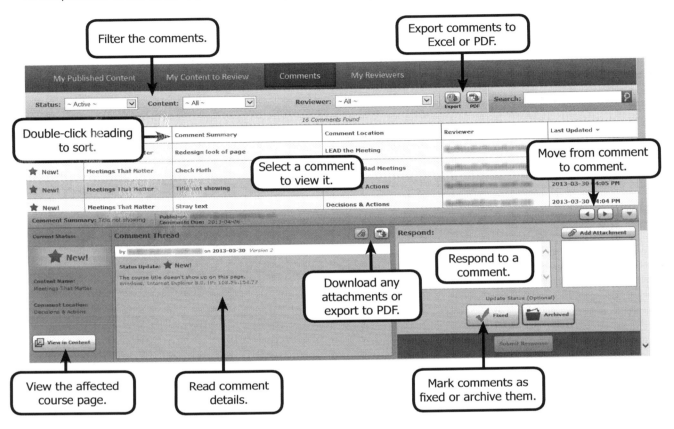

Filter the comments.

Export comments to Excel or PDF.

Double-click heading to sort.

Select a comment to view it.

Move from comment to comment.

Download any attachments or export to PDF.

Respond to a comment.

View the affected course page.

Read comment details.

Mark comments as fixed or archive them.

# Manage Settings in ReviewLink

As the publisher of the course, you have additional tools for managing the comments.

On the **My Published Content** tab:

- To delete a course from ReviewLink, click the **Delete Content** button for that course.

- To close the course for comments, click the drop-down menu and select **Closed**.

- To change the due date for comments, enter a new date in the date field.

- To change permissions for who can view the course, click the **Reviewers** button. From here you can:

    - Change whether one reviewer can see other reviewer's comments.

    - Notify reviewers when content is updated.

    - Send messages to the reviewers.

    - Invite other reviewers.

On the **My Reviewers** tab:

- Use the buttons at the top to import and export lists of reviewers, organize reviewers in groups, and add, remove, or edit reviewers.

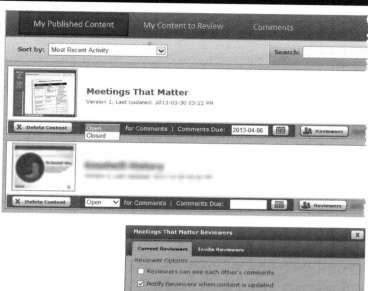

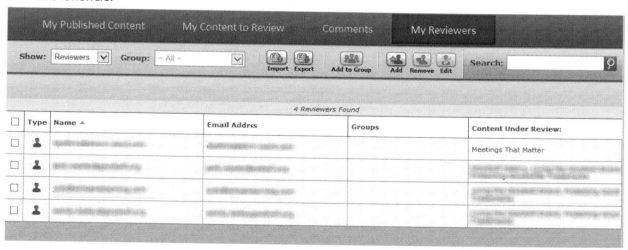

# Title Templates

When you save a title as a template, the title properties and title-level objects are included. When you use that template, a one-page course is created.

Templates (**.awp** files) are saved, by default, in the Lectora program files (**C:/Program Files/Trivantis/Lectora/Templates**).

## Save a Title as a Template

**To save a title as a template:**

1. Go to the **File** tab.
2. Select **Save Options**.
3. Click **Save Title as Template**.
4. Enter a name and description.
5. Click the **OK** button.

 Create a new title from a template, p. 13

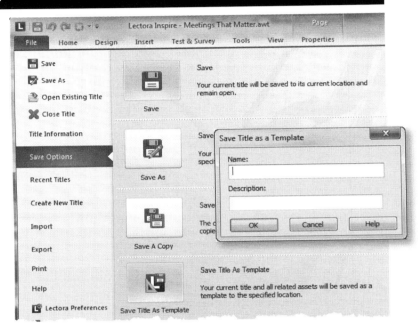

 **TIME SAVER**

You can import and export templates to share them with other developers. From the **Create New Title** tab on the **File** menu, use the **Import**, **Export**, and **Share Online** buttons to share templates.

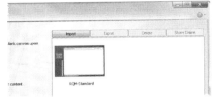

 **DESIGN TIP**

Templates only save title-level objects and properties. To reuse more of a title than that, such as course structure and commonly-used pages, save them as library objects instead.

 Library Objects, p. 221

# Author Control

You can use author control to prevent other authors from changing certain content in your title. First you need to enable author control for the title and set up a password. While this enables author control, it does not actually lock anything. You then need to designate which objects you want to lock. You can lock individual objects such as an image or a text box, or full pages and chapters, such as a test. Author control uses inheritance—so if a chapter is protected, then all content in that chapter is protected as well.

## Enable Author Control for the Title

**To enable author control and set up a password:**

1. Go to the **File** menu.
2. Select **Title Information**.
3. Check the **Enable Author Control** box.
4. Enter your password in the two fields that pop up.
5. Click the **OK** button.

## BRIGHT IDEAS

- Come back to **Title Information** and click the **Change Password** button if you want to change the password.
- If you forget the password, you will need to import your content into another title to be able to edit your content.

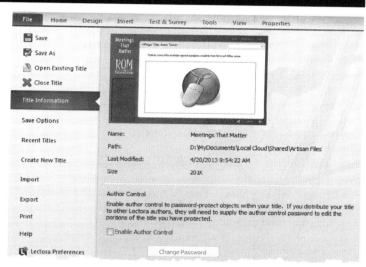

## Turn on Author Control for an Object

**To turn on author control for an object:**

1. Go to the **Properties** tab for that object.
2. Click the author control icon.
3. Click the icon again to unlock the object.

The author control icon is only available if author control is enabled for the title.

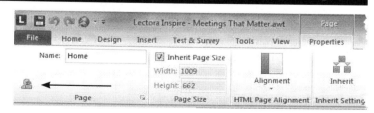

 Locked

 Unlocked

# Notes

# Preferences & Customization

## Introduction

In this chapter, you will learn how to customize Lectora in two ways. First, you'll learn about all the options in the **Preferences** dialog box. Then, you'll learn how to customize the workspace based on how you like to work.

## In This Chapter

- Preferences
- Customizing the Workspace

# Notes

# Lectora Preferences

The **Preferences** dialog box lets you change various settings that help you work more efficiently, turn off features that don't apply to your situation, and customize many of the features.  Lectora preferences affect your license of Lectora rather than a given title.  Therefore, they apply to every title you work in, but do not carry over to someone else's license of Lectora if they open a title you created.

**To change Lectora preferences:**

1. Go to the **File** tab.
2. Select **Lectora Preferences**.
3. Click the category for the type of preference you want.
4. Make your changes.
5. Click the **OK** button.

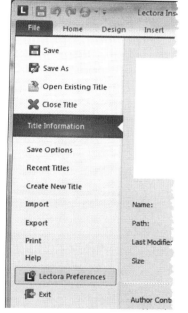

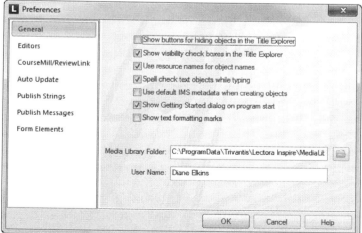

# Preferences: General

### Show Buttons for Hiding Objects in the Title Explorer

If you check this box, an expand/collapse icon appears next to title, chapter, and section level objects. **(A)** Click the icon to hide those objects in the **Title Explorer (B)**, making it a little less cluttered.

### Show Visibility Check Boxes in the Title Explorer

By default, there is a small box **(C)** next to each object in the **Title Explorer** that you can click to show/hide that object in **Edit** mode. Uncheck the box here in **Preferences** if you don't want to see these visibility icons.

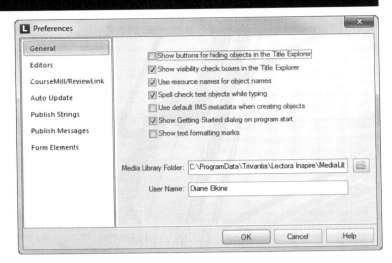

### Use Resource Names for Object Names

When you add an image or media file, the object name in the **Title Explorer** automatically assumes the name of the underlying file. If you don't want that to happen, then uncheck this box, and the object will be automatically named Image 1, Audio 1, etc. (You can always change the name yourself in the **Title Explorer**.)

### Spell Check Text Objects While Typing

Lectora checks for spelling errors as you type, putting a red wavy line under each suspected misspelling. (The lines only show when you are in the edit mode for the text box.) You can turn that feature off by unchecking this box.

### Use Default IMS Metadata When Creating Objects

If you check this box, Lectora automatically adds IMS metadata to your objects, so you don't have to add it manually for each one.

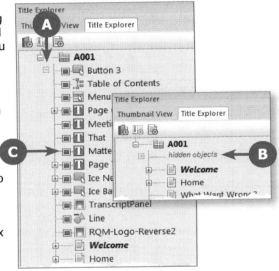

### Show Getting Started Dialog on Program Start

By default, when you start Lectora, a **Getting Started** dialog box **(E)** appears with options for creating or opening titles. Uncheck this box if you don't want to see that dialog box on start-up.

### Show Text Formatting Marks

To see formatting commands in your text, such as spaces, tabs, and hard returns **(D)**, check this box. (You can also show/hide formatting marks by clicking the ¶ button on the **Home** tab.)

### Media Library Folder

When you add an object to **My Library** or add a **Library Object**, it goes to whatever folder is indicated here. By default, this is the Library folder with the Lectora program files on your hard drive. You can change the location here, for example, to a folder on a shared network drive.

### User Name

Whenever you create a note, it is labeled with the user name entered here. The name shows up on the note itself and in the notes report. By default, Lectora uses your system name on your computer, but you can change it to something else here.

## Preferences: Editors

When you add images, audio, video, and other objects to your course, you can set up your preferences to make it easier to edit those objects. Each of those objects has an **Edit** button in its properties. On the **Editors** tab in **Preferences**, you can designate what software is used when you click that **Edit** button.

If you use Lectora Inspire, the links are already set up for Inspire's editing tools. If you do not have Inspire or if you have other software you want to use, such as Photoshop for images or Audacity for audio, then select those programs on this tab.

Click the **Browse** button to find and select the **.exe** for the program you want to use instead (usually found in your **Programs** folder on your hard drive).

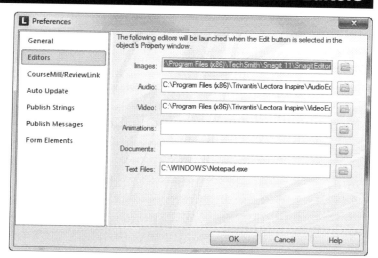

## Preferences: CourseMill/ReviewLink

### CourseMill

If you are using CourseMill, the learning Management system made by Trivantis, you can use this tab to make it easier to upload your files to CourseMill.

In the first field, enter the web address for the CourseMill server. In the second field, enter the location on the server where the course goes. If you are using the default settings for CourseMill, you don't need to change anything here.

 Publish to CourseMill, p. 263

### ReviewLink

If you are using ReviewLink to manage reviews and edits to your title, you can save your log-in information here.

 ReviewLink, p. 232

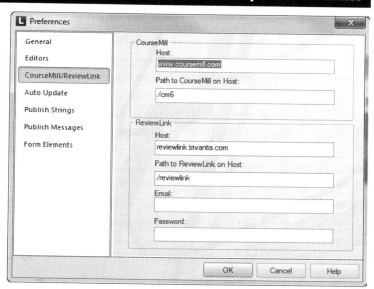

## Preferences: Auto Update

By default, Lectora checks for software updates every seven days. In addition, you have the following options in **Preferences**:

- Uncheck the box, in which case the system will not check for updates.

- Change how often the system checks for updates.

- Come to this tab at any time and click the **Check for Updates Now** to check for updates right then.

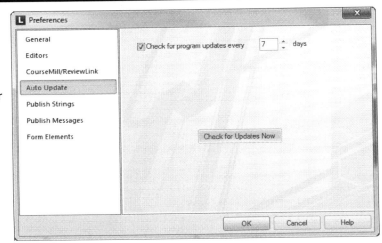

## Preferences: Publish Strings

Lectora automatically generates a number of messages for students when they take your course. If you'd like to change how those messages are worded or translate them into another language, you can do that on this tab by changing the text in the **Value** column. You can change the default settings, or add, import, and export additional sets. That way you can have different sets of messages for different courses or different languages.

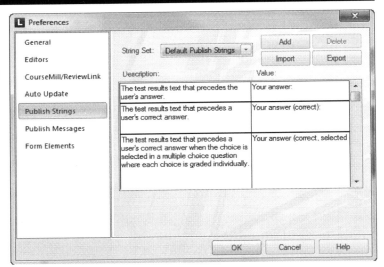

# Preferences: Publish Messages

When you publish or run **Error check**, Lectora checks for a number of different errors. On this tab, you can change some of the options.

### Show Only Errors and Warnings

If you check this box, you only see errors (in red) and warnings (in blue), but not the black informational messages. Leave it unchecked if you want to see all three.

### Show HTML Warnings

If you are publishing to one of the HTML options (including the various LMS options), you'll want to make sure this box is checked so Lectora checks for HTML-specific warnings. If you are publishing to CD or EXE, then you can uncheck this box so you aren't bothered by messages that don't apply.

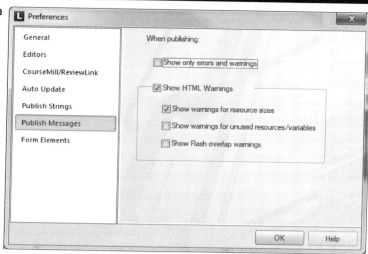

You can use the bottom three check boxes to turn off any of the specific HTML message types that do not apply to you. For example, if are delivering your course on a CD-ROM instead of over a network, you might want to turn off the warnings about resource size.

 Error Check, p. 214

# Preferences: Form Elements

When you add a question, survey question, or form element that involves radio buttons or check boxes, Lectora uses the images indicated on this tab. You can pick from four different options on the drop-down menus or select **Custom Image** to bring in your own image.

Whatever you select here affects all radio buttons and/or check boxes in any new title you create. It does not affect any existing titles unless you check the **Apply to Current Title** button. (You can also make changes to the current title's form elements from the **Test & Survey** tab.)

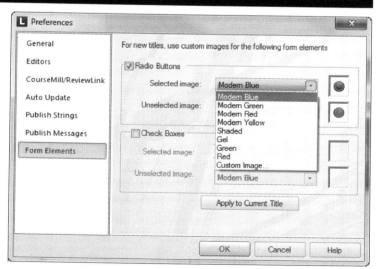

# Customizing the Workspace

To help you be more productive, there are several customizations you can make to the workspace, including customizing toolbars, adding keyboard shortcuts, and rearranging the layout of the interface.

## Customize the Quick Access Toolbar

The **Quick Access** toolbar is the small toolbar at the top-left corner of the interface.  You can add, rearrange, and remove tools from this toolbar so that the features you use most are right at your fingertips.

*Default Quick Access toolbar*

**To add a feature to the Quick Access toolbar:**

1. Right-click the item on one of the tabs.
2. Select **Add to Quick Access Toolbar**. **(A)**

**To move the toolbar below the ribbon:**

1. Click the drop-down arrow on the right side of the toolbar. **(B)**
2. Select **Show Below the Ribbon**.

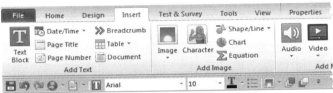

*Customized toolbar shown below the ribbon*

**To manage the Quick Access toolbar:**

1. Click the drop-down arrow on the right side of the toolbar.
2. Select **More Commands**.
3. Make the changes you want in the dialog box. **(C)**
4. Click the **OK** button.

In this dialog box you can:

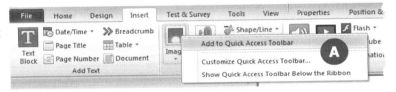

- Add tools by selecting them in the panel on the left and then clicking the double-right arrow button.  Use the drop-down menu at the top to browse through tools on each of the tabs.

- Delete tools from the toolbar by selecting them in the panel on the right and clicking the double-left arrow button.

- Rearrange tools by selecting them in the panel on the right and then clicking the up and down arrow buttons.

- Add separators to organize the toolbar by selecting **<Separator>** at the top of the panel on the left and clicking the double-right arrow button.

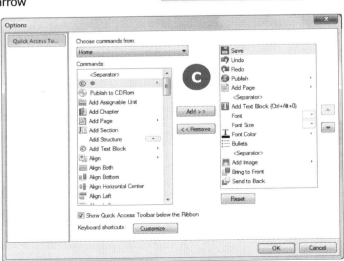

# Add Keyboard Shortcuts

Lectora comes with a large number of keyboard shortcuts already.  But if you want to create your own, you can.

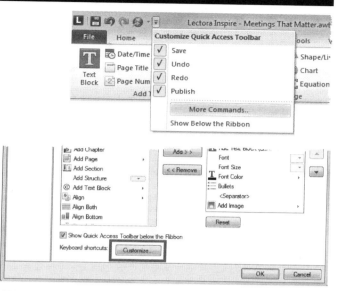

**To add a keyboard shortcut:**

1. Click the drop-down arrow on the right side of the **Quick Access** toolbar.

2. Select **More Commands**.

3. Click the **Customize** button at the bottom of the dialog box.

4. In the **Categories** panel, select a category for the command you want.

5. In the **Commands** panel, select the specific command you want.

6. Click in the **Press new shortcut key** field and type the keyboard shortcut you want to use for that command.

7. Click the **Assign** button.

8. Repeat steps 4–7 for additional shortcuts.

9. Click the **Close** button.

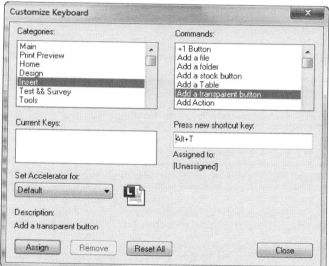

 **BRIGHT IDEA**

There may already be a shortcut for the command you want.  When you select a command, look in the **Current Keys** field. That will show you the current shortcut, if there is one.

 **CAUTION**

Be careful about overriding an existing shortcut. When you type your new shortcut, look just below that field where it says **Assigned to**.  If it shows a command, it means that your new keyboard shortcut is already assigned to a different command.  You can still assign it to the new command, but it's good to know first that's what you are doing.

# Keyboard Shortcuts

Here are some of the most commonly-used keyboard shortcuts.

| Home tab | |
|---|---|
| Add chapter | Ctrl + 1 |
| Add section | Ctrl + 2 |
| Add page | Ctrl + 3 |
| Add text block | Ctrl + Alt + 0 |
| Bold | Ctrl + B |
| Italic | Ctrl + I |
| Underline | Ctrl + U |
| Bullets | Alt + B |
| Cut | Ctrl + X |
| Copy | Ctrl + C |
| Paste | Ctrl + V |
| Paste unformatted | Ctrl + Shift + V |
| Find | Ctrl + F |
| Find next | F3 |
| Publish to HTML | F8 |
| Publish to ReviewLink | Ctrl + F10 |
| Publish to SCORM | Ctrl + F8 |
| Undo | Ctrl + Z |
| Redo | Ctrl + Y |
| Save | Ctrl + S |

| Insert tab | |
|---|---|
| Action | Ctrl + 4 |
| Audio | Alt + 0 |
| Character | Ctrl + Shift + 6 |
| Custom button | Ctrl + Shift + 1 |
| Image | Ctrl + Shift + 5 |
| Video | Ctrl + Alt + 1 |

| Test & Survey tab | |
|---|---|
| Add Question | Ctrl + 8 |
| Add Survey | Alt + 6 |
| Add Test | Ctrl + 6 |
| Add Test Section | Ctrl + 7 |

| Tools tab | |
|---|---|
| Spell check title | Ctrl + F7 |

| View tab | |
|---|---|
| Edit mode | F12 |
| Preview in browser | F9 |
| Preview mode | F11 |
| Refresh | F5 |
| Run mode | F10 |
| Toggle grid | Ctrl + G |
| Toggle guides | Ctrl + E |
| Zoom in | Ctrl + space |
| Zoom out | Alt + space |

| Other | |
|---|---|
| Select all objects | Ctrl + A |
| Next page | Page Down |
| Previous page | Page Up |

# Customize the Interface

You have a few options for customizing the workspace, primarily around the **Title Explorer**. You can:

- Make the **Title Explorer** wider or more narrow by clicking and dragging the right edge of the panel. **(A)**

- Move it to another side of the interface by dragging the **Title Explorer** header bar to one of the other docking spots. **(B)** The docking spots appear as soon as you start dragging. Rather than move the whole **Title Explorer**, you can also drag the tab for just the **Title Explorer** or just the **Thumbnail View**.

- Float the panel by clicking and dragging the header (or one of the tabs) and releasing it outside of the docking spots.

- Turn on auto-hide by clicking the pushpin icon. **(C)** When you do this, the panel disappears and two tabs appear on the side of the interface. **(D)** When you hover your mouse over one of those tabs, the panel reappears. Click the pushpin icon again to turn off the auto-hide feature.

- Keep the **Media Library** at all times by clicking the pushpin icon in the top-right corner of the panel. (Click the icon again to go back to the default auto-hide mode.)

- Change the look of the interface from **Standard** to **Windows 8**, using the drop-down menu on the **View** tab. **(E)**

- Reset the interface by clicking the **Reset Layout** button on the **View** tab. **(F)**

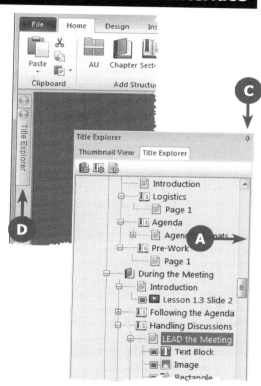

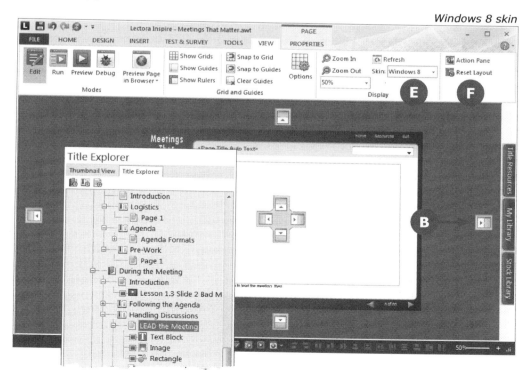

*Windows 8 skin*

# Notes

# Publishing Your Title

## Introduction

As you create and edit your Lectora course, you work in the .awt Lectora title file. But when you are ready to review or share your course, it needs to be published to the appropriate format, based on how you plan to distribute the course.

When you publish your course, a new set of files is created that in some cases looks very similar to your Lectora files. For example, when publishing to any of the Web-based formats (HTML, CourseMill, AICC, or SCORM), you get another copy of your Images folder with all your graphics and another copy of your Media folder, with all of your audio and video. These published files are the ones that you would burn to CD, post to the Web, copy to a shared network drive, or load to an LMS.

Whenever you make changes to your title, you need to republish the title and post/burn/load the new files instead.

In this chapter, you'll learn about how to publish your title into the various publishing formats.

## In This Chapter

- Publishing Formats

# Notes

# Publishing Formats

### ReviewLink

ReviewLink is a free, online platform where reviewers can view and comment on your title.

 ReviewLink, p. 232

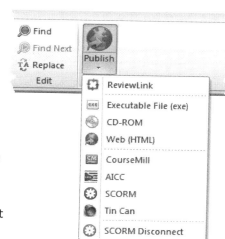

### Executable File (exe)

This format creates a single file that is easy to share and run because the entire course is contained in one file.

### CD-ROM

Use this option to create a set of files that you can burn to a CD-ROM that automatically plays when the student puts the disk in the computer.

### Web (HTML)

The HTML option is useful when you want to post files to a Website or intranet site, but don't need it to track to a Learning Management System (LMS).

### CourseMill

CourseMill is Trivantis' LMS. This publishing option is specifically designed to integrate with the CourseMill LMS.

### AICC

AICC (Aviation Industry CBT Committee) is an e-learning standard that governs how LMSs and e-learning courseware communicate with each other. Use this method to create HTML files that integrate with an AICC-compliant LMS.

### SCORM

SCORM (Shareable Courseware Object Reference Model) is another e-learning standard that governs how LMSs and e-learning courseware communicate with each other. Use this method to create HTML files that integrate with a SCORM-compliant LMS.

### Tin Can

The Tin Can API is often referred to as the next generation of SCORM. It is also a standard for courses to talk to LMSs as well as to Learning Record Stores (LRS). For more information about Tin Can, visit www.tincanapi.com.

### SCORM/Disconnected

Use this option when you want to let the student take a course offline (not connected to the Internet) and then have the course send the information to a SCORM-compliant LMS when a connection becomes available.

# Publish a Title

While the individual settings vary based on what publishing format you choose, the overall process is the same.

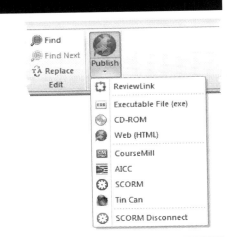

**To publish a title:**

1. Go to the **Home** tab.
2. Click the **Publish** drop-down arrow.
3. Select the publishing format you want.
4. Review and resolve any warnings or errors that need to be addressed.
5. Click the **Publish** button.
6. Configure the publishing settings (explained in the remainder of the chapter)
7. Click the **OK** button.
8. Click the **Done** button.

 Error Checker, p. 214

 **BRIGHT IDEAS**

- Instead of clicking the **Done** button, you can click the Preview button which lets you preview the course in any installed browser or open up the folder with the published files.

- If you are publishing to CourseMill, click the **Send Files** button instead of the **Done** button.

- If you are using the FTP options to automatically send your files to a server, click the **FTP Title** button instead of the **Done** button.

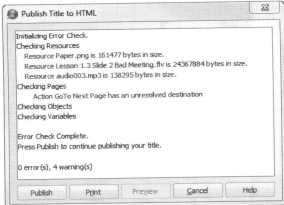

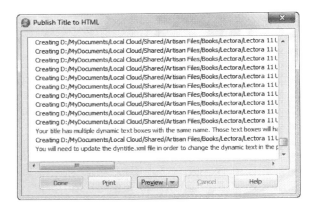

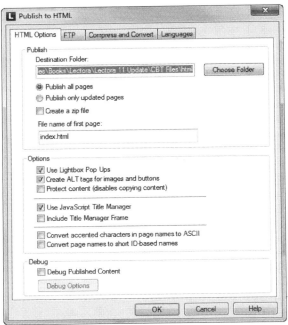

# Executable File (exe)

A single file executable (.exe) puts all course elements in a single file that plays when double-clicked. This makes the file easy to distribute. It can be put on a CD, e-mailed, placed on a network or hard drive, etc.

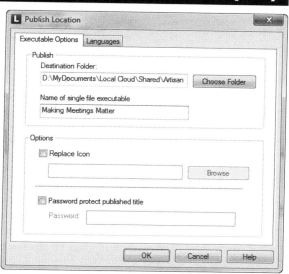

## Executable Options Tab

### Destination Folder

Enter the path where you want to save the file or click the **Choose Folder** button to select the location.

### Name of Single File Executable

Enter the name of the .exe file. By default, it is the same as the Lectora file.

### Replace Icon

By default, the Lectora logo is used as the associated icon for the file. If you want to change this to an icon of your choice (perhaps the company logo), check the box, and then click the **Browse** button to find and select the icon you want to use. Icons must be in **.ico** format.

### Password Protect Published Title

If your course contains sensitive information and you want to protect it with a password, then check the box, and enter a password. When students launch the course, they must enter the correct password to be able to view it.

## Languages Tab

The options on the Languages tab are the same for all publishing types.

 Languages tab, p. 262

 **DESIGN TIP**

If you want to make your own icon, do a web search for **.ico software** to find free or inexpensive software to help you create one.

 **CAUTION**

Some functionality, such as social objects, web windows, and external HTML objects, does not work with this publishing option.

# CD-ROM

When you use the CD-ROM option, Lectora publishes files that you then burn onto a CD. The files include your **.awt** title and associated files, a viewer to view the title, and an autorun file so the course automatically launches when the student loads the disk.

## CD Options Tab

### Destination Folder

Enter the path where you want to save the file, or click the **Choose Folder** button to select the location.

### Publish All Pages/Publish Only Updated Pages

If you have previously published the course, you can choose if you want to publish all the pages and resources or only those that have been updated. If you only publish what has been updated, it is likely to publish more quickly. If you have not previously published the course, it does not matter which option you choose – both result in the same thing.

### Create a Zip File

Check this box if you'd like the published files to automatically be put in a ZIP file for you.

### Replace Icon

By default, the Lectora logo is used as the associated icon for the CD. If you want to change this to an icon of your choice, check the box, and then click the **Browse** button to find and select the icon you want to use. Icons must be in **.ico** format.

### Enable Bookmarking Option

Students can click the icon in the title bar of the course to access a bookmarking option. This saves the current page as a bookmark that the student can go back to at any time from the same menu. Check or uncheck this box to turn this feature on and off.

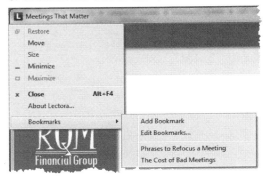

Languages tab, p. 262

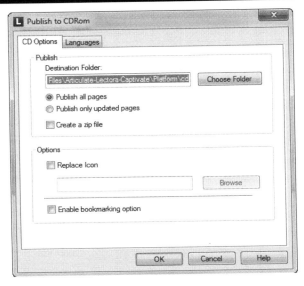

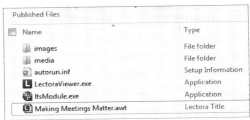

## DESIGN TIP

Students aren't likely to notice on their own that the bookmarking feature exists. Be sure to point out this feature to them if you want them to use it.

## CAUTION

- Putting these course files in a ZIP file makes them easy to archive, store, and transfer. However, if you burn the CD with the ZIP file, it will not autorun.

- When you distribute these files on a CD, you are distributing your **.awt** file. This means that anyone with Lectora could open and use your files. If this is a concern, publish your files to EXE or HTML and use your CD-burning software to set up the autorun feature.

- Some functionality, such as social objects, web windows, and external HTML objects, does not work with this publishing option.

# Web (HTML)

Use the Web HTML option when you want to:

- Post the files on an Internet or intranet page, without going through a learning management system.

- View the course locally on your computer for testing purposes.

- Put the course on a shared network drive for other team members to view.

- Give the files to someone else on a USB drive.

To launch the course from these files, double-click the **index.html** file.  If posting to a website, have the link point to the **index.html** file.

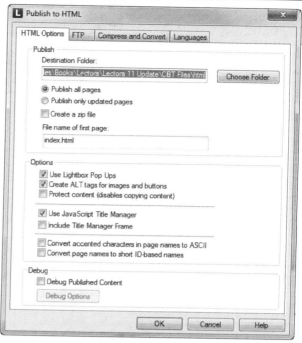

## HTML Options Tab

### Destination Folder

Enter the path where you want to save the file, or click the **Choose Folder** button to select the location.

### Publish All Pages/Publish Only Updated Pages

If you have previously published the course, you can choose if you want to publish all the pages and resources or only those that have been updated.  If you only publish what has been updated, it is likely to publish more quickly.  If you have not previously published the course, it does not matter which option you choose – both result in the same thing.

### Create a Zip File

Check this if you want your published files to be put in a ZIP file.  This is useful for archiving, storing, and uploading your published files.  (The files will need to be unzipped to load onto a server or played locally.)

### File Name of First Page

In this field you can change the name of the first file of the course.  **Index.html** is the web standard for the home page of a website.  It is best not to change this unless there is a specific reason to do so.

### Use Lightbox Pop Ups

Checked by default, this option brings up messages in a lightbox-style window.  Since it is not a new browser window, it will not conflict with pop-up blockers.  Uncheck the box if you want to use standard pop-up windows.  Uncheck this option off for a Section-508 compliant course.

### Create ALT Tags for Images and Buttons

Checked by default, this option uses the object names in the **Title Explorer** to create ALT tags for all images and buttons.  Uncheck it if you do not want ALT tags.

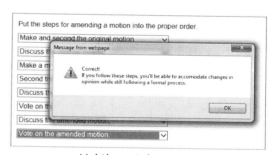

*Lightbox-style pop-up*

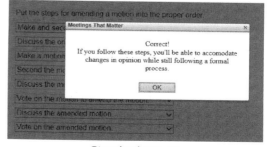

*Standard pop-up*

# Web (HTML) (cont'd)

## Protect Content

If you check this option, certain browser features will be disabled, such as keyboard shortcuts and right-click menu options for cut, copy, and paste, making it difficult for anyone to copy the content.

## Use JavaScript Title Manager

This option is checked by default, but should be unchecked if you are using the option to e-mail either test or survey results.

## Include Title Manager Frame

By default, variable information is stored within cookies in the user's browser. If you check this option, the information is stored on the student's computer instead. This can help a course with a lot of questions and variables run more quickly.

## Convert Accented Characters in Page Names to ASCII

If you have non-ASCII characters in your page names (such as an accented letter), that page name might not work in an Internet browser. If you have any such page names in your title, this option is selected automatically and the characters in question will be substituted for something that is Web-compatible.

## Convert Page Names to Short ID-Based Names

If you have a page name with a multi-byte international character, this option is selected automatically and the page's name is substituted for something that is Web-compatible.

## Debug Published Content

While in Lectora, you can use debug mode to see what is happening "behind the scenes" while previewing the course, making it easier to troubleshoot any problems. If you check this option, you get a similar debug window that appears when you run the published files. Once you check the box, you can click the **Debug Options** button to indicate what you want included in the debug log.

Keep in mind that publishing with this option is for internal use and should not be distributed to your students, who would be confused by the debug log.

 **BRIGHT IDEA**

If you enabled web accessibility in the title options, then some of these fields will be locked to the appropriate setting.

 Title Options, p. 15

# Web (HTML) (cont'd)

## FTP Tab

If you will be posting your course to a web server via FTP (File Transfer Protocol), you can do so right from within Lectora. If you don't set up that option here, you can use your own FTP software or other method to transfer the published files to the FTP site.

To enable the FTP option, check the box at the top of the tab, and then fill in the information provided to you about the FTP site.

The **Initial Remote Folder** field is where you specify what folder to put the files in on the server. To create a new folder, just type the name of it in that field.

When using an FTP to upload your files, you may need to upload through a proxy for security or firewall reasons. If this is the case, use the bottom half of the tab to enter the FTP and security information.

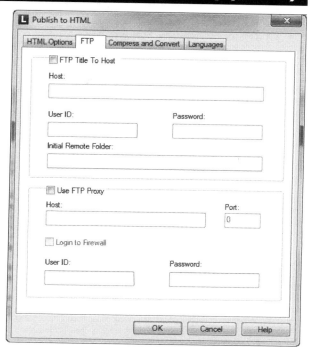

## Compress and Convert Tab

When you publish your course, you have the option of compressing and converting all audio, video, and images in the course. Audio and video files are converted to mobile-friendly **MP3** and **MP4** formats. Images are compressed to **JPG** format.

To compress/convert your images and other media, check the box next to the type(s) you want to compress, and then adjust the slider for the compression level you want. Low compression gives you the highest quality while high compression gives you lower quality.

 **CAUTION**

If you already compressed your images and other media before you brought them into the title, you probably don't want to compress them more here, or you may have quality issues.

FLV audio and video files are NOT converted to MP3 and MP4 format.

 **BRIGHT IDEA**

Remember that you can convert individual audio and video files to **MP3/MP4** format using the **Resource Manager**.

 Resource Manager, p. 222

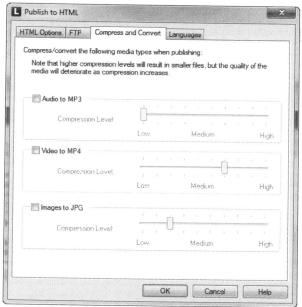

# Web (HTML) (cont'd)

## Languages Tab

If you have several different translations of your title, you can publish them all at once from the **Languages** tab. There are three parts to set up.

- Translation file: The translation tool on the Tools menu results in a rich text file (.rtf) that you can have translated. Attach the translated file here.

- Publish strings: In addition to your title content, there are also system generated messages that need to be translated. You can set up a translated version of these messages (publish strings) in the Preferences dialog box. Here you indicate which publish strings file you want to use for this language.

- Publish folder: Since you will be publishing multiple versions of the course, you need to specify a different file location for each one.

Publish Strings, p. 246
Translation Tool, P. 224

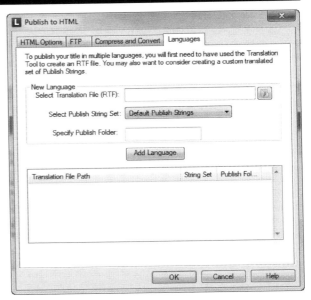

## Published Files

Your published HTML files include an **images** folder and a **media** folder, similar to what is included with your Lectora files. A **files** folder may contain additional files needed for your course to work properly. If you had any additional files in an **extern** folder, they are included and mixed in with the rest of the files, rather than separated out in their own folder.

In addition to an HTML file for every page in the course, there are also a number of files such as XML documents and JavaScript files that Lectora automatically generates to make the course work.

All of these files need to be uploaded, burned, copied, etc. for the course to run properly.

 **CAUTION**

Unless you understand HTML, JavaScript, and any other coding included in your published files, do not change, rearrange, or rename any of your published files.

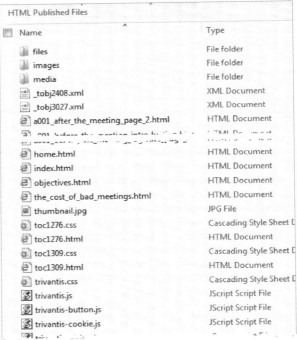

# CourseMill

CourseMill is the learning management system made by Trivantis. Many of the publishing options are the same as for SCORM publishing, with a few differences.

## CourseMill Options Tab

Enter the course ID, instructor ID, and instructor password for this course. Refer to your CourseMill documentation for more information about these fields.

## SCORM Options Tab

Most of the choices on the **SCORM Options** tab are preset and grayed out. You can make three choices.

### Report Test/Survey Question Interaction to the LMS

Check this box if you want to send question-level data to the LMS, such as question text, user's answer, correct/incorrect status, and time data. Note that not all LMSs will accept this data.

### Append Timestamp to Interaction to Create Unique ID

Uncheck this box if you don't want a unique ID created each time the test or survey is taken.

### Prompt the User to Navigate to the Last Viewed Page

When students re-enter a course, the LMS asks them if they want to pick up where they left off. You can disable this feature by unchecking this box.

## HTML Options Tab

This tab is the same as for Web (HTML) publishing. Some of the options are locked to the required setting for CourseMill.

HTML Options, p. 259

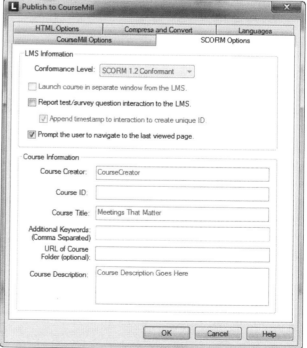

Compress and Convert tab, p. 261
Languages tab, p. 262

# AICC and SCORM

These two formats are HTML files designed for posting on an AICC- or SCORM-compliant learning management system. The **AICC Options** tab and **SCORM Options** tab are very similar to each other, with a few minor differences noted below. Work with your LMS provider to determine the best settings for your situation. The remaining tabs are the same as for regular **Web (HTML)** publishing.

 Web (HTML), p. 259

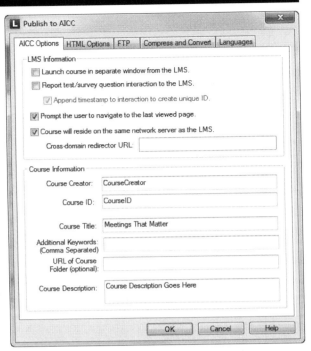

## AICC Options and SCORM Options Tabs

**Conformance Level** (*SCORM only*)

There are several different versions of SCORM. From the drop-down menu, select the one that works best for your LMS. Contact your LMS provider if you do not know which option to use.

**Launch Course in Separate Window From the LMS**

Check this box if the course will open in a separate window than the LMS. By doing this, the student will return to the LMS after closing the course.

**Report Test/Survey Question Interaction to the LMS**

Check this box if you want to send question-level data to the LMS, such as question text, user's answer, correct/incorrect status, and time data. Note that not all LMSs will accept this data.

**Append Timestamp to Interaction to Create Unique ID**

Uncheck this box if you don't want a unique ID created each time the test or survey is taken.

**Prompt the User to Navigate to the Last Viewed Page**

When students re-enter a course, the LMS asks them if they want to pick up where they left off. You can disable this feature by unchecking this box.

**Course Will Reside On the Same Network Server as the LMS** (*AICC only*)

Check this box if the course will be on the same server as the LMS. If it is not, and you are using the JavaScript Title Manager, enter the URL for the script that will redirect the course. See the Lectora User's Guide for more information.

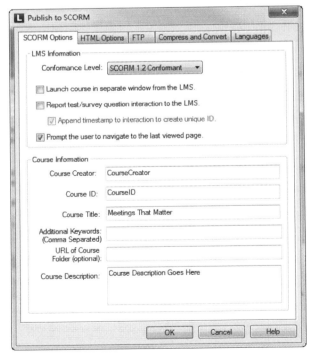

**Course Information**

Enter the course information as you want it to appear in the LMS. In some cases, it is easier to leave this blank and populate this information directly in the LMS. The **URL of Course Folder** field is only required by some LMSs.

# Tin Can

Tin Can API, also known as "the next generation of SCORM," helps a course communicate to a learning management system and/or a learning record store (LRS). Tin Can LMSs and LRSs will be able to keep track of many types of learning experiences other than just courses. Because this is an evolving standard (1.0 release scheduled for Spring of 2013), it is not fully known all the ways that a course and a Tin Can tracking system might be able to interact in the future.

The **Tin Can Options** tab is extremely similar to the **AICC Options** and **SCORM Options** tab. The main difference is that a course is referred to as an activity.

 **BRIGHT IDEA**

Remember that you can add an action to send a Tin Can statement about specific activities, such as answering a question or sharing content.

Tin Can Statement, p. 123

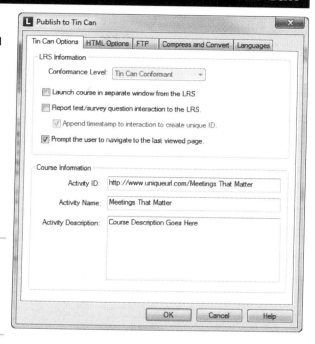

# SCORM/Disconnected

The **SCORM/Disconnected** option lets students complete a course offline (not connected to the Internet), but still keep track of scores and completion status. For example, the course could be distributed on a CD for a student to run locally on a computer. Then, when an Internet connection is available, the course information is sent to the LMS.

The choices on the various publishing tabs are also in the standard SCORM publishing dialog box. However, there are fewer options when publishing to this format.

**BRIGHT IDEAS**

## Tips for Publishing to a Learning Management System

### Title and AU Properties

In addition to the settings in the publishing dialog box, remember to set up the title and AU properties properly. Go to the **Design** tab and click the **Title Options** button to indicate your course will integrate with a learning management system.

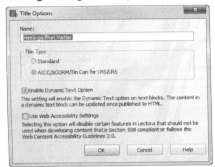

 Title Options, p. 15

Set up the properties for your assignable unit on the **Information** tab.

 Assignable Units, p. 28

### Published Files

Most LMSs require that course files be uploaded as a ZIP file. The option to create a ZIP file upon publishing is checked by default for the various LMS publishing options.

### Posting a Trial Course

When integrating a course with an LMS for the first time, it's best to start testing early. Create a small, sample title to test with the LMS before you get into full development so that you know what specifications and options work best with your particular LMS.

### Required Actions

LMS courses need to have an exit action and a way to mark the course as completed. If you do not, you'll get a red error during the publishing process.

#### Exit Action

Adding an exit action is quite simple—just add an **Exit Title/Close Window** action for the course.

#### Course Completion

The LMS needs to know when the course is complete. You can do that by having a scored test or by modifying the **AICC_Lesson_Status variable** based on the criteria you want. You may need to work with your LMS provider to find the right settings.

 Test Chapter Properties, p. 167

### Modify Variable Method

You can set up an action to modify the **AICC_Lesson_Status** variable using any conditions you want. For example, you can attach that action to run automatically (**On Show**) on the last page of the course or the page the student is directed to upon passing the final test. Or, you could use the **Condition** tab to set up your own criteria for what constitutes completion.

When you set up the action, make sure you are entering the correct value exactly, usually **completed** or **passed** for SCORM and **c** or **p** for AICC.

# Index i

# Index

## Q

**Visit the companion site at:**

www.e-learninguncovered.com

Resources for Rapid Developers

1. Download free resources
2. Access practice files
3. Sign up for our blog
4. Ask about bulk purchases
5. Explore the other books in the series

E-Learning Uncovered
is brought to you by:

Custom E-Learning Development

E-Learning Consulting

E-Learning Team Training

Specializing in:

Articulate, Captivate, Lectora,

and Other Rapid

Development Tools

www.artisanelearning.com

info@artisanelearning.com

(904) 254-2494